INITIATIVE-CENTERED POLITICS

INITIATIVE-CENTERED POLITICS

The New Politics of Direct Democracy

David McCuan

SONOMA STATE UNIVERSITY

and

Stephen Stambough

CALIFORNIA STATE UNIVERSITY-FULLERTON

CAROLINA ACADEMIC PRESS

Durham, North Carolina

Library of Congress Cataloging-in-Publication Data

Initiative-centered politics : the new politics of direct democracy / [edited] by
David McCuan and Stephen Stambough.
   p. cm.
Includes bibliographical references and index.
ISBN 0-89089-280-6 (alk. paper)
1. Direct democracy--United States. 2. Referendum--United States.
3. Political participation--United States. 4. United States--Politics and
government--2001- I. McCuan, David. II. Stambough, Stephen. III. Title.

JF494.I55 2005
328.273--dc22

2005006909

Carolina Academic Press
700 Kent Street
Durham, North Carolina 27701
Telephone (919) 489-7486
Fax (919) 493-5668
www.cap-press.com

Printed in the United States of America

*To our wives, Leslie Janik and Valerie O'Regan,
who put up with our countless chats and endless hours
of discussion for this book. Their support made
this volume possible. And their love for us
made us better spouses.*

CONTENTS

Foreword   xiii

Chapter 1 Progressive Reforms and the Twenty-First Century:
           The New "Parallel Legislature" of Direct Democracy,
           David McCuan and Stephen Stambough   3

The "Parallel Legislature" of Direct Democracy Today:
    A New Progressivism?   5
References   7

           PART I VOTERS, INTEREST GROUPS, AND POLITICAL
                   PARTIES IN DIRECT LEGISLATION

Chapter 2 Voters, Candidates, and Institutions: Can Voters
           Make Sense of Institutions? Can Candidates Make
           Sense of Voters?, *Todd Donovan and Shaun Bowler*   11

Voter Attitudes to Direct and Representative Democracy:
    Is There Any There, There?   13
Candidate and Legislator Attitudes about Voter Opinions   22
Discussion: What Do We Make of These Findings?   26
Appendix—Descriptions of the Data   29
References   30

Chapter 3 Ballot Initiatives and Voter Turnout, *Mark Smith*   33

The Role of Initiatives and Referenda in Increasing Turnout   34
Research Design and Measurement   35

Measuring the Salience of Initiatives   37

The Importance of the Electoral Context   39

Direct Legislation and Turnout   42

Salience, Turnout, and the Electoral Context   45

Conclusions   47

References   48

Chapter 4   Can't Buy Me Love: Interest Group Status and the
             Role of Political Professionals in Direct Democracy,
             David McCuan   51

Research Question: Investigating the Demand for Professional
   Political Services in Direct Democracy—Spillover Effects
   from Candidate Campaigns   52

Theoretical Background   54

Building a Typology of Initiative Contests   55

Type 1 Initiative Contests: "Interest Group Politics"   56

Type 2 Initiative Contests: "Entrepreneurial Politics"   57

Type 3 Initiative Contests: "Client Politics"   57

Type 4 Initiative Contests: "Majoritarian Politics"   58

The Universe of Ballot Measures in the Typology, 1984–1998   58

Hypotheses and Initial Findings on the Extent of Professionalization   67

Interest Groups and Spending on Political Professionals, 1984–1998   69

Conclusion   71

References   73

Chapter 5   The Impact of Campaign Finance on Ballot
             Issue Outcomes, *Richard Braunstein*   77

Resource Bias in Ballot Issue Elections   78

Research Design and Hypotheses   80

   Data Set   81

   Findings: Individual and Organizational Funding Sources   83

   Findings: Campaign Spending and Legislative Type   86

   Findings: Multivariate Analysis   92

Conclusion   94

References   96

**Chapter 6   The Initiative to Party: The Role of Political Parties
in State Ballot Initiatives,** *Dan Smith*   97

The Relationship between Parties and the Initiative Process   98

Why Parties are Taking the Initiative   102

    Increasing Voter Turnout   103

    Ballot Measures as "Wedge" Issues   107

    Ideological Compatibility   108

Conclusion   112

References   113

PART II   ETHNIC MINORITIES AND DIRECT DEMOCRACY

**Chapter 7   The Three Strikes Initiative: The Impact of Racial
and Ethnic Composition on Voting Patterns
and Attitudes Toward Crime,** *Linda Lopez*   121

Party Identification   125

Socioeconomic Status   125

Race and Ethnicity   126

The "Los Angeles Literature"   130

Research Questions   132

Conceptualizing the Variables   133

    Dependent Variables   135

    Hypotheses   135

    Race and Ethnicity   136

    Partisanship   136

    Gender   136

    Age   136

    Income   136

    Education   137

Research Methodology   137

Data Gathering Methodology   138
Survey Polls   138
Analysis   140
Discussion   143
References   144
Appendix 7A: The Jones Three-Strikes Law   150

**Chapter 8   Race, Capitalism and the Media: A Study of
Proposition 209 Editorials,** *Catherine Nelson*   157

Race and Capitalism   158
The Mainstream and Alternative Media   161
Race and Inequality in the Media   163
Data and Methods   167
Questions   169
Results   169
Mainstream Newspapers Supporting Proposition 209   170
Mainstream Newspapers Opposing Proposition 209   172
Ethnic Newspapers Opposing Proposition 209   176
Summary and Conclusion   181
References   183
Editorials Consulted   184

PART III   THE IGNORED INITIATIVE:
DIRECT DEMOCRACY AT THE LOCAL LEVEL

**Chapter 9   Referenda Wars in Cincinnati: The Battle Over
Strong Mayors and Sports Stadiums,** *Clyde Brown
and David M. Paul*   189

Battle #1: The 1995 Strong-Mayor Campaign   191
Battle #2: The 1996 Campaign for Sports Stadiums   195
Battle #3: The 1998 Baseball at Broadway Commons Campaign   200
Battle #4: The 1999 Campaign for a "Stronger Mayor"   204
Discussion   206
References   212

**Chapter 10   Orange Crush: Mobilization of Bias, Ballot Initiatives,
            and the Politics of Professional Sports Stadia,** *Dan Smith* 215

The Privileged Position of Professional Sport Franchises   217

The Bronco's First Drive for a New Stadium   220

Lobbying the Colorado General Assembly   223

The Metropolitan Football Stadium District   225

Lobbying the Legislature, Again   229

The Changing Face of Denver's Mayor   231

The Campaign for a New Stadium   233

Citizens Opposing the Stadium Tax   233

Citizens for a New Stadium   235

The Media and the Stadium   238

Radio Coverage and the Stadium Issue   238

Newspaper Coverage and the Stadium Issue   239

Did the Broncos and the Media Influence Voters?   240

Conclusion   242

References   250

PART IV   BALLOT ACCESS, INITIATIVE REFORM, AND THE QUESTION
          OF REPRESENTATION IN THE "PARALLEL LEGISLATURE"

**Chapter 11   Direct Democracy in the Twenty-First Century:
            Likely Trends and Directions,** *M. Dane Waters and
            David McCuan*   259

"Past is Prologue"   260

The Regulation of the Process and Its Impact on Future Usage   269

Conclusion   271

References   272

Contributors   275

Index   279

FOREWORD

The importance of direct democracy in contemporary politics is no longer in question. Its importance has been well established over the last quarter century and well documented by academic scholars and political journalists. Most of this attention has focused on the effectiveness of direct democracy as a policy tool and its faithfulness (or lack thereof) to the democratic ideals it embodied for its Progressive-era founders.

Our goal in this volume is to bring together a diverse group of scholars who investigate the many aspects of direct democracy across multiple dimensions. Our intention is to build on a recent volume, *Citizens as Legislators* (Donovan, T., S. Bowler, and C. Tolbert. 1998. Columbus: Ohio State University Press). Our volume pays particular attention to trends as we enter an era of "New Progressivism," with direct democracy as a key institution of the new millennium. In our view, direct legislation has become a "parallel legislature" that is a defining feature of how the nation is governed. And as this institution has become an important policy arena, its practices and processes across multiple levels of government have implications for policy outputs. In addition to an emphasis on current trends, we also focus on an often forgotten side of direct democracy—local ballot measures. Finally, we make a case for the expansion of study into a truly comparative nature across issue dimensions and levels of government.

The book expands the focus of direct democracy research in a number of ways. First, we establish the need to develop a comprehensive understanding of the major political players involved in the process. In Part I, a group of scholars explore the changing roles of voters, interest groups, and political parties. We already know that these roles are different than the roles envisioned by the Progressive reformers. Direct democracy was supposed to be a way for the voters to circumvent powerful interest groups and entrenched political party bosses. Many scholars argue that the process is now an additional tool of interest groups and political parties. The true story, however, is not that simple. As much as these groups changed direct democracy, direct legislation also reshaped the strategic decisions and activities of these groups. Part I examines the current relationship between these groups and direct democracy.

Secondly, this book expands our understanding of direct democracy by integrating ethnic politics into its contents. Progressives hoped that the initiative process could serve as a powerful check on entrenched special interests controlling political parties and governmental institutions. When majority and minority are viewed in terms of ethnicity, however, direct democracy enters a whole new dynamic. In Part II, our contributors investigate direct democracy and minority rights, minority voting patterns on certain issues, as well as media coverage of these ballot propositions.

In Part III, we expand our study into an important but often forgotten side of initiative-centered politics. While most research focuses on high-profile state initiative campaigns, most occurrences of direct democracy are at the local level. For every Proposition 13 (California, 1978) there are hundreds of local bond measures. Most are nearly invisible for voters, observers, and scholars. Others are expensive and bitterly fought political battles. In Part III, David M. Paul and Clyde Brown look into an increasing use of direct democracy—stadium measures. Dan Smith, with the assistance of Sure Log, University of Colorado-Boulder, examines the impact of yet another stadium measure in Denver, Colorado. Questions about taxpayer-supported sports facilities are sometimes examined from the viewpoint of economic development or the effectiveness of their celebrity spokespeople (including our current president and former Texas Rangers owner, George Bush).

Finally in Part IV, M. Dane Waters, founder and president of the Initiative and Referendum Institute (<www.iandrinstitute.com>), and David McCuan examine likely directions for direct legislation across multiple institutional settings and at both the state and local levels.

We would like to thank our families, especially Leslie and Valerie, for their patience and guidance with this volume. In addition, we would like to thank the contributors for their patience and contributions. Last, we want to thank Bob Conrow and Keith Sipe of Carolina Academic Press for making this volume a reality. We hope our readers find the work's chapters of value for this important policymaking arena.

David McCuan   Stephen Stambough
Sonoma State University   California State University-Fullerton

INITIATIVE-CENTERED POLITICS

CHAPTER 1

Progressive Reforms and the Twenty-First Century: The New "Parallel Legislature" of Direct Democracy

David McCuan, Sonoma State University
and
Stephen Stambough, California State University-Fullerton

The founding of the democratic experiment known as the United States was an exercise in restraint. The founders designed a republic where representative government would check the power of factions while providing for legislation crafted through the checks and balances of the lawmaking process. However, a century after the nation's founding, the lack of responsiveness coupled with the perception of politics as controlled by elite special interests was seen not as a blessing but as a curse. Indeed, the responsiveness of legislators to the interests of the "common man" was called into question by Progressive reformers intent on bringing forth a system of "direct" democracy where citizens would actively engage in the formulation of public policy. More than two centuries after debates on the form of the national government, and now, after more than a century of experimentation with direct democracy, this group of essays takes stock of how the initiative process has fared and posits future directions for direct legislation in the United States.

In this work, we purposely focus on scholarship that examines the likely future agenda of direct-democracy issues. As direct legislation has come to dominate public policy making across the states, up and down the ballot, in rural states as well as in well populated locales, initiative observers and scholars have failed to take a structured look at differences between areas where direct legislation is common to the ballot and areas where the process less commonly appears on the ballot. States and localities with a long tradition of active direct legislation may have multiple interests operating within the political environment that prove consequential to outcomes. Areas with a less active tradition of direct legislation may have distinct institutional features precluding the level of citizen involvement envisioned by the Progressives. Our theme throughout the volume is that direct democracy in all its forms has become a "parallel legislature," incumbent with the problems and challenges we see in the "sausage-making" process commonly referred to as legislative politics. Similar criticisms can be directed to both the traditional game of legislative politics and the game of the "parallel legislature," known as "citizen" lawmaking. While there are clear and compelling differences in the *processes* associated with each arena, the challenges for democratic governance are largely the same.

The book begins in Part I with an overview of developments in the subfield of initiative research. In this section, the authors tackle some of the most compelling questions concerning the direct legislation debate. What access is provided to citizens? Do ballot measure campaigns restrict access? Or can ballot measure campaigns, referenda, and the like lead voters to pay even closer attention to campaigns and political questions? Does the process of direct democracy affect interests in different ways, working to the benefit of elites at the expense of the "citizens"? The contributions of this section center on questions of the *process* of direct democracy as a "parallel legislative game." How this game is conducted and the repercussions of ballot measure democracy for voters and actors in the process are our focus in this first section of the book.

While at first glance, these questions may seem to have a normative basis, empirical investigation of ballot access, representation, and the protection of citizen interests go to the heart of democratic theory. The protection of minority interests, what Madison referred to as "factions," is a critical component of most research on representation. Additionally, the role of protecting groups and ideas out of the mainstream political discourse (or, in some cases, of assaulting these same groups) has a rich tradition in American political history. The founders sought to guarantee certain rights for specific groups while also guaranteeing some measure of protection from popular preferences. The conflicting and contradictory idea of individual rights conferring legitimacy on our rulers through the transfer of popular sovereignty was limited through the creation of a republican form of government. At once we designed a system protecting the sanctity of individual rights and preferences while minimizing the input of citizens on their government. Attempts to push the pendulum closer to the people, such as the creation of a direct legislation system, struggle maintaining a similar balance between the tyranny of the majority and the protection of minority rights. This has been a debate begun not in the fields of the Great Plains and cities during the Progressive era nor in the town halls of New England, but a debate as rich, old—and conflicted—as the republic itself. Reflecting this pursuit of balancing majority and minority interests, Part II of the text examines the role of ethnic minorities in the "parallel legislature."

While the nature of direct and indirect democracy constitutes an age-old debate, we turn our attention in Part III to more recent developments in direct democracy, that is, what is happening in the local arena. While controversial measures such as Proposition 13 (1978) or Proposition 209 (1996) or the recall of California Governor Gray Davis (2003) capture the media's attention, the rich lineage of the local initiative cannot be ignored. Glitzy media coverage and exhaustive spending may not exist in local initiatives of the "parallel legislature," but the impact on citizens by local ballot measures cannot be understated. In an attempt to shed light on how development, money, power, and values are fought at the local level, we examine battles over the construction of sports stadia in two cities—Cincinnati and Denver.

The "Parallel Legislature" of Direct Democracy Today: A New Progressivism?

The rise of citizen lawmaking has become so pervasive and wide ranging that we might think of its use today as a "parallel legislature." It is open to debate, however, as to whether it was the intent of Progressive reformers that direct legislation should become such a process. Originally designed as a response to entrenched, powerful interests in the political machines and organized interests of the time, Progressives cited the need to reform governmental processes in order to restore control to ordinary citizens (Barnett 1915; Hall 1921; Munro 1912). They hoped to make the political process more responsive to the voting population and citizens' interests.

The debate both within the political science literature on direct democracy and by observers of state practice in direct democracy offers evidence contrary to this democratic view. Generally, a different view has been put forward that direct democracy is unable to overcome the power of special interests and is "captured" by the very interests the system was designed as a safety valve against; in other words, the Progressive, democratic promise of direct legislation has fallen victim to the same abuses it was intended to correct (Bowler, Donovan, and Tolbert 1998; Cronin 1989; Gerber 1999; Magleby 1984; Schrag 1998; California Commission on Campaign Financing 1992).

One senior scholar in the subfield, David Magleby, sums up nicely the points raised by several generations of scholars and observers in his work, *Direct Legislation: Voting on Ballot Propositions in the United States* (1984). Magleby notes that throughout "the history of nearly a century the direct legislation process has been primarily a single-issue-group process" (189). This view is often based on the observation that because organized special interest groups were the principle actors in ballot contests, citizen lawmaking was, in reality, a fiction and subverted the original intentions of its Progressive founders. Cronin (1989) supports this view in a subsequent work, arguing: "Although the direct democracy devices of the initiative, referendum, and recall type are widely available, the evidence suggests it is generally organized interests that can afford to put them to use" (5-6).

This discussion highlights some important developments about the history of direct democracy and how the actual conduct of this game has come to mirror traditional legislative politics. Scholarly debates revolve around normative questions about ballot access and the equity of direct democracy. These concerns arise from the observation that elections—especially those involving ballot measures—are getting more and more expensive. Candidates now are not the only ones spending large amounts of money to win elections. Interest groups—both in support of and in opposition to—initiative measures are involved in this process as well. And while the role of interest groups in politics clearly is not new, the threshold for playing in the parallel legislature is growing.

Historically, the game of initiative politics changed markedly in the wake of Proposition 13. In the 1980s, states across the nation witnessed the emergence of the initiative process as a key component of public-policy battles over property taxes and in California politics. By 1990, the initiative process was believed to be *the* central factor in determining policy outputs in many states (California Commission on Campaign Financing, 1992). And since the passage of Proposition 13 more than two decades ago, initiatives have generated a much higher media profile. The *process* of drafting measures, collecting signatures, and conducting these campaigns changed, too. These changes did not happen overnight, nor were they caused solely by the adoption of Proposition 13 in 1978 or the battles over auto insurance reform or term limits a decade later. Rather, the *process* of direct democracy was altered by changes in the growth of interest group use of the process, the rise of counterinitiatives, the activities of individual "initiative entrepreneurs," and the involvement of more political professionals throughout all stages of the process. All these alterations led to a fundamental shift away from representative government towards the arena of the "parallel legislature" and "democracy by initiative."[1]

There is an additional concern here. While exhaustive spending among just a few measures usually drives initiative campaign spending, we know relatively little about the *process* behind initiative campaigns: how groups conduct their campaigns, what gets on the ballot, and the process in the early stages of the parallel legislative game. We can be certain of some theories. For example, spending money to oppose measures is more successful than supporting or seeking passage of ballot measures (Lowenstein 1982). But even this dynamic is deserving of fuller theoretical exploration. Furthermore, we know even less about the motivations of groups seeking to do battle in direct democracy when the traditional legislative process remains an avenue of opportunity for so many interest groups. How the process of direct democracy varies across institutional settings, state political traditions, and levels of government also remains a glaring theoretical omission in the literature. By taking a step back from these observations, we may *suspect* that direct democracy has changed, but the impact of that change on the *process, actors,* and *institutions* associated with direct legislation is open to speculation. The rise of the process as a "parallel legislative" arena opposite traditional legislative politics presents an opening to our inquiry in this book. It is our hope that the findings presented in this collection spark further interest in this emerging field of study.

References

Barnett, James. 1915. *The operation of the initiative, referendum, and recall in Oregon.* New York: MacMillan Co.

Bowler, Shaun, Todd Donovan, and Caroline Tolbert, eds. 1998. *Citizens as legislators: Direct democracy in the United States.* Columbus: Ohio State University Press.

---

1. See the introductory discussion in California Commission on Campaign Financing. 1992. *Democracy by initiative: Shaping California's fourth branch of government.* Los Angeles: Center for Responsive Government.

California Commission on Campaign Financing. 1992. *Democracy by initiative: Shaping California's fourth branch of government.* Los Angeles: Center for Responsive Government.

Cronin, Thomas. 1989. *Direct democracy: The politics of initiative, referendum, and recall.* Cambridge: Harvard University Press.

Gerber, Elizabeth. 1999. *The populist paradox: Interest group influence and the promise of direct legislation* Princeton: Princeton University Press.

Hall, Arnold. 1921. *Popular government.* New York: MacMillan Co.

Lowenstein, Daniel. 1982. Campaign spending and ballot propositions: Recent experience, public choice theory, and the First Amendment. *UCLA Law Review* 86: 505–641.

Magelby, David. 1984. *Direct legislation: Voting on ballot propositions in the United States.* Baltimore: Johns Hopkins University Press.

Munro, William, ed. 1912. *The initiative, referendum, and recall.* New York: Appleton and Co.

Schrag, Peter. 1998. *Paradise lost: California's experience, America's future.* New York: New Press.

PART I

*Voters, Interest Groups,
and Political Parties
in Direct Legislation*

CHAPTER 2

Voters, Candidates, and Institutions: Can Voters Make Sense of Institutions? Can Candidates Make Sense of Voters?

Todd Donovan, Western Washington University
   and
Shaun Bowler, University of California-Riverside

In a recent survey of public opinion about their state legislature, only one-third of Californians responded that they thought the institution was doing a good or very good job. In a Washington state survey, the comparable figure was 10 percent. Voter regard for the U.S. Congress is similarly low: only 13.5 percent strongly approve of how Congress does its job.[1] For some, these figures are the end point in a long-term decline in popular trust and respect for institutions of representative democracy (Anderson and Guillory 1997; Kaase and Newton 1995; Klingeman and Fuchs 1995; Hibbing and Theiss-Morse 1995; Lispet and Schneider 1983; Citrin 1974). For others, low regard for legislatures or representative government represents the views of an increasingly educated and, hence, increasingly critical citizenry (Norris 1999).

For many such studies, mass opinions about institutions are either taken for granted or are viewed as irrational and flawed. From this latter perspective low regard for the legislature can reflect some fundamental lack of understanding about democracy (Hibbing and Theiss-Morse 1995; 1998) or can

---

1. Data from California are from the California/Field Poll 9806 (1998) and the Public Policy Institute of California Survey #10 (2000). For Washington, data are from the Washington Annual Poll (1999). For Congress, the 1997 National Election Study (NES).

be the product of generalized political anger (Tolchin 1996). Other scholars stress that political legitimacy rests on stable institutions that enjoy popular support (March and Olsen 1984), which implies that discontent with institutions may be a threat to a political system. In order to build an understanding of what attitudes about institutions actually mean, this essay examines the nature of opinions about institutions by asking whether voters actually reason about their political institutions. We assess what voters might think about democratic institutions when responding to questions about the legislature and initiatives. We also investigate what legislative candidates think about voters' opinions. Do they even acknowledge, for example, that anxieties about the legislature are an issue?

Our consideration of a legislative candidate's beliefs stems from long-standing concerns within political science about the views of party elites. The term *elite* is often taken to include legislators and candidates for public office (Erikson, Wright, and McIver 1993). One question of interest concerns the "bottom-up" process of representation and the extent that party elites reflect voter opinions (Erikson, Wright, and McIver 1993, 125). A different research tradition is concerned with the commitment of party elites to democratic institutions and principles in an essentially "top-down" model where elite restraint and tolerance underpins democratic systems. Candidate conceptions of democracy can be seen to be self-evidently important in societies transitioning to democracy, such as that in Russia (Miller, Hesli, and Reisinger 1997). Within established democracies the views of leading members of the political system are also held to be important from the perspective of normative theory (see Parry, 1969, for a review), from literature on toleration and civil liberties (Stouffer 1955), and from a comparative tradition on consensus systems (see Lijphart 1999; 1984; and his earlier work on the "politics of accommodation").

The first (bottom-up) perspective on the relationship between mass and elite attitudes examines how well rival party elites reflect and represent divisions within the electorate. The second (top-down) approach emphasizes consensus among party elites: a consensus that may not, or indeed should not, reflect mass opinions yet is important for the continuation of democracy. In this work, we make a first step towards bringing these two kinds of approaches together by discussing voter and candidate attitudes towards the institutions of democracy. Responses to political institutions are, in principle at least, quite a different topic from mere policy questions, since they invoke concerns over legitimacy and authority. What voters think of institutions has received greater attention in the political science literature of late (Anderson and Guillory 1997;

Anderson and LoTempio 1999; Gordon and Segura 1997; Listhaug and Wiberg 1995). Here we assess how—indeed, *whether*—voters reason about political institutions. Related to this assessment are the questions of how party elites see the same institutions and how they see and understand voter opinions.

The essay is divided into two parts. In the first, we consider voter attitudes to democratic institutions—both direct and representative—in order to establish whether voters do, in fact, have meaningful opinions about institutions that cohere or exhibit evidence of any systematic patterns. From here, we consider candidate attitudes both to the legislature itself and to voters' opinions on the matter.

Voter Attitudes to Direct and Representative Democracy: Is There Any There, There?

Before examining whether legislators and candidates for public office do or do not share voter opinions, we need to establish some basic patterns about voter assessments of representative democracy—partly in order to establish that voter opinions are not just random noise but are, in some sense, meaningful. Establishing that voters *can* reason about institutions means that legislators *ought* to pay attention to them. After all, if voter opinions towards the legislature are simply the grumblings *de jour,* then legislators could hardly be expected to respond to them.

To some extent, there is little theory concerning how voters reason about political institutions. According to one view, institutions are mere vehicles for aggregating fixed, preexisting preferences about policies (Tiebout 1956; Riker 1982). According to another, institutions have an important social function: helping people learn their preferences about policies (March and Olsen 1984). Gerber and Jackson (1993) and Carmines and Stimson (1989) illustrate how the political process itself helps voters take cues from parties while forming policy preferences. Carmines and Kuklinski (1990) demonstrate that positions taken by congressional leaders can shape the policy opinions of citizens and shape confidence in the leaders' positions. Lupia and McCubbins (1998), Lupia (1994), and Zaller (1992) also demonstrate the importance of cue taking in policy preference formation. None of these perspectives, however, explain directly how people form preferences for and opinions about political institutions. Furthermore, legislators and the public may have fundamentally different (if not adversarial) perspectives about the nature of democratic institutions that can inhibit the ability of elite positions to shape mass attitudes on the subject.

There are reasons for thinking that voter opinions about institutions are even less well considered or meaningful than opinions on specific policy issues. It is not obvious, for example, that the figures reported in the very first sentence of this essay carry much meaning at all. When citizens are asked their opinion of a legislature, they are typically asked to express it in absolute terms. They are asked whether they think the legislature is doing a good or a bad job in isolation from any explicit yardstick or benchmark. They are not asked, for example, whether the legislature is doing a good or bad job in comparison to legislatures of the past, to some mythic legislature described in their civics courses, to legislatures of other states, or to nonlegislative processes.

It is not clear, then, what kind of comparison voters are making when responding to such a question, or whether all voters are making the same comparison and using the same yardstick; some voters could be comparing the state legislature to the U.S. Congress, others to the "good old days" of Jesse Unruh or Willie Brown. This lack of any common yardstick matters because citizens are pretty much stuck with the legislature *as an institution*. For good or ill—and for any foreseeable future short of armed insurrection—the legislature is here to stay. Thus, interpreting voter assessments of the legislature has some of the same drawbacks of assessing voter responses to the weather: their assessment isn't something that they can change very readily. This being the case, it is possible to read far too much into the surveys reporting that x percent responded that the legislature is doing a good job and y percent that it is doing a bad job. A more concrete sense of the limits to measures of these opinions may be gained from the figures in Table 2.1.

Table 2.1 displays responses to survey questions asked of both voters and legislative candidates in two states (Washington and California) concerning their respective state legislatures. The figures show that nonincumbent candidates had a much more negative opinion of the legislature than voters and incumbent legislators. Only 16 percent of Washington voters and 14 percent of California voters rated their legislatures as poor or very poor in 1998 and 1999. Comparable figures for major party candidates (and challengers) were 40 percent for both California and Washington. Sixty percent of incumbent legislators, in contrast, rated the legislature as very good or good. Incumbents were twice more likely to make this rating than Washington legislative challengers, three times more likely than California voters and challengers, and six times more likely than Washington voters.

Part of the differences here might be due to the fact that candidates and legislators have more defined opinions than voters. This is fully in line with the conventional wisdom that "elites," or at least incumbents and candidates

Table 2.1   Evaluations of State Legislatures: Voters and Legislative Candidates

	California voters 1996 / 1998	All CA chall. 1998	CA maj. party chall. 1998	WA voters 1999	All WA chall. 1998	WA maj. party chall. 1998	All incumbent legislators 1998
Very good / Good	23 / 33	19	22	10	32	34	60
Fair	45 / 44	26	32	69	26	26	23
Poor / very poor	22 / 14	50	40	16	40	40	12
DK / No opinion	10 / 9	4	6	6	2	2	5
Number of cases	599	133	72	401	50	48	61

Note: Cell entries are percentages. Response categories differ by survey. Candidates and legislators were offered 6 categories (VG, G, F, P, VP, and no opinion). CA voters were read the same 5 initial categories, with "no opinion" recorded but not offered. WA voters were read 4 categories (VG, F, P, VP) with "no opinion" recorded but not offered.

Sources: 1996 California voters, California/Field Poll 9606; 1998 California voters, California Field Poll 9805; 1998 California and Washington candidates, authors' mail survey; 1999 Washington voters, Washington Annual Poll, Applied Research Northwest.

for public office, have more definite opinions than do "masses" (Converse 1964). Voters are much more likely than candidates to give the legislature a "fair" grade—such a neutral response that it may be roughly equivalent to a nonresponse. The concentration of voter responses in this neutral category gives limited meaning to voter opinions on institutions and raises a question about the nature of the survey response: Is such an opinion at all thoughtful or systematic? If voter opinions about political institutions are more or less random, we have little reason to expect candidates to reflect their views, let alone to try to understand them.

Couching the topic in this way also raises standard concerns about voter competence. Although the "reasoning-voter" literature has done much to help reassess the picture of voter ignorance built up over much of the postwar period, it has mostly done so with regard to policy areas, not with regard to institutions (Lupia and McCubbins 1998; Bowler and Donovan 1998; Zaller 1992; Sniderman, Brody, and Tetlock 1991; Popkin 1991; conversely see Delli Carpini and Keeter, 1996). Voter responses to institutions may require a much greater level of sophistication than responding to policy appeals, and assessments of legislative institutions, even by reasoning voters, may be suspect. Absent any yardstick or means of calibrating opinions, we should treat general voter opinions about legislative institutions with some caution.

In most western states, however, the presence of the initiative process does allow voters to compare direct and representative legislative forms of governance and thus provides a common institutional reference point for both voters and politicians. Evidence from these comparisons provides some basis for claiming that voters are indeed able to form sensible and coherent responses to institutions. We can show this in several ways, albeit indirectly, using available cross-sectional data.[2]

First, by comparing mass attitudes toward representative and direct democracy, we can see opinions shift in response to the type of question being asked. We test if opinions shift in readily interpretable ways that suggest voters might be reasoning about institutions. Second, we test if there is some consistency among the ways voters link their attitudes about "direct" and "representative" democracy. This allows us another way of determining if voter attitudes about institutions are more than mere random noise. Third, we examine if the attitudes of both voters and candidates are formed in similar ways. If the struc-

---

2. Time series data may well be more useful in helping to answer some of these questions. General affect/opinion questions have been examined using time series but the kinds of specific evaluations we are interested in here are not available.

Table 2.2   Evaluations of Representative versus Direct Democracy:
California Voters

	Elected Representatives %	Voting Public %	Other*
Who do you feel generally enacts more coherent and well-thought-out government policies?	38	44	18
Which do you feel is better suited to decide upon highly technical or legal policy matters?	49	37	16
Which do you feel gives more thorough review to each particular aspect of a proposed law?	46	39	15
Which do you feel is better suited to decide upon large-scale government programs and projects?	30	55	15
Which do you feel is more influenced by special interest groups?	57	29	16
Which do you feel can be trusted more often to do what is right on important government issues?	19	64	17

Source: Field Research California Poll 9606 N=1023.
Note: Cell entries are percentages.
*Other responded "both," "neither," or "don't know."

ture of mass attitudes about institutions is similar to that of elites, we have additional evidence that voters make sense of political institutions.

We begin by looking at responses to questions that allow voters to assess representative democracy in relation to direct democracy. Here, then, we see opinion about a legislature expressed in relation to a common benchmark.

Table 2.2 reveals that voter opinions make distinctions about the relative strengths and weaknesses of representative versus direct democracy. The California public, at least, is not uniformly hostile to representative government, nor is it uniformly supportive of direct democracy. The table also displays patterns of public opinion that are quite consistent with the views of the early Progressives (Mowry 1951). Although—as a whole—the voting public seems to believe elected representatives are capable of making detailed decisions and also of reviewing legislation, when it comes to matters of broad principle, voters see themselves, not legislators, as more likely to make the "right" choice and be relatively uninfluenced by "special" interests. The point here is not that voters are willing to criticize legislatures but that many are also willing to say good things about legislatures and their abilities. Voter opinion plainly shifts in response to different questions. Such evidence is hardly sufficient to claim that every voter is as sophisticated as Madison in his or her analysis of legislative institutions, but it does suggest that voters can and do think about what legislatures can and cannot do well.[3]

We found similar patterns of discriminating opinions in voter responses to various reform proposals that would grant the legislature greater influence over citizen initiatives (frequencies not reported here). In general, voters are very supportive of direct democracy. The question: "Are statewide ballot proposition elections a good thing or a bad thing for your state?" generally elicits the response, "a good thing," from the overwhelming majority of voters in both California and Washington.[4] But this is not to say that voters do not see flaws in the initiative process and would not like to see changes. Many do see flaws and at least some would like to see changes, such as greater use of the indirect initiative or more legislative discretion in amending initiatives.

The attitudinal structure that predicts voter support for these reform proposals is one place to look for evidence that the public reasons about political institutions. Statistical models estimating voter attitudes about reforming the initiative process reflect that mass attitudes about direct and legislative process are linked in some logically consistent ways. One reform proposal, for example, is to open up the citizen initiative process to amendment by politicians either *ex post* via amendment or *ex ante* via the indirect initiative. Consistency in opinion would demand that if voters do not think very highly of the legislature, they are unlikely to want to favor either reform. Table 2.3 reports results from a simple logit model in which the dependent variable (0,1) is seen

---

3. While evidence of voter opinion shifting in response to the questions being asked is not sufficient to show that voters understand institutions, it is at least evidence that is necessary for an argument of voter understanding of institutions to hold.

4. Sixty-eight percent of California voters, and 80 percent of Washington voters said ballot propositions were good for the respective states.

Table 2.3   Opinions about the Legislature and Reform of the Initiative: California and Washington Voters

	Should Adopt Indirect Initiative	Legislature Should Amend Proposals Once Passed	Legislature Should Amend Proposals Once Passed (WA)
Democrat	.24	.49*	-.23
	.26	.27	.3
Gender	-.28	-.71**	—
	.25	.26	
Minor party	-.33	.1	1.1
	.35	.44	.95
Age	-.002	-.01**	.06
	.007	.008	.04
Education	-.02	.02	.007
	.05	.06	.06
Anglo	.29	.32	-.13
	.28	.3	.36
Opinion of Leg. (1)	-.35+	—	-0.38+
	.24		.24
Opinion of Leg. (2)	—	-.43**	—
		.16	
Constant	.13	.78	-.9
% Correct	58	72	80
N	284	327	371
	Cal Poll	Cal Poll	WA state poll
	Panel A	Panel B	

Source: California, Field Research Cal Poll 97-03 (1997). Washington, Washington Annual Poll (1999).

Note: Dependent variables: 1=support reform, 0=other. Logistic regression coefficients. Standard errors below coefficients. The California sample was split and slightly different questions were asked of each panel regarding the legislature. The "opinion of leg." variable is coded 1 if respondents claimed the voters were better at making policy than the legislature.

**= significant at .05 level 2 tailed
*=significant at .10 level 2 tailed
+=significant at .10 level 1 tailed

as support for an institutional reform that grants the legislature more influence over initiatives. Support is modeled as a function of a standard set of control variables, with the key variable of interest here being attitudes towards the legislature. The models are estimated with opinion data from California and Washington. We see that voters who are leery of the legislature are less likely to want to give the legislature the power to amend citizens' initiatives. Although this pattern is hardly definitive evidence that voter opinions about institutions make sense, it is at least evidence consistent with that conjecture.

Another way of approaching the question of whether voters reason about democratic institutions is to compare the causal factors underpinning voter attitudes toward the initiative process with the causal factors underpinning candidate attitudes. One way of establishing whether the mass opinions presented in Table 2.1 result from reasoning is to see whether a broadly similar model of opinion formation captures how both candidates (elites) and voters think about institutions. If we see similar patterns, then we may have some evidence of similar thinking among both voters and candidates.

Table 2.4 displays results from similar models estimating the opinions of Washington voters and legislative incumbents and candidates. The dependent variable here is a dichotomous measure of whether or not the respondent thinks ballot propositions are a good or bad for their state (where 1=bad, 0=good or "makes no difference"). Among key independent variables are the party identity of respondents (identification for voters, party label for candidates) and a summary measure of how many specific good points they agree were associated with initiatives, minus the number of specific bad points. The—admittedly simple—goal underpinning this specification is to see whether or not the same kinds of concerns structure the opinions of voters and candidates/legislators. If there are some commonalties, then we can say voters and legislative candidates seem to reason about institutions in similar ways.

Clearly, we need to build some differences in model specification for the two populations. Voters cannot, for example, be incumbent legislators, but it is reasonable to expect that incumbency colors legislative views of the initiative process (Bowler et al. 1999). Similarly, the voters' views of legislative ability (are legislatures or voters better at making overall policy?) might color their views of the initiative process. Our expectation is that, even after accounting for the different sources of opinion for candidates and voters and after accounting for simple (but theoretically uninteresting) demographic traits, we should see some similar patterns of opinion formation among voters and candidates.

As can be seen from Table 2.4, there are similarities in the structure of opinions across voters and candidates. The division of opinions along party lines—

Table 2.4   Attitudes toward the Initiative Process:
WA Voters and Legislative Candidates

	WA Voters	WA Voters	WA Candidates	WA Candidates
Opinion of Leg.[a]	1.53** .79	1.84** .63	—	
Age	.0008 .13	-.04 .11	-.21** .08	-.04 .03
Anglo	.36 1.15	.87 1.08	-3.82* 2.3	-1.2 1.1
Democrat	2.14** .79	1.67** .64	3.4[+] 2.2	2.3** 1.11
Education	.06 .16	.08 .14	-.3 .49	-.21 .23
Good / Bad Points	-1.03**	—	1.31**	—
Scale	.22		.48	
Incumbent	—	—	.78 2.3	.3 1
Leader	—	—	2.4 2	.2 .96
Constant	-6.1 1.77	-5.9 1.5	5.7 5.4	1.49 2.4
N	395	395	57	57
% Correct	97	97	95	84

Source: Voters, Washington Annual Poll (1999); Candidates, author's survey of legislative candidates in California, Oregon, and Washington (1998).

Note: Dependent variables: 1=think initiative process a bad thing, 0=otherwise. Logistic regression coefficients. Standard errors below coefficients.

[a] Response to question: Who can make policy better: the legislature or voters?

with Democratic elites being notably more likely to see direct democracy as a bad thing—is mirrored among voters. We can also see that the variable tapping the balance between specific good and bad points of the initiative process works in the same way for voters as for candidates. For voters and elites, those who found more good points about citizens' initiatives were less likely to see that ballot propositions were generally a bad thing. If voters cannot reason, then the results of Table 2.4 would suggest that candidates cannot, either. But if, as it seems reasonable to assume, candidates for public office can reason about institutions, then so, too, can voters.[5]

Putting the evidence of Tables 2.2, 2.3, and 2.4 together, we argue that we have accumulated some basis for thinking that voter opinion about legislative institutions is not simply noise: There is, as the phrase puts it, "some there, there." Depending on the questions asked, voters do not automatically respond with a cynically chic negative view of legislators. Voter support of granting the legislature a greater role in the initiative process is colored in predictable ways by voter views of the legislature and, finally, the structures of both voter and candidate opinions share at least some common features. While this collection of evidence may not be compelling, it is at least consistent with the conjecture that voters reason about legislative institutions in some meaningful ways.

Candidate and Legislator Attitudes about Voter Opinions

After having established some basis for thinking that voters' opinions have a thoughtful component, we examine candidate and legislator perceptions of how voters understand legislative institutions. Our basic hypothesis, outlined in more detail in a previous paper, is essentially a variant on "where you stand depends on where you sit" (Bowler et al. 1999). The candidates' position inside the political system is likely to color candidate views of the political sys-

---

5. We have not addressed, and indeed cannot do so with currently available data, whether voters share or simply mimic the attitudes of elites. It is quite likely that elites have considerable influence in opinion formation, but it is uncertain how thorough that influence actually is. It seems unreasonable to expect voters to act as perfect mirrors of elite opinion with no scope for their own views. Major examples of voter independence in the face of elite opposition on matters of institutional reform include popular support for term limits (Donovan and Snipp 1994) and the open primary (Bowler and Donovan 1998). In any event, for purposes of the current argument, the origin of voter attitudes is not our topic of interest as much as the internal consistency and meaning of voter attitudes. But the topic of elite influence on voter attitudes toward institutions is one we intend to address in future work, not least because of the importance of normative work which accords the constructive role of elite attitudes in building support for democratic institutions. What is especially intriguing here is whether voters may be picking up elite hostility to some democratic institutions.

tem for no other reason than the current arrangements have made some candidates winners and others losers. An overarching argument concerning the effect of "where you stand…" is virtually an expression of relatively narrowly drawn self-interest. Candidates inside the political system are likely to have a much more favorable view of the legislature and its processes than those outside the system. Furthermore, insider candidates (incumbent legislators and those who have held office previously) are less likely to attribute the flaws of the legislature to themselves but are more likely to attribute them to outside forces.

Table 2.5 displays results from simple models estimating candidate responses to two questions, with data drawn from a survey we conducted in 1998 (Bowler et al. 1999). One question asked how widespread candidates thought popular discontent with the legislature was. Response categories ranged from 1 ("most are dissatisfied") through 5 ("very few are"). Overall, 40 percent of legislative candidates replied that "most" or "a majority" of the public is dissatisfied "with the way the legislature is working." Another 42 percent replied that "some" voters are dissatisfied. A second question asked candidates themselves to rate the legislature's job performance, with response categories ranging from 1 ("very poor") through 5 ("very good"). Responses to this question are listed in Table 2.1. Models used to estimate these opinions account for incumbent status, party, race, age, gender, education, state, and the respondent's status as a party leader in the legislature (see Bowler et al. 1999, for a discussion of these models). Of interest here is the respondent's opinion of the legislature and how it is related to the respondent's views of how voters perceive the legislature.

As can be seen, the two opinions are strongly related. Results from the first estimation demonstrate that elites who thought the legislature's job performance was good also thought that voters view the legislature in positive terms. This suggests elites find some meaning in mass opinions about the legislature and see public satisfaction and discontent with the institution, at least in part, as a function of how the legislature does its job.

The second column demonstrates the structure of elite opinions about the legislature. Not surprisingly, we see that legislative "insiders" (incumbents and party leaders) are more sanguine about the legislature's performance than other respondents. The third column of Table 2.5 estimates the difference between the respondent's perceptions of the public's view of the legislature and his or her own personal view. A positive score for this dependent variable means the respondent thinks voters see the institution in a more positive light than the candidate does; a negative score means that the candidate thinks voters see the institution as even more negative than the candidate does. Here we

Table 2.5   Evaluations of State Legislatures: Legislative Candidates'
Perceptions of Voter Opinion and Their Personal Opinion
of the Legislature

	Candidates' Perception of Voters' View of Legislature (high=positive)	Candidates' Own Opinion of Legislature (high=positive)	Difference (high score=thinks voters' view more positive than own view)
Rating of Legis.	.31**	—	—
	.05	—	—
Incumbent	.05	.59**	.85**
	.13	.16	.25
Democrat	0	.32**	-.4*
	.1	.13	.2
Minor Party	.02	-1.23**	-1.6**
	.14	.15	.24
White	.02	-.24*	-.29
	.11	.13	.21
Over 50	.11	-.05	.19
	.09	.11	.17
Female	.09	.23*	.35*
	.1	.12	.2
College Education	.2+	.01	.16
	.12	.15	.24
Party Leader	.21	.33	.63*
	.2	.24	.37
Washington	.28**	-.01	.27
	.11	.13	.21
Constant	3.24	3.15	-.48
N	303	309	303
Adj. R^2	.22	.28	.28

Note: Dependent variables in first two columns are presented according to a five-point scale. Dependent variable in final column is the difference between these (according to a nine-point scale). OLS coefficients. Standard errors beneath coefficients.

Source: Author's survey of candidates for state legislature in California, Oregon, and Washington, 1998.

find that incumbents and legislative party leaders—who have relatively positive views of the legislature—are likely to claim that most voters think even better of the legislature than they do. Women legislative candidates are also more positive in their assessments (column 2), both in absolute terms and relative to their perception of popular opinion (column 3). In contrast, minor party candidates—who are invariably legislative "outsiders"—see the legislature in negative terms either absolutely or in relation to popular sentiment. So, too, do Democrats.

These general patterns hold when we turn to examine which candidates respond to various explanations for voter discontent. Our survey of candidates offered questions drawn from two broad groups of explanations about why voters might think ill of the legislature. On the one hand, legislative candidates might see voter discontent as driven by the legislature's own faults. Examples include perceptions of a legislator's being tied to "special interests" or suffering from the fallout of various legislative scandals. On the other hand, legislative candidates might see public discontent as generated by factors outside the public's direct control. Its legislature could suffer from overly critical media attention, from the fact that voters may simply be unable to understand what it takes to make legislation (a variant on the Hibbing/Theiss-Morse thesis), or from state legislatures suffering from critical attention directed at the U.S. Congress. Table 2.6 reports candidate responses to these questions. The data reveal that most candidates are sympathetic to the idea that voters see legislators listening to special interests rather than voters. We also find substantial support for the view that the media coverage stirs up and magnifies discontent about the legislature and for the idea that voters confuse healthy bargaining with partisan bickering.

Table 2.7 reports the estimations of some simple logit models where the dependent variable is set at 1 if the respondent agreed that a particular cause underlay voter discontent with the legislature, and 0 if otherwise. That is, we ask, in turn, whether candidates think special interests are to blame, or scandals, media coverage, voter confusion/misunderstanding, and so on. The main conjecture here is that "insiders" will see voter discontent as driven by factors outside the legislature; "outsiders" will blame the legislature itself. In fact, this is the broad pattern we find. In particular, we find that incumbents believe— along with Hibbing and Theiss-Morse (1995)—that low regard for the legislature results from voters failing to understand the legislative process and having their discontent mobilized by a hostile media. Incumbents are also significantly less likely to see voter disdain as caused by the influence of "special interests." On the other hand, candidates from minor parties and from the De-

Table 2.6   Legislative Candidates' Perceptions of the Cause of Voter Dissatisfaction with the State Legislature

	Agree	Disagree	no opin.	N
Voters feel the legislature listens to "special interests" and not the average voter.	80	13	8	322
Voters are reacting to recent scandals.	23	57	20	322
Voters confuse healthy bargaining and compromise in the legislature with partisan bickering.	47	33	20	276
Media commentators stir up and magnify discontent.	65	24	11	278
The reputation of the state legislature suffers as a result of voter anger with Congress.	44	36	20	265

Note: Cell entries are percentages. The questions were prefaced with the following: "Now some questions regarding why voters become dissatisfied with the legislature."

Source: Author's survey of candidates for state legislature in California, Oregon, and Washington, 1998.

mocratic Party see the explanation of voter discontent lying largely in the legislature's own hands and being driven by ties to "special interests." Interestingly, respondents with a college education were less likely to blame the media for public dissatisfaction with state legislatures.[6]

Discussion: What Do We Make of These Findings?

Clearly, much work remains to be done, especially on the mechanisms by which mass and elite views on institutions are related to each other. Two

---

6. Overall then, the patterns in our findings differ quite markedly from academic theories that see voter opinion as tracking elite opinion. As we noted earlier, debates on institutional reforms such as term limits do show some fairly dramatic differences of opinion between voters and party elites.

Table 2.7 Estimations of Legislative Candidates' Perceptions of the Cause of Voter Dissatisfaction with the State Legislature

	Special Interest	Legisl. Scandal	Confusion Regarding Process	Media	Confused with U.S. Congress
Incumbent	-.72*	-.23	1.21*	1.13**	.11
	.38	.38	.4	.47	.37
Democrat	1.08**	-.66*	-.04	-.24	-.05
	.35	.32	.29	.31	.29
Minor Party	1.15**	-.51+	-.96**	-.41	-.85**
	.43	.37	.35	.34	.36
White	.68*	-.16	.35	.09	.23
	.34	.32	.31	.31	.31
Over 50	.3	.34	.31	.22	.12
	.3	.27	.25	.26	.25
Female	.54+	.27	-.35	.3	-.22
	.37	.31	.29	.31	.29
College Education	.46	.46	-.43	-.78**	-.16
	.37	.39	.35	.38	.35
Washington	-.51+	.67**	-.14	.61*	.37
	.35	.32	.32	.35	.31
Party Leader	.04	.08	.36	.3	.8
	.56	.57	.54	.71	.55
Constant	-.02	-1.51**	-.03	.9*	-.28
	.4	.44	.45	.47	.44
N	322	322	276	278	265
% Correct	83	76	65	67	62

Note: Dependent variable=1 if respondent agreed item was cause of voter dissatisfaction. Logistic regression coefficients. Standard errors below coefficients.

Source: Author's survey of candidates for state legislature in California, Oregon, and Washington, 1998.

points stand out from the data and analyses we set out above. First, there are notable differences between what voters think of the performance of state legislatures and what state legislators think, and there are differences between the definitions of voter and elite attitudes (Table 2.1). These findings are consistent with some political science literature regarding the differences between the relative coherence and consistency of mass and elite views (Converse 1964). A sizeable proportion of legislative candidates also display attitudes reflecting that voter evaluations of legislatures are somehow flawed. Many candidates claim, for example, that voters do not understand what goes on inside representative institutions—or they claim that voter attitudes and understanding are based on media distortions of representative processes (Table 2.6). The patterns we identify also suggest that elites—particularly incumbent legislators—may not necessarily share the public's concerns about the legislative process (Table 2.5, Table 2.7). Elites, furthermore, are divided about the causes of mass dissatisfaction with the legislature (Table 2.7).

Second, and in contrast with these views of some elites, the evidence from the first part of our paper suggests that voters may, in fact, be able to reason about democratic institutions (Table 2.2, Table 2.3) and may do so in ways that reflect a structure of opinions that is broadly similar to that of legislative candidates (Table 2.4). Although voters still do not have as clearly defined a conception of institutions as candidates do, we have seen that voters hold some ideas about how institutions function. Their attitudes about direct democratic institutions, moreover, are linked to their attitudes about representative institutions (Table 2.4).

These findings raise important questions concerning both divisions among candidates and between them and voters. On the one hand, we might note that many voters' (mass) views about institutions could mirror candidates' (elite) views. Following Zaller (1992), this would suggest that attitudes about democratic institutions reflect the unity or divisions that exist among elites. Finding divisions in opinions within elites and between voters and elites is entirely consistent with the idea that the mass attitudes about institutions echo cues from elites (Key 1966)—particularly those who share their partisan predispositions (Zaller 1992, 9).

Previous studies of support for institutional reforms such as term limits clearly establish that voters' opinions are structured by partisan contacts (Donovan and Snipp 1994) and by knowledge of the positions of party elites (Karp 1998). A large amount of variation in mass attitudes about democratic institutions, however, is probably shaped by factors that operate independently of elite positions. It seems unreasonable to expect voters to act as perfect mirrors of elite opinion, with no scope for their own views. Major examples of voter independence in the face of elite opposition on matters of institutional reform include popular support for term limits and the open primary initiative (Bowler and Donovan n.d.).

The empirical nature of the mass-elite relationship has consequences for normative questions about democracy. If public satisfaction or discontent with democratic institutions simply reflects responses to elite divisions, as per Zaller, then institutional rules might easily become regularly contested partisan terrain. Our results illustrate that elite divisions are apparent and the history of ballot initiatives in the West demonstrates that these divisions are often expressed over questions about political reforms. A critical question is thus not whether such divisions exist but what limits there might be to attempts at reshaping institutions. Rather than expressing the permanence and "stickiness" that some observers see as essential to a well- functioning democracy (Riker 1982; March and Olsen 1985; Hibbing and Theiss-Morse 1998), institutions can be arenas where elites rally voters to change rules for their groups' advantage. If elites show restraint, however, the stickiness of institutions is possible.

This raises another key question: How much might public attitudes about institutions be shaped by factors independent of elected elites? If the divisions we identify between elites and the public exist at some deep, core level of mass attitudes, then elite attempts at directing the public to change or maintain institutions may be for naught. This would imply, however, that elite efforts to restrain attempts at changing institutions might also be for naught.

Appendix—Descriptions of the Data

Table A1   Response to question, "How widespread is dissatisfaction with the legislature?" Used as second dependent variable in Table 2.5

	All CA Candidates	CA Major Party Candidates	All WA Candidates	WA Major Party Candidates
Most voters are dissatisfied.	12	16	5	6
Majority are dissatisfied.	31	28	19	18
Some are dissatisfied.	44	46	53	53
A minority are dissatisfied.	9	7	20	21
Very few are dissatisfied.	2	3	3	3

Source: Author's survey of candidates for state legislature in California, Oregon, and Washington, 1998.

References

Anderson, C., and C. Guillory. 1997. Political institutions and satisfaction with democracy: A cross-national analysis of consensus and majoritarian systems. *American Political Science Review* 91, no. 1: 66–81.

Anderson, C., and A. LoTempio. 1999. Winning, losing and political trust in America. Paper presented at the meeting of the American Political Science Association in Atlanta GA.

Bowler, S., and T. Donovan. n.d. Political reform via the initiative process: Proposition 198 as an example. In *California's open primary*, edited by Bruce Cain and Elizabeth Gerber. Berkeley: IGS/University of California Press.

_____. 1998. *Demanding choices: Opinion and voting in direct democracy.* Ann Arbor: University of Michigan Press.

Bowler, S., T. Donovan, M. Neiman, and J. Peel. 1999. Elite attitudes about direct democracy. Paper presented at the meeting of the Western Political Science Association in Seattle, WA.

Carmines, E., and J. Kuklinski. 1990. Incentive, opportunities, and the logic of public opinion in American political representation. In *Information and democratic processes*, edited by J. Ferejohn and J. Kuklinski. Urbana: University of Illinois Press.

Carmines, E., and J. Stimson. 1989. *Issue evolution: Race and the transformation of American politics.* Princeton: Princeton University Press.

Citrin, J. 1974. Comment: The political relevance of trust in government. *American Political Science Review* 68: 973–88.

Converse, P. 1964. The nature of belief systems in mass publics. In *Ideology and discontent*, [edited by] David Apter. New York: Free Press.

Delli Carpini, M., and S. Keeter. 1996. *What Americans know about politics and why it matters.* New Haven: Yale University Press.

Donovan, T., and J. Snipp. 1994. Support for legislative term limitations in California: Group representation, partisanship and campaign information. *Journal of Politics* 56: 492–501.

Erikson, R., G. Wright, and J. McIver. 1993. *Statehouse democracy: Public opinion and policy in the American states.* Cambridge, MA: Cambridge University Press.

Gerber, E., and J. Jackson. 1993. Endogenous preferences and the study of institutions.*American Political Science Review* 87, no. 3: 657–65.

Gordon, S., and G. Segura. 1997. Cross national variation in the political sophistication of individuals: Capability of choice? *Journal of Politics* 59, no. 1: 126–47.

Hibbing J., and E. Theiss-Morse. 1995. *Congress as pubic enemy: Public attitudes toward American political institutions.* Cambridge, MA: Cambridge University Press.

_____. 1998. Too much of a good thing: More representative is not necessarily better. *PS: Political Science and Politics* 30: 28–31.

Kaase, M., and K. Newton. 1995. *Beliefs in government.* Oxford: Oxford University Press.

Karp, J. 1998. The influence of elite endorsements in initiative campaigns. In *Citizens as legislators: Direct democracy in the United States,* edited by S. Bowler, T. Donovan, and C. Tolbert. Columbus: Ohio State University Press.

Key, V. O. 1966. *The responsible electorate.* Cambridge, MA: Harvard University Press.

Klingeman, H., and D. Fuchs. 1995. *Citizens and the state.* Oxford: Oxford University Press.

Lijphart, A. 1984. *Democracies: Patterns of majoritarian and consensus government in twenty-one countries.* New Haven: Yale University Press.

_____. 1999. *Patterns of democracy: Government forms and performance in thirty-six countries.* New Haven: Yale University Press.

Lipset, S., and William Schneider. 1983. *The "confidence gap": Business, labor and government in the public mind.* New York: Free Press.

Listhaug, O., and M. Wiberg. 1995. Confidence in political and private institutions. In *Citizens and the state,* edited by Hans-Dieter Kilgemann and Dieter Fuchs. Oxford: Oxford University Press.

Lupia, A. 1994. Shortcuts versus encyclopedias: Information and voting behavior in California insurance reform elections. *American Political Science Review* 88: 63–76.

Lupia, A., and M. McCubbins. 1998. *The Democratic dilemma.* Cambridge, MA: Cambridge University Press.

March, J., and J. Olsen. 1984. The new institutionalism: Organizational factors in political life." *American Political Science Review.* 78: 734–49.

Miller, A., V. L. Hesli, and W. Reisinger. 1997. Conceptions of democracy among mass and elite in post-Soviet societies. *British Journal of Political Science 27*, no. 2: 157–90.

Mowry, G. 1951. *The California progressives.* Berkeley: University of California Press.

Norris, P. 1999. *Critical citizens: Global support for democratic governance.* Oxford: Oxford University Press.

Parry, G. 1969. *Political elites.* New York: Praeger University Series.

Popkin, S. 1991. *The reasoning voter: Communication and persuasion in presidential campaigns.* Chicago: University of Chicago Press.

Riker, W. 1982. *Liberalism against populism: A confrontation between the theory of democracy and the theory of social choice.* San Francisco: W. H. Freeman.

Sniderman, P., R. Brody, and P. Tetlock. 1991. *Reasoning and choice: Explorations in political psychology.* Cambridge, MA: Cambridge University Press.

Stouffer, S. 1955. *Communism conformity and civil liberties.* New York: Doubleday.

Tiebout, C. 1956. A pure theory of local expenditure. *Journal of Political Economy 64*: 416–24.

Tolchin, S. 1996. *The angry American: How voter rage is changing the nation.* Boulder: Westview Press.

Zaller, J. 1992. *The nature and origin of mass opinion.* Cambridge, MA: Cambridge University Press.

CHAPTER 3

Ballot Initiatives
and Voter Turnout

Mark Smith, University of Washington

During the 1996 presidential election, only 49 percent of voting-age Americans showed up to cast a ballot. Two years later, in the 1998 midterm elections, the proportion voting was only 36 percent. These percentages extended the recent pattern of decreasing voter turnout during both presidential and midterm elections. Though certain election years, such as 1992, were exceptions, the downward trend began after the Kennedy-Nixon contest of 1960 and has continued unabated since then.

The seeming inability of the American political system to attract more people to the polls regularly stimulates lamentations from scholars and political commentators alike. Several concerns are often raised in this context. First, the fall in voter turnout seems to crystallize public dissatisfaction with how politics is conducted. Because the downward trend has corresponded with parallel declines in political efficacy and trust in government, many observers have suspected some kind of connection among them. Moreover, low turnout is often seen as threatening the legitimacy of electoral results. When fewer than half of eligible citizens vote, it is the active minority who is determining which candidates win. The candidates endorsed by voters may differ from those favored by the more passive majority. Legislative decisions designed to appeal to voters may be out of sync with what nonvoters want, undermining common notions that policies should reflect the will of the people at large.

A diverse range of reforms have been advocated in recent years to counter the decline in turnout. Relaxing registration laws has often attracted attention as a potential solution (Wolfinger and Rosenstone 1980; Piven and Cloward 1988). Donald Green and Alan Gerber (1999) extol the possibilities of nonpartisan get-out-the-vote messages, while Wattenberg (1998) proposes making election day a national holiday. Lipjhart (1997) contends that compulsory voting should be considered as an option.

The Role of Initiatives and Referenda in Increasing Turnout

Initiatives and referenda, too, are often proposed as a means to increase turnout. Many party activists, interest group leaders, journalists, and political consultants have long believed that initiatives can attract to the polls some citizens who otherwise would not vote. Politicians as diverse as Richard Gephardt, Jack Kemp, and Mark Hatfield have supported a national initiative in part as a means to boost turnout among those alienated from contemporary politics. The Direct Democracy Center, which advocates greater usage of the initiative and referendum in existing states and their spread to new states and the national level, bemoans the widespread political apathy and the low and declining voter turnout in the United States. The group's Web site asserts that with more extensive usage of initiatives, "Voter apathy will vanish" and be replaced by "people participating in their future."[1] The Initiative and Referendum Institute makes similar claims through "Talking Points" posted at its Web site. They argue that when initiatives appear on the ballot, turnout rises because they give voters "a reason to participate in the electoral process and a reason to believe that their vote counts."[2]

While the notion that direct legislation can stimulate greater turnout has received renewed attention in recent years, the basic claim is not new. Around the time that states first adopted constitutional amendments to permit citizen-initiated legislation, advocates like Cree (1892) and Sullivan (1893) contended that direct democracy would invigorate citizenship, overcome distrust with how politics was conducted, and ultimately increase voter participation. Throughout the history of direct legislation in the United States, advocates have consistently pointed to the effects on voting rates as one of the strongest arguments in favor of the initiative process.[3]

---

1. The Direct Democracy Center. 2000. Available [Online]: <http://www.realdemocracy.com> [14 May 2000].

2. Initiative and Referendum Institute. 1999. "Talking Points." Available [Online]: <http://www.iandrinstitute.org/> Select: I&R Fact Sheets, Talking Points [14 May 2000].

3. See, for example, the 1977 hearings on a constitutional amendment to allow a national initiativeconducted by the Senate Subcommittee on the Constitution.

Beneath all of these claims rests the implicit comparison to candidate races. Given the focus of many candidate campaigns upon personal qualities rather than policy issues and the tendency for the mass media to treat elections as horse races, contests for public office may fail to engage some citizens. Initiatives and referenda could provide a remedy by allowing those citizens to vote on policy directly. Through campaigns by both sides to pass or defeat these measures, extensive information about them would be disseminated to the public. The resulting attention and wide-ranging debates could encourage higher election-day turnout among citizens for whom gaining a voice on those issues represents an important incentive to vote.

Any changes in turnout brought about by initiatives could also have larger implications. In the United States, elections are often won or lost based upon which side has better mobilized its base, and party leaders and candidates often see initiatives as tools that can activate their strongest supporters (Smith 1999). Initiatives can mobilize people for whom the candidate races alone are not a strong enough draw; if so, those people will likely vote on candidate races anyway once they arrive at the polls. If their preferences concerning those races are different from the rest of the electorate, which will often be the case, their presence can change the outcomes of those races. This is the "spillover" effect that Schmidt (1989), among others, has stressed as a consequence of placing initiatives on the ballot. The potential for this spillover effect provides an additional reason for understanding the relationship between direct legislation and turnout.

This chapter seeks to uncover the bounds of that relationship. Several different kinds of elections—presidential, midterm, primary, and off-year—will be examined to determine how the effects vary across these alternative contexts.

Research Design and Measurement

For a linkage that has been so frequently and loudly asserted, systematic evidence to evaluate the effects of direct legislation on turnout remains in surprisingly short supply. To the extent that the linkage has been studied, most evidence has questioned its validity. In one approach, survey research has been used to determine whether direct legislation increases rates of voting participation. Magleby (1984, 96) cites polling data suggesting that California ballot propositions in 1962 and 1978 had, at most, a very weak effect on turnout. Cronin (1989, 174-75) presents the contradictory results of a national survey in which most respondents claimed they would be more likely to vote if issues appeared on the ballot.

However, given the differences between responding to public opinion surveys and actually showing up to vote, surveys cannot resolve the matter definitively. The most widely cited scholarly attempt to answer the question has been Everson's (1981) cross-sectional analysis of aggregate data. Everson found that among nonsouthern states, turnout rates from 1960 through 1978 did not differ in either presidential or midterm elections between states with and without the initiative process. Magleby (1984) subsequently extended this basic analysis through the 1980 elections, finding similar results. This evidence suggested that advocates of the initiative had misread the turnout relationship.

Given the prominence of Everson's conclusions, the methodology those conclusions rest upon becomes all the more important. In constructing a dummy variable to separate initiative and noninitiative states, Everson implicitly treats as equal all twenty-three (now twenty-four) states whose constitutions allow the initiative. Such an assumption could be problematic because some states, such as Oregon and California, use the initiative frequently to address high- profile issues, while other states, such as Illinois and Oklahoma, rarely use the initiative and, when they do, they normally address issues of low salience. Moreover, even within states that heavily use the initiative, the salience of the initiatives varies considerably over time. One would expect, for example, that California's set of initiatives in the general election of 1996, which included Proposition 209 to ban most existing forms of affirmative action, would be more important and better known by voters than the low-profile initiatives appearing on the ballot in 1976.

Determining whether initiatives can lead to increases in turnout is thus a more complicated question than it appears upon first glance. Venturing an answer requires one to consider the reasons why initiatives might lead more citizens to vote. The key factor is probably not the provision in a state's constitution that allows the initiative, for it should be the usage of the initiative—not its mere possibility—that provides the impetus to participation. Similarly, simply having an initiative on the ballot would not be expected to make a difference if most voters know and care little about the topic being addressed. What matters most, it can be hypothesized, is the salience to citizens of the initiatives appearing on the ballot. A set of initiatives that attract widespread interest and concern from citizens could provide a spark for voter participation. By contrast, a set of initiatives receiving little attention from the electorate would not be expected to increase turnout. This leads us to Hypothesis 1:*The greater the salience of the initiatives on the ballot, the larger their effect on turnout.*

The foregoing discussion suggests that the critical concept to be measured is the salience to citizens of ballot initiatives across states and over time. With a suitable measure of salience, one can compare states to distinguish among those that use the initiative to address prominent issues, those whose initiatives cover matters less important to the electorate, and those that do not allow initiatives at all. Similarly, one can compare within each state to distinguish elections when particularly salient initiatives appeared from those where initiatives were more "pedestrian." Devising a means for making these comparisons is not easy, for it requires collecting data over many states and elections.

Measuring the Salience of Initiatives

One way to capture the salience of initiatives is to measure the volume of media attention given to them. Scholars studying the mass media recognize that, as profit-seeking businesses, news outlets choose their stories, in part, with an eye toward the impacts on circulations and ratings (Gans 1980; Bennett 1996). Stories that are believed to interest readers, listeners, and viewers get covered more extensively and in more prominent locations (like the front page of a newspaper or the beginning of a newscast) than stories deemed uninteresting. The content of the mass media is significantly shaped by the judgments of reporters and editors as to the kinds of stories needed to keep their audiences engaged, for the size of the audience, in turn. strongly affects the amount of advertising revenue and ultimately the profits that will be collected.

This principle applies to all kinds of issues, including those resolved through ballot initiatives. When a ballot initiative important to citizens comes along, such as California's Proposition 13 in 1978, the mass media will cover it extensively. This is true whether the owners and editors of a particular news organization support or oppose the initiative in question; in either case, the incentives of profit seeking will lead to a high volume of coverage and to placing the coverage in the most prominent locations. Similarly, an initiative most people care little about will attract a low volume of coverage, and when it does get coverage, that will typically occur on the back pages of newspapers and at the ends of newscasts.

The volume of media attention given to ballot initiatives, then, can provide a valid indicator of their salience. To develop a research procedure that can measure salience, I first identified all states and years with initiatives and popular referenda on the ballot from 1971 through 1997. A list provided by the Initiative and Referendum Institute was used for this purpose. For each time an initiative appeared on a state's ballot, I made photocopies of the front pages of leading newspapers in that state for the day following the election. In each case the newspaper with the largest circulation was used, along with all others having a circulation of at least half that amount. Reflecting California's size and importance to the study of initiatives, a cutoff point of one-fifth was used for that state. After all newspapers had been collected, I read the front pages and coded the content of each text paragraph. I recorded the number of paragraphs focusing on that state's initiatives and popular referenda, allowing me to construct a measure of salience.[4] For the duration of the chapter, I use the term "initiatives" to refer collectively to both initiatives and popular referenda.

The measure of salience for each state and election is defined as the average number of paragraphs discussing initiatives divided by the total number of paragraphs. Each newspaper's contribution to the average is weighted by its circulation. The measure has a theoretical range of 0 to 1. A score of 0 is achieved if the state in question does not allow initiatives or if the state had no initiatives for a particular election. Similarly, observations take the value 0 on the salience scale if the direct legislation that did appear on the ballot was not interesting enough to citizens for reporters and editors to deem it worthy of front-page coverage. This outcome occurred fairly frequently; of all instances where the ballot included one or more initiatives, 18 percent did not receive any paragraphs on the front page. Examples include initiatives regarding when Memorial Day will be observed (South Dakota, 1986), reducing the size of the legislature (Illinois, 1980), and ending restrictions on the selling of dentures (Washington, 1994). On the high end, theoretically it is possible for an initiative to so dominate a state's news that it would absorb all the paragraphs on the front page on the day following the election. As a practical matter that never happens, but on some occasions the direct legislation in a state attracted a third or more of the paragraphs.

The set of initiatives with the highest salience during a presidential-year general election came in Arizona in 1996, where a pair of initiatives on gambling and drug laws received top billing. During a midterm-year general election, the set of initiatives scoring highest occurred in Alaska in 1978, when three initiatives, dealing with relocating the state capital, requiring deposits on bottles, and selling state lands, grabbed extensive attention. Among the rel-

---

4. Both initiatives and popular referenda are included, for they share the critical characteristic of reaching the ballot only through citizen petitions. Legislative referenda and bond questions, which are placed on the ballot by legislatures, are not included. The debate about direct democracy and turnout centers on citizen-initiated propositions, not ones proposed by legislatures, so only the former kinds are incorporated into this study.

atively few states and years allowing initiatives during primary elections, the highest salience occurred in California in 1978, where Proposition 13's successful effort to roll back property taxes captured a stunning 56 percent of all paragraphs in the state's largest newspapers. The highest salience during an odd-year general election came in Washington in 1991, when four initiatives, dealing with physician-assisted suicide, abortion, term limits, and property taxes, collectively generated extensive attention.

Table 3.1 shows the state rankings over the period 1971-1997. In the first two columns that show the results for presidential and midterm general elections, Oregon ranks first, and the states of Colorado, California, and North Dakota also score high. All of these states are well known as national leaders in both the frequency of initiative use and the importance of the issues placed on the ballot, so their ranking on the measure of media salience provides a kind of construct validity. Very few states allow initiatives during primary elections; among those that do, California (as seen in the third column of Table 3.1) has by far the highest average salience. Initiatives during off-year elections, when neither the Congress nor the presidency is contested, also occur only in a handful of states. Among those states, Maine's initiatives reach the highest average salience. In fact, the most salient issues Maine has addressed through initiatives—such as repealing the income tax and restricting the usage of nuclear energy—have appeared during off-year elections. When all four kinds of elections are averaged together, Oregon, California, and Maine are the leaders, as seen in the fifth column of Table 3.1.

The Importance of the Electoral Context

While the salience of initiatives is the central independent variable under study, the dependent variable to be explained is state-level turnout. For as long as voting statistics have been kept, observers have recognized differences in turnout across various kinds of elections, and these differences remain stark in recent decades. Presidential elections routinely draw the largest number of voters to the polls. Primary, special, and off-year elections produce a much smaller turnout, as low as 10 percent in certain instances. The kinds of races on the ballot, then, affect the propensity of citizens to show up in the first place. Elections with the highest-profile races inspire the highest turnout, resulting from the substantial expenditures and efforts by campaigns to reach citizens, the coverage by the news media, and ultimately the amount of voter interest.

Table 3.1   Average Salience of Direct Legislation for Different Kinds of Elections, 1971–1997

State	Rank for Presidential General Elections	Rank for Midterm General Elections	Rank for Off-Year Elections	Rank for Primary Elections	Rank Overall	Average Salience Across All Elections
Oregon	1	1	T5	T5	1	.12
California	3	5	4	1	2	.1
Maine	22	9	1	4	3	.09
Colorado	2	4	T5	T5	4	.08
North Dakota	8	3	T5	2	5	.07
Idaho	11	2	T5	T5	6	.07
Ohio	9	20	2	T5	7	.06
Montana	6	8	T5	T5	8	.06
Arizona	4	12	T5	T5	9	.05
Washington	18	15	3	T5	10	.05
Alaska	23	6	T5	3	11	.04
South Dakota	7	13	T5	T5	12	.04
Florida	19	7	T5	T5	13	.04
Missouri	14	10	T5	T5	14	.04
Michigan	24	18	T5	T5	15	.04
Utah	10	11	T5	T5	16	.04
Arkansas	12	19	T5	T5	17	.03
Massachusetts	15	16	T5	T5	18	.02
Wyoming	20	14	T5	T5	19	.02
Nebraska	16	17	T5	T5	20	.02
Maryland	13	T23	T5	T5	21	.02
Nevada	17	21	T5	T5	22	.01
Oklahoma	21	22	T5	T5	23	.01
Illinois	24	T23	T5	T5	24	0
New Mexico	T25	T23	T5	T5	T25	0
Mississippi	T25	T23	T5	T5	T25	0
Kentucky	T25	T23	T5	T5	T25	0

Note: "T" indicates a tie with an average salience of 0, which occurred if the state either does not permit initiatives or popular referenda during a given kind of election or if none of the initiatives or popular referenda received coverage on the front page of the state's leading newspapers on the day following the election. The final column provides the average salience across all elections, calculated by summing the average salience for the four kinds of elections and dividing by four. Decimal places beyond those shown in the table are used to determine the rankings.

In a related way, recent research has found that the electoral context shapes the effect, if any, a given candidate race will have on turnout. Robert Jackson (1997) finds that the turnout boost attributable to senatorial and gubernatorial races depends upon when they are decided. During presidential-election years, according to Jackson's data, those races make very little difference in turnout because the presidential contest has already stimulated voting by those citizens who can be activated through campaign-related messages. Adding another race to the ballot, even a high-profile race for senator or governor, leads to only a minor, if any, additional increase in turnout. The picture looks very different, though, for midterm elections. Without the draw of a presidential race on the ballot, the presence of a senatorial or gubernatorial race makes a noticeable difference in the number of citizens who choose to cast a ballot.

The same principle ought to apply to initiatives, meaning that their effects should depend upon what else is on the ballot. The weakest effects should occur during presidential elections, when turnout is highest and the presidential election dominates media and public attention. The effects of initiatives should be stronger during midterm elections. That is, a high-salience piece of direct legislation should lead to a noticeable increase in turnout during midterm elections but a small, if any, increase during presidential elections. This line of reasoning should apply with even greater force to other elections. Special, primary, and odd-year elections have average turnouts lower than those for midterm general elections. With fewer prominent candidate races on the ballot, the presence of direct legislation should make an even stronger impact on turnout.

This set of claims can be stated succinctly as Hypothesis 2: *The lower the normal turnout for an election, the greater the impact that initiatives will have on raising turnout.* Testing this hypothesis requires one to observe multiple instances of several kinds of elections. The covariation between the presence of initiatives and the resulting turnout can then be assessed for each kind of election, allowing the effect sizes to be compared to each other. This would be difficult to do for special elections, though, because they are such unique events. That is, it is difficult to compare two special elections within a single state, let alone across states, because the races being contested change for each one. It is possible, however, to find a set of elections where the offices being voted upon stay roughly constant over time, allowing a baseline to be established. Four such instances are presidential general elections, midterm general elections, primary elections, and off-year general elections. These four kinds of elections will form the focus of the empirical analysis.

Direct Legislation and Turnout

I will first consider low-turnout primary elections where very few states allow initiatives. Even among the handful of states that allow them, voting on direct legislation is still a rare event. Alaska, Maine, North Dakota, and Oklahoma have all voted on direct legislation during a primary election in the last three decades, but each of these states have done so four times or fewer. The small number of observations makes systematic comparisons difficult. Only one state, California, has regularly voted on initiatives during primary elections. In California, nearly every primary election witnesses the presence of one or more initiatives, thereby providing an extensive record for analysis. Given the existence of abundant data only for California, I will restrict my analysis to that state. The estimation seeks to determine whether turnout rises when high-salience initiatives appear on the ballot.

The dependent variable is the total number of ballots cast, as provided by the office of the California secretary of state, divided by voting-age population. The data gathered include those from each primary election from 1970 to 1996; in California there is only one statewide primary election every two years. The central independent variable to be examined is the salience of initiatives, as described earlier in the chapter, which ranges from 0 in 1992 and 1994 to a high of 0.56 in 1978. The statistical model also includes the lagged dependent variable, taken from the most recent primary election when the same basic set of candidate races appeared on the ballot. Including the lagged dependent variable should account for temporal dependence in the model. In addition, the model includes dichotomous variables for the presence of presidential, gubernatorial, and senatorial contests both to determine whether they increase turnout and to provide a basis of comparison for the effects attributable to initiatives.

The empirical results are shown in the first column of Table 3.2. The coefficient on the salience of initiatives, 20.18, has the expected sign and is statistically significant at the .05 level. Its magnitude indicates that the highest observed salience of initiatives during this period, which occurred with the passage of Proposition 13 in 1978, led to an increase in turnout of 11.3 points. Exit polls taken after that election suggested that Proposition 13 led to an increase in turnout of 7 points, as 7 percent of the respondents answered yes to the question of whether they would not have voted had Proposition 13 not been on the ballot (Magleby 1984, 96). This survey-based estimate of a 7 percent boost in turnout is close to the estimate based on aggregate data developed here, providing greater confidence in it. My estimates also reveal the lim-

Table 3.2   The Relationship between Initiatives and Turnout

Variable	Primary Elections[a]	Off-Year Elections[b]	Midterm Elections[c]	Presidential[c] Elections
Constant	1.33 (5.58)	33.72** (5.09)		
Lagged Turnout	.71** (.13)	-.16 (.15)	.15 (.15)	.18 (.19)
Salience of Initiatives	20.18* (7.93)	19.3** (7.81)	9.18* (4.1)	-.18 (3.63)
Presidential Race	8.96 (6.54)			
Gubernatorial Race	3.63 (5.85)		3.85 (3.27)	.91 (1.65)
Senatorial Race	-1.11 (3.05)		1.90** (0.73)	.14 (.47)
N	13	41	300	350
Adjusted R^2	.75	.97	.73	.78

p<.05**p<.01

Note: Table entries are unstandardized regression coefficients. Standard errors are in parentheses.

[a] Estimates are from a time series analysis of California.

[b] Estimates are from a pooled time-series-cross-sectional analysis of ME, OH, and WA. Separate intercepts for OH and WA are not shown.

[c] Estimates are from a pooled time-series-cross-sectional analysis of all 50 states. Separate intercepts for each state are not shown.

itations of initiatives as a means to stimulate turnout; in most primaries, when the salience of initiatives is 0.1 or lower, the increase in turnout is no more than 2 percent.

A similar analysis can be conducted for off-year elections. Many states hold elections during odd years, when no seats for Congress are contested. Some states, such as Kentucky, New Jersey, and Virginia, put statewide contests on those ballots. Only three states, however, routinely decide initiatives during off years. Maine, Ohio, and Washington had initiatives on the ballot 13, 7, and 9 times, respectively, during the off-year elections between 1971 and 1997.[5] Accordingly, these states provide a sufficient number of observations for analysis. The analysis seeks to determine whether turnout in Maine, Ohio, and Washington rises, relative to its expected value, when a high-salience initiative is decided.

As before, the dependent variable is turnout, with the denominator measured as voting-age population and the numerator measured as the total number of ballots cast in the state that collects the data (Washington) and as the number of ballots cast for the highest-ranking contest in the other two states (Maine and Ohio). The central independent variable is the salience of initiatives. A separate intercept is estimated for each state, as is normally done when one uses pooled time-series-cross-section data (Stimson 1985). As before, the lagged dependent variable is included to account for the dynamics.

The second column of Table 3.2 summarizes the results of the estimation. The estimated coefficient on the salience of initiatives, 19.30, is positive, as expected, and is statistically significant at the .05 level. The data developed here, then, support the hypothesis that high-salience initiatives draw additional citizens to the polls during off-year elections. Thus, statistically significant effects of initiatives on turnout have been detected for primary and off-year elections; all that remains to analyze is midterm and presidential elections.

For midterm and presidential elections, turnout is measured as the number of votes cast for the highest-ranking contest on the ballot, divided by voting age population. All fifty states will be included in the model because, unlike primary and off-year elections, comparable data can be gathered for each of them during midterm and presidential elections. This allows for a pooled time-series-cross-sectional analysis. The model specification controls for the presence of gubernatorial and senatorial contests, which provides a basis of comparison for whatever effects initiatives are estimated to have. The lagged dependent variable is included to account for the dynamics of the model, and separate intercepts are estimated for each state. Preliminary analysis detected the presence of heteroskedasticity across states, which is addressed by calculating panel-corrected standard errors (Beck and Katz 1995).

The results for midterm general elections are summarized in the third column of Table3.2. We can see that both the salience of initiatives and the presence of a senatorial contest are statistically significant predictors of turnout.

---

5. California, the only other state to decide an initiative during an off-year, did it only twice during the period under study and is therefore excluded from this analysis.

The coefficient of 9.18 indicates that a high-salience initiative attracting 30 percent of the front-page paragraphs—a level achieved twenty times during the period under study—will boost turnout by about 3 points. That increase is larger than the 1.9-point increase that results from having a senatorial contest the same year.

We can see from the fourth column of Table 3.2 that a different pattern emerges during presidential elections. The fourth column shows that the coefficient on the salience of initiatives actually has the wrong sign (-0.18) but is nowhere close to statistical significance. At the same time, the presence of gubernatorial and senatorial races also have no statistically discernable relationship to turnout. These results parallel those of Jackson (1997), who finds that contests for other offices do not boost turnout during presidential elections.

Salience, Turnout, and the Electoral Context

One can get a greater sense of the magnitude of the effects across the different kinds of elections by examining Table 3.3. In addition, this table will help us evaluate Hypothesis 2, which asserts that the size of the effect increases as the normal level of turnout falls.

The first column of Table 3.3 shows the average turnout from 1971 through 1997 for the four kinds of elections. Not surprisingly, presidential elections rank first, with an average of 54.7% percent of voters participating.[6] Midterm elections average about 14 points lower, at 40.6 percent. Off-year elections show an average turnout of 34.3 percent in the three states that regularly vote on initiatives in them. Finally, the average turnout during California primaries is 32.4 percent, the lowest level achieved in the four types of elections.

If Hypothesis 2 is accurate, the effects on turnout attributable to initiatives should fall as we move down through presidential general elections, midterm general elections, off-year general elections, and primary elections. Columns 2 through 4 uncover precisely this pattern. Consider first the high-salience initiatives summarized in column 2, defined here as those ranking in the top decile of all initiatives voted upon during the period under study. Such a level was achieved if the set of initiatives on the ballot received 30 percent or more of the paragraphs on the front page. High-salience initiatives are estimated to

---

6. The averages are calculated across states. Because many states with small populations have higher-than-average turnout, the average turnout calculated across states is slightly higher than the national turnout.

Table 3.3   The Increase in Turnout According to the Salience
of Initiatives and the Type of Election

Type of Election	Average[a] Turnout	Turnout Increase,[b] High-Salience Initiatives	Turnout Increase,[b] Average-Salience Initiatives	Turnout Increase,[b] Low-Salience Initiatives
Presidential	54.7	0	0	0
Midterm	40.6	2.8	1.3	.4
Off-Year	34.3	5.8	2.7	.8
Primary	32.4	6.1	2.8	.8

[a] Cell entries are average turnout from 1971–1997. For presidential and midterm elections, all states are used to calculate the averages. For off-years, the averages are based only on ME, OH, and WA. For primary years, the averages are based only on California.

[b] Cell entries are the estimated point increase in turnout attributable under each set of circumstances.

have no effect upon turnout during presidential elections. However, the estimated effect rises to 2.8 points during midterm elections, 5.8 points during off-year elections, and 6.1 points during primary elections. The elections with the lowest turnout, then, are the ones where initiatives make the most difference. In the elections with the highest turnout—presidential elections—initiatives appear to have no effect at all. These results provide strong support for Hypothesis 2: the lesser the prominence of the candidate contests on the ballot and the lower the normal turnout, the greater the impact of the initiatives. A high-salience initiative during off-year or primary elections brings about 6 percent more people to the polls than an initiative of less prominence. However, when the presidential race appears and dominates the attention of both the media and the public, initiatives do not lead to increases in turnout.

Table 3.3 also confirms the accuracy of Hypothesis 1. This can be seen as we compare columns 2, 3, and 4. Column 3 shows the results for average-salience initiatives, defined as those at the mean for the period under study, when 14 percent of the front-page paragraphs discussed initiatives. Column 4 shows the results for low-salience initiatives, defined as the bottom decile, where initiatives garnered 4 percent or less of the paragraphs. As we move from high-salience to average-salience to low-salience initiatives, the relationship between initiatives and turnout declines. During midterm elections, for example, the effect size falls from 2.8 points to 1.3 points to 0.4 points. During primary elections, the effect size falls from 6.1 points to 2.8 points to 0.8 points. That is exactly the pattern that Hypothesis 1 predicts. Initiatives of average salience lead to voter turnout that is considerably lower than that generated by initiatives of high salience, while initiatives of low salience lead to barely any effect on turnout at all.

Conclusions

Debates over the desirability of initiatives have often considered their effects on voting participation. Previous research has found that, contrary to the claims of advocates of direct legislation, placing initiatives on the ballot has no effect on turnout. This chapter, however, supports the opposite view. Once we distinguish initiatives according to their salience to citizens and distinguish the kind of election under study, the relationship emerges quite clearly. The relationship is strongest for low-turnout elections like off-year and primary elections but declines all the way to zero for presidential elections. High-salience initiatives generate sizable impacts on turnout of about 6 points during off-year and primary elections, with smaller effects seen for average-salience initiatives and only tiny effects for low-salience initiatives.

What do these results imply for the low and declining voter turnout in the United States? It is clear that, at least in their present form, initiatives do not create effects large enough to reverse the trend or to alleviate concerns related to low turnout. As currently used, initiatives should be considered a partial but far from total solution to low levels of turnout. The use of initiatives as a *total* solution appears to be an instance where, as Cronin (1989—see especially Chapter 9) notes concerning other aspects of direct legislation, advocates of the initiative process have overstated their case. On the other hand, the results cannot speak directly to what would happen if the initiative was extended to the national level and given much attention by citizens, parties, interest groups, and the media. It seems fair to assume that the effects on turnout would be larger than those reported here, but how much larger is open to debate.

It is important to keep in mind that sizable effects of initiatives occur only during midterm, primary, and off-year elections. The implications of this finding can be interpreted in multiple ways. On the one hand, it is the low-turnout elections that are most in need of a boost. With rates of voting participation of twenty points or more below that in presidential elections, it is clear that midterm, primary, and off-year elections could benefit from any institution or reform that could shrink that gap. Because of the threat that the minority casting a ballot is unrepresentative of the larger population, these are the elections most vulnerable to concerns about the legitimacy of the results. Research has generally supported the proposition that the lower the turnout, the more different voters are from nonvoters (Rosenstone and Hanson 1993—see especially Chapter 8; Magleby 1984—see especially Chapter 6). The people most likely to be falling out of the voter ranks when we move from presidential to other kinds of elections are those who are lowest in socioeconomic status and in political skills and resources. If turnout in these other elections could be increased, the attitudes and characteristics of those who vote probably would more closely resemble those of the population at large. Placing initiatives on the ballot is one way to achieve that increase in turnout.

There is a limit, though, in how far this argument should be pushed. Initiatives, as currently used, reduce but do not eliminate the gap in participation between presidential and other elections. Thus, shifting more initiatives into the lower-profile elections would bring mixed results. Overall turnout would increase, often making the electorate more representative of the population. Yet, in turn, initiatives would surely inherit, to some degree at least, the same problems with democratic theory as candidate races in low-turnout elections. That is, initiatives decided during midterm, primary, and off-year elections would be decided by a narrower pool of citizens than would be the case if the initiatives appeared on the ballot during presidential years. The chances would increase of a deviation between the choices made by actual voters on an initiative and what the entire body of citizens would have chosen. This Catch-22 means that moving more initiatives to elections other than presidential ones, as a partial remedy to low turnout, would carry real costs. As with much of the debate over ballot initiatives, definitive evaluations of the consequences they create for turnout yield to mixed and often complicated answers upon closer scrutiny.

References

Beck, Nathaniel, and Jonathan N. Katz. 1995. What to do (and not to do) with time-series-cross-section data. *American Political Science Review* 89: 634–47.

Bennett, W. Lance. 1996. *News: The politics of illusion*. 3rd ed. New York: Longman.

Cree, Nathan. 1892. *Direct legislation by the people*. Chicago: A. C. McClurg.

Cronin, Thomas E. 1989. *Direct democracy: The politics of initiative, referendum, and recall*. Cambridge: Harvard University Press.

Everson, David H. 1981. The effects of initiatives on voter turnout: A comparative state analysis. *The Western Political Quarterly* 34: 415–25.

Gans, Herbert. 1980. *Deciding what's news*. New York: Vintage.

Green, Donald P., and Alan S. Gerber. 1999. Does canvassing increase voter turnout? A field experiment. *Proceedings of the National Academy of Sciences of the United States* 96: 10939–43.

Jackson, Robert A. 1997. The mobilization of U.S. state electorates in the 1988 and 1990 elections. *The Journal of Politics* 59: 520–37.

Lijphart, Arend. 1997. Unequal participation: democracy's unresolved dilemma. *American Political Science Review* 91: 1–14.

Magleby, David B. 1984. *Direct legislation: Voting on ballot propositions in the United States*. Baltimore: The Johns Hopkins University Press.

Piven, Frances Fox, and Richard A. Cloward. 1988. *Why Americans don't vote*. New York: Pantheon Books.

Rosenstone, Steven J., and John Mark Hansen. 1993. *Mobilization, participation, and democracy in America*. New York: Macmillan.

Schmidt, David D. 1989. *Citizen lawmaking: The ballot initiative revolution*. Philadelphia: Temple University Press.

Smith, Daniel A. 1999. The initiative to party: The role of political parties in state ballot initiatives. Paper presented at the annual meeting of the Western Political Science Association, Seattle, Washington.

Stimson, James A. 1985. Regression in space and time: A statistical essay. *American Journal of Political Science* 29: 914–47.

Sullivan, J. W. 1893. *Direct legislation by the citizenship through the initiative and referendum*. New York: True Nationalist Publishing.

Wattenberg, Martin P. 1998. Should Election Day be a holiday? *The Atlantic Monthly*, October, 42–51.

Wolfinger, Raymond, E., and Steven J. Rosenstone. 1980. *Who votes?* New Haven, CN: Yale University Press.

CHAPTER 4

Can't Buy Me Love: Interest Group Status and the Role of Political Professionals in Direct Democracy

David McCuan, Sonoma State University

The resurgence in direct democracy activity at the ballot has understandably led to increased attention by scholars of American politics. More accurately, attention has shifted to how interest groups and political actors use the tools of direct democracy to further their own goals. This attention has included a focus on the role of political professionals and the techniques of modern campaigns, including the employment of political consultants, pollsters, signature gatherers, political law attorneys, and the like by ballot measure committees. The focus of this chapter rests on the interaction between interest groups and their direct democracy actors, the political professionals.

While political scientists argue that all levels of electoral politics today witness the use of modern campaign techniques coupled with a greater presence of political professionals (Magleby and Patterson 1998a; 1998b), the role of these professionals and the reasons for their use among initiative campaigns are less well known. We believe more of these professionals exist, but we are not sure why they exist or where they came from. How do groups, both proponents and opponents, use political hacks in their campaigns? This chapter sets out to answer these questions.

Research Question: Investigating the Demand for Professional Political Services in Direct Democracy—Spillover Effects from Candidate Campaigns

The expanded role of political professionals in direct democracy presents important questions for social scientists. The initiative process was designed as a process for amateurs to work around powerful, entrenched interests (Shultz 1996; Cronin 1989; Magleby 1984). Professionalization of this process poses questions about changes in the practice of direct democracy. That is, how did a supposedly "amateur" process evolve into battles among interest groups where the campaigns include more and more political professionals? Most ballot measures today are characterized by the frequent use of signature-gathering crews, pollsters, and media consultants over the course of a campaign. These "political professionals" pose an interesting paradox for scholars of direct democracy since the initiative process was designed to enable ordinary citizens access to the ballot. If that access is blocked via traditional legislative channels and by high entrance fees associated with costs to hire political professionals, direct democracy itself may merely represent a branch of government with all of the barriers to entry that are incumbent on other forums rather than an effective conduit for citizen participation. If this is the case, it also suggests that political professionals are not merely passive service providers engaged in assisting those who hire them.

Indeed, if the use of professionals is now pervasive, in a broader sense, changes in the process of direct democracy are consequential for the viability of the process as a forum representing "the interests of the citizenry." The initiative process, as an element of a broader democratic society, has many challenges confronting democratic government. For example, democracies face a dilemma when constructing institutions that reflect some degree of involvement by citizens in the formation of public policy. This dilemma is often framed by discussion of whose interests prevail in debates over policy action. Battles over whose interests prevail occur in the context of competitive elections. And control of the policy agenda is most commonly granted to victorious parties soon after an election is held. However, in our system of checks and balances, the ability of the majority to stifle minority preferences is blocked to a certain degree by rules that govern the majority's conduct. For example, rules and procedures common to legislative organization prevent the majority from trampling on certain rights of the minority.

Direct democracy has fewer of these protections in place and this compounds the democratic dilemma. In cases of direct citizen participation on matters of policy, these protections may actually prove to be less stringent when measures are passed by an overwhelming majority of voters (Tolbert 1998). While common to the political cultures of many more states since the turn of the century, direct democracy was designed as a method of popular involvement in order to circumvent representative government (Barnett 1915; Hall 1921). As the tools of the Progressives became more important over the last twenty-five years or so, normative concerns about whose interests are actually served by direct democracy became an important theme in the literature of the field. This theme receives prominent attention because direct democracy is deemed to lack the "checks and balances" of legislatures.

The rise of ballot activity often is reflected by periodic expressions among scholars and observers critiquing the "democratic & representative" nature of direct democracy (California Commission on Campaign Financing 1992; Magleby 1994; Thomas 1989). These pontifications derived from one of two concerns. First, is the process sufficiently "democratic"? In other words, does the actual practice of initiative politics reflect the policy concerns of "the People"? A second view follows a different path. The excessive use of the initiative process leads to the frequent refrain: "Are we suffering from too much democracy?" This latter view is expressed as too much direct democracy coming at the expense of a deliberative process common to legislatures. This argument is often linked with a general critique of what the initiative process accomplishes "that is not already being accomplished by a representative government whose members are subject to periodic elections[.]" (Campbell 1997, 2). In this study, the focus on professionalization of the initiative process attempts to link the rise of ballot measure activity within the framework of these broader questions.

This chapter takes the first view into consideration by analyzing the types of initiatives that appeared on the California ballot from 1984 through 1998 in light of a typology borrowed from Wilson (1980) on the costs and distribution of benefits of proposed ballot measures. I also build on the database of initiatives analyzed by Bowler, Donovan, and Tolbert (1998). The data set includes all popular initiatives (placed on the ballot through the petition process) that appeared on the California ballot from 1984 through 1998. The typology is then supplemented by analysis of how campaigns actually spend campaign dollars. The categories for this spending include media and print advertising, expenditures for professional consulting, dollar transfers to other campaigns, and other categories noted below. The goals are to assess the types of popular initiatives appearing on the ballot and their frequency of appearance and success and to link these findings with campaign expenditure data provided in previous works. Through this effort, I hope to clarify theoretical approaches about the role of interest groups in direct democracy and how ballot measure campaigns spend their money. By combining information on the types of benefits that groups seek through the initiative process with how campaigns allocate their campaign resources, I hope that scholars can obtain a broader understanding of interest groups and direct democracy. Central to this goal are theoretical expectations about the level of professional involvement in ballot measure campaigns based on the typology provided by Wilson (1980). Before discussing the hypotheses, I will provide some theoretical context for both interest group policies and the role of political professionals in direct democracy. The basic argument is that, based on the perceived costs and benefits of popular initiatives, the distribution of campaign expenditures differs for specific categories of professional services. These expenditure variations exhibit different patterns as the interests and sponsors of ballot measures work to get different "types" of voters to the polls during the primary- and general-election periods.

Theoretical Background

The argument herein is that one of the consequences of the professionalization of initiative elections is that groups spend campaign dollars in different ways. The theoretical approach necessarily draws from the literature on campaigns and elections. I ask if the general conclusions of this literature are generalizable to contests other than those for candidate campaigns?

As a starting point, let us define the process of "professionalization" by an "initiative industry." When speaking of the "professionalization" of the initiative process, I am referring to the activities of consultants and firms who engage in tasks common to the practices of political-candidate campaigns. These tasks include professional political services germane to initiative measures, from the drafting of ballot language by political-law attorneys to the collection of signatures administered by professional signature-gathering firms. The tasks include other specialties common to candidate campaigns, such as the use of survey-research and direct-mail consultants.

Contrary to the claims of the literature on candidate-centered campaigns, initiative campaigns differ in the degree of professionalized assistance utilized by each campaign. This is so because different types of players in initiative politics provide differing levels of resources for campaigns. These players determine the level of professionalization as "learning" occurs by groups throughout direct democracy. Therefore, groups bring both differentials in resources and the learning experiences of other players to the game of initiatives.

This argument is made because interest-group players drive the professionalization of the initiative process. As professionalization is perceived to be successful, the process will spread. In other words, as professionals serve winning interests or succeed in defeating ballot measures (a "win" in the view of opponents of a measure), we should see an increase in the hiring of professionals. The campaign literature asserts this view. If we think of these political professionals as campaign resources, the differential use of resources becomes more distinct. In this version of the process, the focus is on the "narrow" players, such as politicians and interest groups who use the initiative process over and over, who drive the professionalization of the initiative process. These "narrow" groups (and their campaigns) use professionals because they have had previous experience and have "learned" from this experience, and they control an important campaign resource—money. These groups are also more likely to receive direct economic benefits from a given initiative. The initiative process manifests itself in the form of professionals hired to navigate a proposal through the different requirements at each stage of the process—from its early stages, prequalification and qualification, and later into the campaign stage. This paper asserts that only certain players and their campaigns will use political professionals and will utilize broadcast services to a large degree. It is these players who drive the subsequent professionalization of all measures, across all players in direct democracy. I expect that the use of professionals differs according to the requirements of initiative campaigns and the resources groups bring to bear on the process. In order to demonstrate this view, I classify initiatives into types of contests based on the groups that organize to support or defeat ballot measures.

Building a Typology of Initiative Contests

To adequately investigate the logic, and at the very least, the patterns of the California initiative process, I borrow the typology (Bowler, Donovan, and Tolbert 1998; Wilson 1980) that separates initiatives into quantifiable categories. These categories can then be used to demonstrate the types of initiatives that are more likely to pass or fail and, further, to demonstrate the kinds of proponents and opponents who receive beneficial effects from professionalization. The method of classification utilized for this work is drawn from Bowler, Donovan, and Tolbert (1998), and like them, we also draw upon the initial work of Wilson (1980) to create the typology.

The divisions of the typology are based upon the conception of "players" in an initiative game. These players represent either a broad or a narrow interest, and their behavior and resources are modified to assist either the few or the many in their respective quests. The identification of a proponent/opponent as either broad or narrow is an imperative in our study, for the questions, "Who benefits?" and "Who pays?" appear to have important effects on the conceptions of the voters and, hence, on the success of the initiative.

Type 1 Initiative Contests: "Interest Group Politics"

The first type of initiative is narrow versus narrow—or "Interest Group Politics" (Wilson 1980; Bowler, Donovan, and Tolbert 1998). This refers to legislation (or ballot measures in this case) where both the costs and the benefits of the initiative are narrowly distributed, such as a subsidy or regulation benefiting a small/narrow group at the expense of another small/narrow group (Wilson 1980; Bowler, Donovan, and Tolbert 1998). Thus, the public is not interested in the success or failure of the proposal, and the involved groups are therefore forced into hiring professionals and spending immense amounts of money to attract attention. Examples of narrow groups versus narrow groups include cases where trial attorneys and insurance companies battle each other—for example, Propositions 201 and 202 (on the 1996 California primary election ballot), as well as Propositions 207 and 211 (on the 1996 California general election ballot). These contests involved policy battles over attorney's fees, class-action suits, and limits on damages. Another interesting consequence of the public's attention is that this type of initiative is extremely unlikely to pass; from 1984 to 1998, only one initiative in this category was voted into law. The conflicts in this arena are often spillovers from a legislature unable to decide among several dueling interest groups, but they also tend to include battles between lawyers and insurance companies/corporations (Bowler, Donovan, and Tolbert 1998). My expectation is that these contests will use the services of political professionals freely and professionalization will be highest among such contests because of the resource capabilities of the parties involved. For the period between 1984 and 1998, eleven contests were characterized as Type 1 battles.

Type 2 Initiative Contests: "Entrepreneurial Politics"

The second type of initiative is that of a broad proponent challenging a narrow interest. Often collectively referred to as "Entrepreneurial Contests," this type of policy proposal usually requires the skill of a popular entrepreneur who can successfully organize the public around a crisis or scandal while simultaneously associating the legislation with cross-cultural, feel-good values, such as keeping children safe or promoting clean air (Wilson 1980). The opponent is put on the defensive from the outset, yet, because of its size and resource capabilities, the opponent is well-organized and well-funded enough to put up a worthy fight. This category pits two players against one another: the broad proponent with a large volunteer base (although funds are usually limited) against a narrow opponent with lower levels of public support but ample resources available to use for professionalized services. On its face, this type of contest appears to be the fairest of fights in the initiative wars, for the frequency of victory is roughly equal for either side (Bowler, Donovan, and Tolbert 1998). Examples of Type 2 contests include wildlife protection measures such as Proposition 117 (on the 1990 California primary election ballot), tobacco taxes such as Proposition 99 (on the 1988 California general election ballot), and Proposition 103, regarding auto insurance rates (on the 1988 California general election ballot). For the period between 1984 and 1998, twenty-two contests were characterized as Type 2 battles.

Type 3 Initiative Contests: "Client Politics"

The third category of initiative, known as "Client Contests," is the narrow group challenging the broad, diffuse group. The benefits of a proposed piece of legislation for this narrow group are concentrated, while the costs are widely distributed. In fact, the costs tend to be so widely distributed over the population that it has little reason to object; the perceived cost is low enough to the voter to prevent him/her from automatically rejecting the proposal (Wilson 1980). However, the narrow group is faced with a serious complication in this arena, for, although it must spend an immense amount to attract support, it must also attempt to maintain a level of secrecy. That is, if the narrow group reveals itself as the primary beneficiary of a self-drafted proposal, the voting populace tends to mistrust the motives of the group and thereby to defeat the initiative. Not surprisingly, therefore, groups in this type of initiative contest often attempt to remain as discreet as possible. Thus, my expectations for success in Type 3 battles are quite low (Bowler, Donovan, and Tolbert 1998). Examples of Type 3 initiative contests include efforts to balance the federal budget such as Proposition 35 (which qualified for the 1984 California general election ballot but was subsequently removed from the ballot by a court order), pesticide regulation (Proposition 135 on the 1990 California general election ballot), and Proposition 185, concerning public transportation funds (on the 1994 California general election ballot). For the period between 1984 and 1998, fifteen ballot measures were characterized as Type 3 contests.

Type 4 Initiative Contests: "Majoritarian Politics"

The final type includes "Majoritarian Contests." Such a contest is a challenge of a broad group by a broad group, and, thus, both costs and benefits are widely distributed across the population. Within this category, both industry and interest-group attention is low because of the lack of specific winners and losers; and there is a noted absence of professional, high-spending organizations (Wilson 1980). The public is left to its own devices to gather support for or opposition to proposed legislation, and, without the money available to narrow, well-organized groups, the public often relies upon free media to attract attention. This category includes a plurality of initiatives and appears the most controversial, as well as most successful, type of contest (Bowler, Donovan, and Tolbert 1998). Type 4 contests include the state lottery measure such as Proposition 37 (on the 1984 California general election ballot), school - funding initiatives such as Proposition 98 (on the 1988 California general election ballot), and Proposition 227, regarding the English language in public schools (on the 1998 California primary election ballot). For the period between 1984 and 1998, forty-five ballot measures were characterized as Type 4 contests.

The Universe of Ballot Measures in the Typology, 1984–1998

Popular initiative measures were coded into each of the four categories given above, and each category was given the lineup of proponents and opponents engaged in each contest. The division of initiatives into each category of the typology is presented in Table 4.1.

Table 4.1   California Initiatives by Result and Type of Measure, 1984–1998

Initiative	Prop. No.	Year	Election	Type	Approved ?	% Vote For	Type of Contest
Legislature—Rules and Procedures	24	1984	PRMY	IS	Y	53.1	2
Balanced Federal Budget	35	1984	GENL	IS	REMOVED	–	3
Taxation	36	1984	GENL	ICA	N	45.2	3
State Lottery	37	1984	GENL	ICA/IS	Y	57.9	1
Voting Material—English Only	38	1984	GENL	IS	Y	70.5	4
Reapportionment	39	1984	GENL	ICA/IS	N	44.8	4
Campaign Contribution Limits	40	1984	GENL	IS	N	35.5	4
Welfare and Public Assistance	41	1984	GENL	IS	N	37	4
Defendant Tort Damages	51	1986	PRMY	IS	Y	62.1	1
Public Employee Compensation	61	1986	GENL	ICA/IS	N	34.1	2
Taxes—Local Gov't and Districts	62	1986	GENL	IS	Y	58	4
English as Official Language	63	1986	GENL	ICA	Y	73.2	4
AIDS	64	1986	GENL	IS	N	29.3	4

Table 4.1   California Initiatives by Result and Type of Measure, 1984–1998 (*continued*)

Initiative	Prop. No.	Year	Election	Type	Approved ?	% Vote For	Type of Contest
Toxic Exposure and Water Discharge	65	1986	GENL	IS	Y	62.6	4
Legislative Campaigns—Spending	68	1988	PRMY	IS	Y	52.8	4
AIDS	69	1988	PRMY	IS	N	32	4
Wildlife and Coast Bond Act	70	1988	PRMY	ICA	Y	65.2	2
Appropriations Limit	71	1988	PRMY	ICA	N	48.9	4
Emergency Reserve	72	1988	PRMY	ICA	N	38.5	4
Campaign Funding	73	1988	PRMY	IS	Y	58.1	4
Hunger and Homeless Funding	95	1988	GENL	IS	N	45.2	2
Communicable Disease Tests	96	1988	GENL	IS	Y	62.4	4
State OSHA	97	1988	GENL	IS	Y	53.7	2
School Funding	98	1988	GENL	ICA/IS	Y	50.7	4
Tobacco Tax and Benefit Fund	99	1988	GENL	ICA	Y	58.2	2

Table 4.1   California Initiatives by Result and Type of Measure, 1984–1998 (*continued*)

Initiative	Prop. No.	Year	Election	Type	Approved ?	% Vote For	Type of Contest
Insurance Rates	100	1988	GENL	IS	N	40.9	1
Auto Accidents and Rate Claims	101	1988	GENL	IS	N	13.3	3
Reporting Exposure to AIDS	102	1988	GENL	IS	N	34.4	4
Auto Insurance	103	1988	GENL	IS	Y	51.1	2
Auto Insurance	104	1988	GENL	IS	N	25.4	3
Disclosures to Consumers	105	1988	GENL	IS	Y	54.5	2
Attorney Fees and Limits	106	1988	GENL	IS	N	46.9	1
Criminal Justice	115	1990	PRMY	ICA/IS	Y	57	4
Rail Transportation	116	1990	PRMY	IS	Y	53.3	4
Wildlife Protection	117	1990	PRMY	IS	Y	52.4	2
Reapportionment	118	1990	PRMY	ICA/IS	N	33	4
Reapportionment	119	1990	PRMY	ICA/IS	N	36.2	4

Table 4.1   California Initiatives by Result and Type of Measure, 1984–1998 (*continued*)

Initiative	Prop. No.	Year	Election	Type	Approved ?	% Vote For	Type of Contest
Environment and Public Health	128	1990	GENL	IS	N	35.7	2
Drug Enforcement and Treatment	129	1990	GENL	ICA/IS	N	27.7	4
Forest and Timber Acquisition	130	1990	GENL	IS	N	47.9	2
Term Limits and Campaign Finance	131	1990	GENL	ICA/IS	N	37.8	4
Marine Resources	132	1990	GENL	ICA	Y	55.8	1
Drug Enforcement and Treatment	133	1990	GENL	IS	N	31.9	4
Alcohol Surtax	134	1990	GENL	IS	N	31	2
Pesticide Regulation	135	1990	GENL	IS	N	30.4	3
State and Local Taxation	136	1990	GENL	ICA	N	47.9	4
Initiative and Referendum Process	137	1990	GENL	ICA	N	45	4
Forest and Timber Programs	138	1990	GENL	IS	N	28.8	3
Prison Inmate Labor and Tax Credits	139	1990	GENL	ICA/IS	Y	54.1	4

Table 4.1 California Initiatives by Result and Type of Measure, 1984–1998 (*continued*)

Initiative	Prop. No.	Year	Election	Type	Approved ?	% Vote For	Type of Contest
Term Limits and Operating Costs	140	1990	GENL	ICA	Y	52.2	4
Physician Assisted Death	161	1992	GENL	IS	N	45.9	4
PERS	162	1992	GENL	ICA	Y	51	3
Food and Candy Taxation	163	1992	GENL	ICA/IS	Y	66.6	3
Congressional Term Limits	164	1992	GENL	IS	Y	63.6	4
Budget Process and Welfare	165	1992	GENL	ICA/IS	N	46.6	4
Basic Health Care Coverage	166	1992	GENL	IS	N	30.8	2
State Taxation	167	1992	GENL	IS	N	41.2	2
School Vouchers	174	1993	GENL	ICA	N	30.4	4
Parks and Wildlife Land Conservation	180	1994	PRMY	IS	N	43.3	2
Increased Sentences—Three Strikes	184	1994	GENL	IS	Y	71.9	4
Public Transportation Funds	185	1994	GENL	IS	N	19.5	3

Table 4.1   California Initiatives by Result and Type of Measure, 1984–1998 (*continued*)

Initiative	Prop. No.	Year	Election	Type	Approved ?	% Vote For	Type of Contest
Health Services and Taxes	186	1994	GENL	ICA/IS	N	26.6	2
Illegal Aliens and Public Services	187	1994	GENL	IS	Y	58.9	4
Smoking and Statewide Regulation	188	1994	GENL	IS	N	29.3	3
Open Primary and Elections	198	1996	PRMY	IS	Y	59.5	4
Mobile Home Rent Control	199	1996	PRMY	IS	N	39.2	4
No-Fault Auto Insurance	200	1996	PRMY	IS	N	34.8	4
Attorney Fees–Class Actions	201	1996	PRMY	IS	N	40.7	1
Attorney Fees and Limits	202	1996	PRMY	IS	N	48.8	1
Attorney Fees and Limits	207	1996	GENL	IS	N	34.2	1
Campaign Funding	208	1996	GENL	IS	Y	61.3	4
Preferential Treatment	209	1996	GENL	ICA	Y	54.6	4
Minimum Wage Increase	210	1996	GENL	IS	Y	61.5	2

Table 4.1 California Initiatives by Result and Type of Measure, 1984–1998 (*continued*)

Initiative	Prop. No.	Year	Election	Type	Approved ?	% Vote For	Type of Contest
Attorney Fees and Security Fraud	211	1996	GENL	IS	N	25.7	1
Campaign Funding	212	1996	GENL	IS	N	49.2	4
Limitation on Recovery to Felons	213	1996	GENL	IS	Y	76.8	4
Health Care, Consumer Protection	214	1996	GENL	IS	N	42	1
Medical Marijuana Use	215	1996	GENL	IS	Y	55.6	4
Health Care, Consumers and Taxes	216	1996	GENL	IS	N	38.8	1
Top Income Tax Brackets	217	1996	GENL	IS	N	49.2	2
Taxation—Voter Approval Limits	218	1996	GENL	IS	Y	56.6	4
School Spending Limits—Administration	223	1998	PRMY	IS	N	45.5	1
State Funded Design and Engineering	224	1998	PRMY	ICA	N	38.2	2
Term Limits—Congress	225	1998	PRMY	IS	Y	52.9	4
Political Contributions by Employees	226	1998	PRMY	IS	N	46.7	2

Table 4.1   California Initiatives by Result and Type of Measure, 1984–1998 (*continued*)

Initiative	Prop. No.	Year	Election	Type	Approved ?	% Vote For	Type of Contest
English Language—Public School	227	1998	PRMY	IS	Y	60.9	4
Wildlife Traps and Animal Poisons	4	1998	GENL	IS	Y	55.6	3
Indian Gaming and Tribal Gambling	5	1998	GENL	IS	Y	61.5	3
Prohibitions on Horsemeat	6	1998	GENL	IS	Y	59.3	3
Air Quality Improvement	7	1998	GENL	IS	N	42.7	2
School Class Size and Site Councils	8	1998	GENL	IS	N	38.4	3
Electric Utilities Assessments	9	1998	GENL	IS	N	27	2
State and County Tobacco Surtax	10	1998	GENL	ICA/IS	Y	50.5	3
Totals:	93	GENL #: 69 PRMY #: 24			Y #: 40 N#: 52	46.5% Mean Vote "Yes"	

Figure 4.1   Expectation for Professional Services by Type of Interest Group Contest

	Narrow	Broad, Diffuse
Narrow	Type 1 Contest	Type 3 Contest
	"Interest Group Politics"	*"Client Politics"*
	Trial Attorneys vs. Insurance Companies	Repeal of Smoking Regulations
	(Professionalization is Highest)	(Prof. is Higher Than Type 2)
Broad, Diffuse	Type 2 Contest	Type 4 Contest
	"Entrepreneurial Politics"	*"Majoritarian Politics"*
	Environmental Measures Minimum Wage	Political Reform and Criminal Justice Measures
	(Prof. is Lower Than Type 3)	(Professionalization is Lowest)

Table 4.1 illustrates the number of measures that were qualified for the ballot overall (N = 93) as well as the number of measures that appeared on the primary election ballot (N = 24) versus the number that appeared on the general election ballot (N = 69). Merely 40 of the 92 measures that ultimately appeared on the ballot passed—a passage rate of 43.5 percent.

Hypotheses and Initial Findings on the Extent of Professionalization

Figure 4.1 lists the typology of and the expectations for the extent of professionalization in all four types of contests.

Given this typology and the expectations for professionalized services, I investigate the following hypotheses:

Hypothesis 1: In the case of Type 1 campaigns, or "Interest Group Politics," the use of political professionals will be at its highest as these campaigns reflect groups who have the resources to contract with political professionals for the services they offer.

Table 4.2   California Ballot Measures by Type of Interests Involved, 1984–1998

Type of Initiative Contests	Mean % Yes Vote	% of All Measures that Pass	N
Narrow Proponent, Narrow Opposition (*Type 1 Contests*)	44.1	5	12
Diffuse Proponent, Narrow Opposition (*Type 2 Contests*)	43.1	20	22
Narrow Proponent, Diffuse Opposition (*Type 3 Contests*)	40.7	15	15
Diffuse Proponent, Diffuse Opposition (*Type 4 Contests*)	49.4	60	44
Average/Totals:	**44.3**	**100**	**93**

Hypothesis 2: In the case of Type 4 campaigns, or "Majoritarian Politics," the use of political professionals will be at its lowest as these campaigns reflect groups who possess fewer resources to contract with political professionals.

In the case of Type 2 ("Entrepreneurial Politics") and Type 3 ("Client Politics") races, predictions about the use of political professionals are less robust because of the muddied nature of the interests that operate in these contests. Consequently, we are less convinced that theory can adequately predict the level of professionalization in these campaigns other than to argue that it is mixed and likely to fall between the extremes of Type 1 and Type 4 races.

Based on the typology listed in Figure 4.1, I arrive at a schedule that illustrates the success and failure of initiative contests in the state between 1984 and 1998.

Table 4.2 illustrates the success and failure of measures based on the typology offered by Wilson (1980) and Bowler, Donovan, and Tolbert (1998). As we can see, Type 4 contests are the most frequent during this period (N = 44) and consist of 60 percent of all popular initiatives that passed between 1984 and 1998. The mean percentage "Yes" vote for these contests was 49.4 percent.

Type 1 contests, where we expect professionalization to be at its lowest, constitute but 5 percent of all measures that passed during this period. The lack of measures on the ballot at this time may be somewhat surprising, given the frequent criticisms of direct democracy as a playground only for affluent interests. However, these interests are involved in the process often as opponents to a given measure. The mean percentage "Yes" vote for Type 1 contests was 44.1 percent. As a final note, Type 3 contests have the lowest mean percentage "Yes" vote among all four categories of the typology. The mean percentage "Yes" vote for Type 3 contests was 40.7 percent. This factor is highlighted later—in the discussion of how differing interests allocate funds in direct democracy campaigns.

Interest Groups and Spending on Political Professionals, 1984–1998

One of the most telling trends of campaign spending involves dollar transfers among ballot committees. Independent expenditures for ballot measures are an unregulated activity. This is an unforeseen consequence of current regulations that require reporting of expenditures, but it is generally believed that "transfers" by supporters and opponents help capture the extent of independent expenditure activities.[1] When we analyze how different initiative contests spend money, dollar transfers prove insightful as a category of interest especially for Type 3 contests.

Table 4.3 presents an analysis of initiative spending according to the types of contests between players. As expected, we see larger expenditures by Type 1 campaigns for categories of expenses that rely on political professionals. Not surprisingly, costs related to broadcast advertising are the highest expenditure for Type 1 players. If we add this category of broadcast spending to the categories of professional consultants, signature-gatherers, and pollsters, as well as to the category of dollar transfers to other campaigns, we account for al-

---

1. This may be changing, however. In the last three election cycles—1994, 1996, and 1998—there has been a rise in multiple (more-than-one-ballot-measure) committees that channel dollars for support and opposition of more than one initiative. The ability to track where dollars are contributed and spent has been problematic as a result. Usually, tracking these expenditures includes dividing expenditures of joint committees evenly across the measures of concern. See also Tobin 1997, especially pp. 32–34.

Table 4.3   Initiative Contests and Campaign Budgets—
Where Does the Money Go?

	Narrow	Broad, Diffuse
Narrow	Type 1 Contest *"Interest Group Politics"* **(Professionalization is Highest)** % Spending-Broadcast: 34.4 % Spending-Prof. Cons.: 28.4 % Spending-Sigs./Surveys: 11.1 % Spending-Dollar Transfers: 23.7 % Spending-Literature & Mail: 2.6 % Spending 'Other:' 0.7%	Type 3 Contest *"Client Politics"* **(Prof. is Higher Than Type 2)** % Spending-Broadcast: 25.6 % Spending-Prof. Cons.: 24.1 % Spending-Sigs./Surveys: 9.8 % Spending-Dollar Transfers: 29.6 % Spending-Literature & Mail: 4.3 % Spending 'Other:' 6.8
Broad, Diffuse	Type 2 Contest *"Entrepreneurial Politics"* **(Prof. is Lower Than Type 3)** % Spending-Broadcast: 36.4 % Spending-Prof. Cons.: 23.5 % Spending-Sigs./Surveys: 10.7 % Spending-Dollar Transfers: 23.1 % Spending-Literature & Mail: 7.2 % Spending 'Other:' 5.3	Type 4 Contest *"Majoritarian Politics"* **(Professionalization is Lowest)** % Spending-Broadcast: 20.2 % Spending-Prof. Cons.: 16.7 % Spending-Sigs./Surveys: 10.7 % Spending-Dollar Transfers: 22.1 % Spending-Literature & Mail: 6.1 % Spending 'Other:' 25.3

most 98 percent of expenditures in the typical "Interest Group Politics" initiative battle. By comparison, we expect Type 4 contests to demonstrate the lowest amount of spending for professional political services overall. This rate of reliance on professional consulting seems to hold true when we examine the percentage of spending devoted to professionals.

While the theoretical expectation that professionalization is highest among Type 1 contests holds true, a focus on this element alone misses an important part of the data. Type 3 contests, where "narrow" interests challenge "broad, diffuse" groups, use the transfer of campaign dollars at a much higher rate than the other types of contests. While my expectation is that the arena of "Client Politics" will exhibit mixed levels of professionalization, clearly one strategy of this type of battle is funneling dollars (or transferring funds) to other campaigns. Although evidence of this phenomenon is not presented here, there is a general view that this transfer of dollars occurs as "narrow" proponents work to move their own ballot measures as well as other measures through the various stages of the process—from their formulation and the collection of signatures to qualification and onto the campaign stage. That is, instances of dollar transfers seem highest in cases of "Client Politics."

Conclusion

The use of a typology such as that of Wilson (1980) and Bowler, Donovan, and Tolbert (1998) is fraught with peril. Policy distinctions are problematic as narrow groups frequently pursue a strategy of opposing initiatives rather than proposing them. This is further compounded by definitional questions concerning the categorization of groups who sponsor initiatives and the assessment of a particular measure's consequences (see, for example, Campbell 1997). This typology, however, relies on definitional parameters that differ from scholar to scholar. To ameliorate this concern, I provide a list of which measures were placed into each category in the Appendix. I freely acknowledge the limitations of a typology and the concerns it raises. Nevertheless, one way to deal with these concerns is to analyze campaign expenditures in light of this typology in order to illuminate the spending patterns of supporters and opponents. This work examines initiative expenditures in the context of how the costs and benefits of ballot measures play out and is thus intended to inform our theory building about the nexus between interest groups' and political professionals' behaviors.

There is at least one area of concern left unresolved by this work. Some scholars suggest that a spending differential between proponents and opponents of ballot measures may explain some of the imbalance between players in direct democracy (see Lowenstein 1982). Furthermore, Bowler, Donovan, and Tolbert (1998) argue that the advantages of "moving second" may be a factor in resources brought to bear throughout the stages of direct democracy. I have not tackled either of these criticisms in a substantive manner.

However, the chapter does argue that one way of distinguishing the difference between narrow groups and grassroots groups is by virtue of the kinds of benefits each seeks from policy proposals. Narrow groups are likely to seek divisible benefits distributed in a concentrated way, while grassroots groups are likely to seek a broader distribution of benefits and can conceivably seek collective goods. This means that groups such as labor unions, no matter how broad the membership base, tend to pursue narrowly sectional interests. On the other hand, consumer groups and environmental-issues groups are examples of those that tend to promote broader causes.

A number of points can be made in light of this simple classification. First, this approach deals with the subject matter of propositions implicitly, not explicitly. We justify this on the grounds that much of the criticism of the process of direct democracy is structured this way; that is, "narrow" interests pursue "narrow" ends. Therefore, the important task is to identify whether narrow interests are at work, since we "know" (or at least critics assume) that these groups will pursue their own interests at the expense of the public good. Over and above this, we do recognize the difficulty of placing propositions into unique, single categories. For example, even a relatively straightforward measure like a liquor tax can be classified as either a tax issue or as a moral issue. Similarly, school vouchers can be seen as both an educational and a tax issue.[2]

A final point is necessary. One element that seems clear from the data compiled throughout the project and confirmed through both interviews with political professionals and campaign expenditure reports is that campaigns involve political professionals earlier and earlier in the process. In addition, there seems to be some anecdotal evidence that as groups continue through the campaign stage with these political professionals, they are more likely to generate professionalized opposition. This occurs because of two conditions: Either the interests involved are capable of raising sufficient sums of money to pay for political professionals, and/or past experience with ballot measures results in sufficient "learning" by proponents and opponents to warrant the hiring of political professionals. The final condition is met when proponents and

---

2. See Lowenstein (1982) for further information on the "single-subject" problems of ballot measures.

opponents seek guidance in the nonpartisan field of initiative politics. The services provided by consultants can therefore assist both "veterans" and "rookies" of the initiative wars with navigation through the many stages of the process.

References

Barnett, James. 1915. *The operation of the initiative, referendum, and recall in Oregon.* New York: MacMillan.

Bowler, Shaun, Todd Donovan, and Caroline Tolbert, eds. 1998. *Citizens as legislators: Direct democracy in the United States.* Columbus: Ohio State University Press.

California Commission on Campaign Financing. 1992. *Democracy by initiative.* Los Angeles: Center for Responsive Government.

Campbell, Ann. 1997. The citizen's initiative and entrepreneurial politics: Direct democracy in Colorado, 1966–1994. Paper Presented at the annual meeting of the Western Political Science Association, Tucson, AZ, March.

Cronin, Thomas. 1989. *Direct democracy: The politics of initiative, referendum, and recall.* Cambridge: Harvard University Press.

Donovan, Todd, and Shaun Bowler. 1998. An overview of direct democracy in the American states. In *Citizens as legislators,* edited by Shaun Bowler, Todd Donovan, and Caroline Tolbert. Columbus: Ohio State University Press.

Donovan, Todd, Shaun Bowler, David McCuan, and Kenneth Fernandez. 1998. Contending players and strategies: Opposition advantages in initiative campaigns. In *Citizens as legislators,* edited by Shaun Bowler, Todd Donovan, and Caroline Tolbert. Columbus: Ohio State University Press. Columbus: Ohio State University Press.

DuBois, Philip, and Floyd Feeney. 1992. *Improving the California initiative process: Options for change.* University of California: California Policy Center Report.

Gerber, Elisabeth. 1996. Legislative response to the threat of popular initiatives. *American Journal of Political Science* 40: 99–128.

Hall, Arnold. 1921. *Popular government.* New York: MacMillan.

Kelley, Stanley. 1956. *Professional public relations and political power.* Baltimore: The Johns Hopkins University Press.

Appendix—Characteristics of Initiative Sample by Type of Contest

	Type 1	Type 2	Type 3	Type 4
Number of Measures in a Primary Election	4	6	0	14
Number of Measures in a General Election	8	16	15	30
Number of Initiative Statutes	10	17	12	27
Number of Initiative Constitutional Amendments	1	3	2	8
Number Classified as Both IS/ICA	1	2	1	9
Highest % Vote "Yes"	62.1 (Prop. 51 1986)	65.2 (Prop. 70 1988)	66.6 (Prop. 163 1992)	76.8 (Prop. 213 1996)
Lowest % Vote "Yes"	34.2 (Prop. 207 1996)	26.6 (Prop. 186 1994)	13.3 (Prop. 101 1988)	29.3 (Prop. 64 1986)
Mean % Vote "Yes"	44.9	43.1	40.7	49.6
Electoral Success, 1984–1990*	Passed: 3 Rejected: 2	Passed: 7 Rejected: 5	Passed: 0 Rejected: 5	Passed: 12 Rejected: 15
Electoral Success, 1992–1998	Passed: 0 Rejected: 7	Passed: 1 Rejected: 9	Passed: 6 Rejected: 3	Passed: 11 Rejected: 6
Overall Success, 1984–1998	Passed: 3 Rejected: 9	Passed: 8 Rejected: 14	Passed: 6 Rejected: 8	Passed: 23 Rejected: 21

*Prop. 35 removed by the CA Supreme Court from the 1984 G.E. ballot and is not included.

Lascher, Edward, Michael Hagen, and Steven Rochlin. 1996. Gun behind the door? Ballot initiatives, state policies and public opinion. *Journal of Politics* 58: 760–75.

Lowenstein, Daniel. 1982. Campaign spending and ballot propositions: Recent experience, public choice theory, and the First Amendment. *UCLA Law Review.* 86: 505–641.

Magleby, David. 1984. *Direct legislation: Voting on ballot propositions in the United States.* Baltimore: Johns Hopkins University Press.

Magleby, David, and Kelly Patterson. 1998a. Consultants and direct democracy. *PS* 31: 160–69.

_____. 1998b. The art of persuasion: Consultants and the rise of direct democracy. Paper presented at the annual meeting of the American Political Science Association, Boston, MA, September.

McCuan, David, Todd Donovan, Shaun Bowler, and Kenneth Fernandez. 1998. California's political warriors: Campaign professionals and the initiative process. In *Citizens as legislators,* edited by Shaun Bowler, Todd Donovan, and Caroline Tolbert. Columbus: Ohio State University Press. Columbus: Ohio State University Press.

Munro, William, ed. 1912. *The initiative, referendum, and recall.* New York: Appleton and Co.

Schmidt, David. 1989. *Citizen lawmakers: The ballot initiative revolution.* Philadelphia: Temple University Press.

Schrag, Peter. 1998. *Paradise lost: California's experience, America's future.* New York: New Press.

Shultz, Jim. 1996. *The initiative cookbook: Recipes and stories from California's initiative wars.* San Francisco: The Democracy Center.

Smith, Daniel. 1998. *Tax crusaders and the politics of direct democracy.* New York: Routledge.

Thomas, Tom. 1989. Corporate political strategy and influence in the California initiative process. Ph.D. diss., University of California, Berkeley.

Tobin, Mitch. 1997. Campaign spending and California ballot measures, 1924–1994. Master's thesis, University of California, Berkeley.

Tolbert, Caroline. 1998. Changing rules for state legislatures: Direct democracy and governance policies. In *Citizens as Legislators: Direct Democracy in the United States,* edited by Shaun Bowler, Todd Donovan, and Carolyn Tolbert. Columbus, OH: Ohio State University Press.

Wilson, James. 1980. *The politics of regulation.* New York: Basic Books.

CHAPTER 5

The Impact of Campaign Finance on Ballot Issue Outcomes

Richard Braunstein, University of South Dakota

Much of the contemporary research on direct democracy has concluded that campaign spending is the best predictor of the success of ballot measures. From media accounts to academic literatures in political science and law, many feel that spending by well-financed interests dominates the politics of initiative and referendum voting. This, as is commonly argued, leaves little opportunity for ordinary citizens to use direct democracy to construct laws of their own choosing, laws that would qualify as democratic because they were first proposed and then approved by the public that has to live under the obligations those laws impose.

The contemporary research has not, however, offered clear answers to the question of whether different sources of campaign finance have distinct impacts on final voting outcomes. Much of the research moves from the observed effect of campaign spending to the conclusion that money, not citizens, controls these processes. What is missing is a study of where the money comes from. For instance, we know that 78 percent of ballot campaigns were won by the side that spent the most money (Cronin 1989, 215; Zisk 1987). We also know that campaign spending is particularly influential when money is spent in opposition to ballot measures (Magleby 1984, 146-47; Lowenstein 1982). What we do not know is the source of money involved in these efforts.

Contemporary wisdom suggests that because money rules, citizens lose. But what if it was found that citizens fund many of the political committees responsible for supporting and opposing ballot measures? Additionally, how would we view the process if we were able to determine that many of the measures supported by organizational interests pursued inclusive legislation benefiting the entire community? Presumably, these findings would reduce our fears of special-interest capture, because it was the public, not corporations or other narrowly interested groups, reaping the benefits of direct legislation regardless of who advanced the funding necessary to secure its passage. Here, our understanding of the role of campaign spending is framed in a different light. We must evaluate the source of campaign finance and substantive outcomes to better understand the impact of money in ballot issue elections, and, moreover, the character of direct democracy.

The current research seeks to address these essential questions by empirically challenging commonly held perceptions in this area of American politics research. The project disaggregates the source of contributions to California and Colorado ballot issue committees from 1992 through 1998 to determine the percentage of campaign spending coming from individual citizens and organizations. Additionally, the source of contributions is juxtaposed with the type of legislation resulting from ballot issue elections to examine the relationship between spending behavior and substantive outcomes. Ultimately, the goal is to build a better understanding of the role citizens play in direct democracy elections.

Resource Bias in Ballot Issue Elections

Although it is difficult to generalize about direct democracy as an institution of state lawmaking because of the tremendous variation among the states that permit direct democracy, the procedures adopted to regulate the ballot contests, the professionalization of campaigns, the media coverage of campaigns, and the propositions' subject matter, researchers have observed a number of specific instances where well-funded, organized groups have dominated these contests (Broder 2000; Smith and Herrington 2000). And while it is generally noted that campaign spending is not, in itself, a guarantee of ballot success, many have concluded that "the odds are with the big spenders" (Cronin 1989).

In particular, contemporary researchers have discovered that groups with access to financial resources are particularly successful in opposing ballot measures. Daniel Lowenstein (1982) noted that one-sided spending[1] by propo-

---

1. According to Lowenstein, one-sided spending occurs when at least $250,000 is spent and when that spending is at least twice as much as the other side. However, this was defined for research in California, which is not likely to be consistent with campaign spending in other states with these procedures (e.g., Colorado, Nevada, South Dakota, etc.).

sition opponents to block a proposed measure was successful in 90 percent of contests, suggesting that groups with the capacity to spend large sums of money not only have the potential to pursue desired legislation but also to block proposed measures contrary to their interests. This conclusion was corroborated by David Magleby (1994), who found that when opposition groups spent as much as, or more than, the proposition's initiators, they were successful in blocking 80 percent of measures.

Studies of the petition stage of ballot contests have revealed similar findings. Groups with the financial resources to hire professional-consulting, petition-gathering, and campaign fund-raising firms have an advantage in qualifying a proposition for the ballot. A primary source of this advantage is the fact that these firms own organized lists of potential supporters and detractors and thus can efficiently pursue ballot qualification with lower startup costs (California Commission 1992; Cronin 1989, 217; Berg and Holman 1989).

Finally, it has been suggested that resource bias may be stronger in direct democracy than in other types of elections where variables such as candidate charisma, incumbency, party identification, and general media coverage can mitigate differences in financial resources. Voting cues in these cases are limited to what is provided by supporting and opposing campaign committees. This is particularly relevant for the less educated voters, who are "inhibited by the unnecessarily complex and lengthy propositions" presented on the ballot (Magleby 1984, 183). Thus, the groups behind the committees serve a particularly important role insofar as they are the principal source of information for the electorate. Therefore, an effective use of the media may be singly responsible for a successful or unsuccessful ballot campaign, which is contingent upon a group's ability to purchase media time.

Moreover, ballot issue committees are not subject to the same campaign finance regulations that candidate committees are, further increasing their impact on public policy making. Even though the federal government and many state governments have instituted limitations on contributions to candidate campaigns, there are no limits whatsoever on contributions to ballot issue committees in the United States.

Each of these factors shares a common focus on resource bias as a prominent source of direct democracy's perceived failures, but none concern who actually funds campaigns for and against these ballot measures. One sees a great deal of discussion about what happens when a proponent or opponent spends more, but little is said about who those proponents and opponents are. As a result, a series of incomplete assumptions is developed. For instance, it is assumed that because of the noted resource bias, the public (e.g., citizen groups or individual citizens) does not benefit from the use of initiative or referendum contests. Further, it is assumed that only legislation reflecting the narrow interests of well-funded groups can be secured through these contests. Finally, it is assumed that representative institutions are considerably more responsive to citizen interests and should be used, rather than initiatives or referenda, to pursue desired legislation. While some of these assumptions may be correct, there is a strong need to reconsider their empirical validity with more updated and sophisticated research than has been offered to date.

In any case, it is not the intention of this research to dismiss the role of resource bias in direct democracy contests. Instead, the current research is concerned with studying whether the specific incidence of resource bias in direct democracy contests carries with it the implications assumed by many observers of direct democracy. To engage in a more complete study, we must disaggregate total spending to see where the money being spent actually comes from. Clearly, if the breakdown of contributions includes a variety of actors beyond the well-financed interest group, many of the conclusions offered in contemporary literatures need to be reconsidered.

Research Design and Hypotheses

Two hypotheses tested in this research were designed to continue the discussion of the role of money in ballot issue elections. Each hypothesis, which can be understood more generally as a question in an ongoing dialogue, is based on the underlying assumption that contemporary use of direct democracy has been dominated by well-funded organizational interests.[2] The questions are framed in the context of expectations generated in the existing literature so that we may fairly evaluate their merit given the scope of the current data. The questions are as follows:

---

2. This conclusion is based exclusively on studies of the aggregate amount of contributions available to campaign committees in support of or opposition to specific propositions (Lowenstein 1982; Magleby 1984; Zisk 1987; Cronin 1989). This introduces two concerns for the present research. First, is it accurate that overwhelming support for ballot issues comes from well-funded interests rather than individual or grassroots sources? Second, is there a correlation among funding sources, funding amount, and final voting outcomes?

H1 = Organizational contributions to ballot issue committees determine a ballot measure's success or failure at the ballot.

H2 = Organizational contributions to ballot issue committees are directed at the passage of ballot issues offering narrowly concentrated benefits to particular interests within the community.

Data Set

Campaign spending data were collected from the 1992 through 1998 elections in California and Colorado, two states that rely heavily on direct democracy to pursue public policy (Tolbert 1996). Data were obtained from the California and Colorado secretary of states' reports for all ballot issue committees registered for each of these elections.[3] Once obtained, the records were disaggregated to determine their source (i.e., individual citizens or organizations) and intended use (i.e., whether they were designated to support or oppose issues).

The dependent variable employed in this research is PASSFAIL, a dummy variable coded 1 if a ballot measure passed and 0 if the measure failed. PASSFAIL was used to study the impact of several independent variables on a proposition's success at the ballot. The analysis began with several bivariate correlations designed to consider the effect of the campaign spending and, later, legislative typology variables. Because some of these variables were introduced for the first time, a wide range of correlations were tested to insure the relevance of these variables to the current analysis. These correlations have the advantage of adding both simplicity and detail to this research.

The analysis continued with a series of multivariate logistic regressions. The logistic model contributes to the current research by estimating the effect of independent variables on the probability of a measure's success. A logistic regression, or probability model, works particularly well with dichotomous dependent variables, such as whether a ballot measure passed or failed. A logistic model can estimate the likelihood of predicting a successful ballot measure, which will help corroborate (or contradict) the observations taken from the bivariate correlations, as well as facilitating a more reliable prediction of what contributes to a ballot issue's electoral success.

---

3. In California, that data was collected from the Political Reform Division of the Secretary of State's Office, and in Colorado, it was collected from the Elections Division of the Secretary of State's Office.

The list of independent variables includes measures of campaign spending and legislative typology. FUNDSOUR focuses on the main source of monetary contributions for the entire campaign. FUNDSOUR has three values coding the source of campaign contributions: (1) individual, (2) mixed(when there was less than a 20 percent difference between funding sources) and (3) organizational.[4] FUNDSUPP measures the funding source of supporting campaign committees, and FUNDOPP measures the funding source of opposing committees. Values for both FUNDSUPP and FUNDOPP are the same as the values for FUNDSOUR.

In addition to the campaign spending variables, an independent variable measuring the type of legislation was included to test whether the different sources of contributions (individual and organizational) are correlated with the type of substantive laws put before voters. TYPE considers two types of proposed legislation, inclusive and exclusive.[5] The use of this variable allows us to consider whether individuals and organizations are more likely to contribute in support of ballot issues offering widely accessible benefits than in support of ballot issues that offer narrowly distributed benefits accessible to select members of the community. Clearly, the common expectation is that organizations are more likely to support narrowly scripted laws that benefit select members of the community. From the analysis below, we will be able to consider whether this expectation is empirically valid, while at the same

---

4. Differentiating organizational from individual contributions was quite simple in both states, as the source of each contribution of more than $100.00 must be declared in California and more than $25 in Colorado to comply with statutes governing campaign procedures. One need only look at the name of record on the disclosure form to determine the source. Individuals noted on the contributions form were treated as individuals and all others (e.g., corporations, political parties, professional associations, interest groups) were treated as organizations.

5. In order for a ballot measure to be defined as inclusive, the benefits that result from the public policy created must be accessible to the entire community without exception. This is not to suggest that the entire community *must* benefit but that they must have, at minimum, the potential to benefit. If the benefits of legislation are accessible to the individuals who must live under the laws that ballot measure would create if passed, then we may consider that legislation inclusive. By contrast, when the benefits derived from ballot propositions are narrowly distributed (i.e., offering no potential benefits to identifiable segments of the community regardless of their proportional size), that law must be categorized as exclusive legislation. This label is justified by the fact that only distinct segments of the public can benefit from the policies produced in ballot issue elections. Thus, exclusive measures exist when the public, understood in the broadest terms, does not have access to the potential benefits of legislation.

time increasing our understanding of what contributes to the probability of a ballot measures success.

Findings: Individual and Organizational Funding Sources

H1 = Organizational contributions to ballot issue committees determine a measure's success or failure at the ballot.

To analyze this widely held view that well-funded organizations dominate the politics of direct democracy, it was necessary to disaggregate ballot issue committee revenues by the source of contributions. Here, a distinction was drawn between individual contributions and organizational contributions. The expectation, based on popular perception, is that organizational contributions far outpace individual contributions, making it difficult for citizens to "make a difference." The data show that this is not always the case. Individual spending outpaced organizational spending in 17 percent of the ballot issues studied here, or in 13 of 78 measures. Additionally, we saw parity between individual and organizational spending in 5 percent of the ballot issue campaigns. Still, the observation that 22 percent of ballot issues received financial support from individuals greater than or equal to the amount received from organizations does not contradict the expectation that organizational contributions constitute a majority source of campaign finance.

However, a closer look at the data reveals a less obvious trend in contributions behavior that challenges existing assumptions. Perhaps the most interesting observation of this research concerns the intended use of individual contributions versus that of organizational contributions. For the 78 ballot measures analyzed here, individuals gave a majority of their contributions in support of ballot measures, while organizations gave a majority of their contributions to oppose measures. Although the organizational strategy of blocking ballot measures has been well documented, the literature has largely ignored the role of individual citizens in supporting measures. The difference in the contribution patterns of individuals and organizations is an indicator of the role citizens play in ballot issue elections. Specifically, individuals are more active in supporting measures than their organizational counterparts. When one considers that 45 percent of all ballot issues included in this research were successful, a more exacting focus on contributions behavior in support of measures is justified.

Figure 5.1 shows the contribution source breakdown for supporting committees. Thirty-one percent of committees supporting the adoption of a bal-

Figure 5.1   Contribution Sources for Supporting Committees

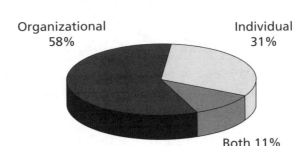

Figure 5.2   Contribution Sources for Opposing Committees

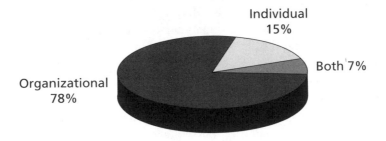

lot issue received a majority of their contributions from individual donors, while organizational donors gave a majority of support for 58 percent of the measures. The remaining 11 percent of supporting committees had roughly the same support from both individuals and organizations. There was less balance in the contributions breakdown of opposition committees. Figure 5.2 shows that only 15 percent received a majority of funding from individual contributors; 79 percent received a majority from organizational contributors; and 6 percent received a majority from both.

It is clear from this analysis that individuals are participating as financial supporters with greater frequency and, perhaps, with greater effect than typically thought. When total contributions to ballot issue committees are disaggregated by both source and purpose, we begin to see a clearer picture of the comparative impact of individual and organizational contributors. We recall that overall contributions to committees were heavily biased by organizational

Table 5.1   Ballot Issue Success by Contributor Source

	Individual	Mixed	Organization
Fail	4 (30.8%)	2 (50%)	38 (62.3)
Pass	9 (69.2%)	2 (50%)	23 (37.7%)
Total	13 (16.7%)	4 (5.1%)	61 (78.2%)

Pearson's R = -.237, p < .05

contributions; however, the nuances of the relationship between contributions and a ballot measure's electoral success show a weakness in drawing conclusions based on aggregate data alone.

That individual contributions to supporting committees made up nearly 40 percent of the funds used to advocate passage of ballot measures tells us a great deal about the role of individual contributors. Furthermore, the passage rate for ballot measures receiving a majority of funding from individual contributors was 33 percent greater than for those receiving a majority of their funds from organizations. Table 5.1 shows that 70 percent of all individually funded measures passed, while only 37 percent of organizationally supported measures passed. Still, it is difficult to determine whether the electoral success of ballot measures can be explained by financial support from citizens, noting a direct relationship between the two variables, or whether the relationship between citizen contributions and ballot success is obscured by an independent phenomenon (e.g., the subject matter of a measure, its substantive benefit to the community, or its controversial nature).[6]

However, when we recall that 45 percent of measures included in this analysis were approved by voters[7] and that almost 40 percent of the committees sup-

---

6. See discussion concerning Table 5.2 below for a more detailed review of this relationship.

7. Also relevant is the fact that the passage rate for all measures during the last thirty-four years (1964-1998) was substantially higher—at 58 percent. Although data prior to 1992 was not available for this research, the pre-1992 passage rate suggests that individual contributions may have played an even greater role in past ballot issue elections.

porting ballot measures secured a majority of their funds from individuals, we can not help concluding that organizations do not dominate in the way that has previously been thought. If we accept the literature's assertion that contributions are the primary reason why measures succeed and fail, the conclusion that contributions from individual citizens have a strong impact on electoral outcomes seems quite reasonable after a review of the data.

Although it may seem obvious to many, it is important to note that ballot measures funded by individual citizens do exist and that these are better received by voters than organizationally funded measures. The presence of individual contributions, particularly in committees supporting ballot measures, challenges the conventional wisdom articulated in both popular and academic literatures that campaign finance for ballot measures is dominated by organizational sources. In short, there is a difference in the observed electoral behaviors of individually and organizationally funded ballot measures. Therefore, it is not possible to accept *H1*—"*Organizational contributions to ballot issue committees determine a measure's success or failure at the ballot*—as a valid explanation of ballot issue politics in the two states under study here.

When considered together, the above observations show that individuals have a greater role in ballot issue elections than is often suggested. More precisely, it seems that the weakness of the contemporary wisdom is found in its inability to capture the complexity of the campaign spending issue, not in its more general observation that money matters. This is not to say that organizational contributions do not have an impact on ballot issue outcomes. We must not, however, overlook the impact of individual contributions to ballot issue campaigns by focusing narrowly on the impact of aggregate spending. In this researcher's view, this narrow focus has been a mistake. Still, the general conclusion that campaign spending by well-funded organizations has a strong impact on ballot issue outcomes cannot be refuted by the data considered here.

Findings: Campaign Spending and Legislative Type

H2 = Organizational contributions to ballot issue committees are directed at the passage of ballot issues offering narrowly concentrated benefits to particular interests within the community.

The analysis now moves to a study of the relationship between funding behavior and the substantive type of legislation proposed in ballot issues. As noted above, it is difficult to identify the independent effect of campaign spending, unraveling it from the effect of the substantive type of legislation proposed in the ballot measure, its subject matter, the presence of similar/competitive measures on the ballot, the mood of the electorate, or a number of other factors that may influence final outcomes. The current analysis examines these factors further, particularly as they relate to the connection between contributions behavior and the substantive type of legislation proposed—the first of the independent variables mentioned above. Further investigation is essential to our understanding of the role of campaign spending in direct democracy. Additionally, the current research offers an alternative to spending as a predictor of ballot issue success.

As indicated previously, the legislative typology variable used to ascertain the impact of the substance of the measure, the variable TYPE, was introduced to analyze the distribution of benefits produced by a proposed ballot issue. Depending upon the benefits they create, measures were broken down into two values, inclusive and exclusive. Inclusive measures create legislation with benefits accessible to the entire community without exception; exclusive measures create legislation with benefits accessible only to specific members of the community.

Given the conclusions found in much of the literature on the subject, we expect to see greater organizational resources dedicated to the passage of exclusive legislation. This expectation is based on the common view that organizations will use their limited resources to their greatest advantage, which is found in the passage of legislation benefiting their narrow interests alone.[8] The use of organizational resources, especially corporate- or interest-group funding, for the purpose of supporting public policy benefiting the entire community is viewed as economically irrational. Thus, we expect to see organizational contributions flooding into exclusive ballot campaigns and largely absent from efforts to support inclusive measures. We expect to see organizational resources spent in both opposition to and support of exclusive ballot issue contests, as opponents will align themselves on both sides of an issue, but only on the opposing side of inclusive measures. The public, however, is expected to support inclusive meas-

---

8. The term "narrow interests" includes what is commonly referred to as "public interests." This research acknowledges the difficulty of separating the public from the special interest, as pointed out by social-choice theorists. Thus, although groups like the Sierra Club or the League of Women Voters might consider their advocacy in the interest of the entire community, this research does not treat their interest as such. They were coded as organizations like more narrow groups, such as professional associations, corporations, single-issue groups, and labor unions—groups traditionally identified as special interests. The purpose here is to identify the impact of citizens and well-funded organizations on the process, necessitating this kind of broad-stroke coding.

ures as a means to choose the laws citizens must live under in their communities. These expectations are represented by the following hypothesis, *H2*.

> *H2 = Organizational contributions to ballot issue committees are directed at the passage of ballot issues offering narrowly concentrated benefits to particular interests within the community.*

In testing *H2*, there is virtually no difference in the source of funding for exclusive and inclusive measures. Organizational funds were distributed similarly across both legislative types, as were individual funds. Although there were more than twice as many exclusive measures than inclusive measures in the data set,[9] the percentage of campaigns dominated by organizational spending was virtually identical for both types (see Table 5.2 below). Of exclusive measures, 78.2 percent received a majority of funds from organizational sources, compared with 78.3 percent of inclusive measures. This alone points to a misconception that organizations only contribute to measures that forward their narrow interests.

There was variation, however, in the electoral response to the different funding sources when layered with legislative typology (see Table 5.2). Although there is considerably more support among the electorate for inclusive measures generally—74 percent of inclusive measures were approved, compared with only 31 percent of exclusive measures—there is even greater support among the electorate for inclusive measures funded by individual contributors. Of these measures, 100 percent were approved by voters, whereas of inclusive measures supported by organizational contributors, 66.7 percent passed. It should be noted that there were only three cases of individually funded inclusive measures in the data set, too small a number upon which to base any generalizations. Still, the potential trend should not be ignored. The fact remains that 100 percent of inclusive measures funded by individuals were adopted.

Moreover, the relationship between funding source and voter response, when layered with the inclusive type, was statistically significant at the .05 level. However, the relationship between funding support and voter response, when layered with the exclusive type, was not statistically significant ($p=.114$). Even though the correlation coefficients for both types were moderate, -.227 for inclusive and -.182 for exclusive, the significance of the relationship for inclusive measures points to the electorate's preference for measures with widely accessible benefits supported by their fellow citizens. Seventy-five percent of exclusive measures funded by organizations were rejected by voters (see Table 5.2).

---

9. 55 exclusive measures and 23 inclusive measures.

Table 5.2   Success Rate of Funding Source, By Legislative Type

Row pct. Column pct.	Individual	Mixed	Organization	Total
Inclusive*				
Fail	0	0	6 (100%) (33.3%)	6 (100%) (26.1%)
Pass	3 (17.6%) (100%)	2 (11.8%) (100%)	12 (70.6%) (66.7%)	17 (100%) (73.9%)
Total	3 (13.0%) (100%)	2 (8.7) (100%)	18 (78.3%) (100%)	23 (100%) (100%)
Exclusive**				
Fail	4 (10.5%) (40.0%)	2 (5.3%) (100%)	32 (84.2%) (74.4%)	38 (100%) (69.1%)
Pass	6 (35.3%) (60.0%)	0	11 (64.7%) (25.6%)	17 (100%) (30.9%)
Total	10 (18.2%) (100%)	2 (3.6%) (100%)	43 (78.2%) (100%)	55 (100%) (100%)

* Pearson's R = -.2.96, p < .10
** Pearson's R = -.263, p > .10

These observations demonstrate the electorate's preference for a certain type of measure, namely inclusive measures supported by individual citizens. The combination of public accessibility to benefits resulting from the proposed legislation and the citizen base of support can be a powerful tool to generate a positive voter treatment, which is exactly what the norms of democratic politics dictate. That this combination has the potential to deliver victory to the proponents of a ballot measure suggests that direct democracy is working in accordance with our collective goals for this institution of lawmaking.

It is likely, however, that individual financial support was secured for these measures because of a substantive interest among the public, which had a secondary effect of motivating voter support. While this is inconsistent with the view that individual financial support was a cause of voter approval, both cases can be distinguished from the electorate's behavior in response to organizationally funded measures. Clearly, the unanimous support for inclusive ballot measures that received a majority of financial support from individuals suggests that the public is responsive to the difference between inclusive and exclusive measures, to the source of financial support, or to some combination of the two. In any case, the findings here cast serious doubt on the validity of *H2*. From what we have observed thus far, we know that organizational contributions are not solely directed toward the passage of narrow legislation as *H2* suggests.

The dynamic discovered here was also witnessed when the variables SPENDMORE, measuring whether a majority of contributions was raised in support or opposition, and PASSFAIL were layered with legislative type (see Table 5-3). Seventy percent of the inclusive measures were funded by supporting committees, compared with 58 percent of the exclusive measures. Also, an inclusive measure with a majority of campaign finances spent in support of its adoption enjoyed a greater success rate (81 percent) than a similarly funded exclusive measure (37 percent). This suggests that the substantive type of legislation has a strong impact on ballot issues, perhaps stronger than campaign spending. We will, however, reserve these inferences for the following section, employing multivariate analysis.

In addition to suggesting a spending trend biased towards inclusive measures, Table 5.3 shows the impact that oppositional spending has on exclusive measures. This is a more specific component of the general observation, offered in much of the literature, that spending against a measure has a great impact on ballot outcomes. In fact, we learn from Table 5.3 just where the impact of oppositional spending is greatest. The effect observed by Magleby (1984), Lowenstein (1982), and others is stronger for exclusive measures than inclusive measures. When we disaggregate ballot issues by legislative type, we see that oppositional spending is associated with the defeat of 78 percent of proposed exclusive measures but of only 43 percent of inclusive measures. Again, this finding uncovers the explanatory power of the legislative type variable, suggesting that the substantive type of a measure may have a greater impact on final votes than the source or amount of funding it receives. Only 5

Table 5.3   Passage Rate and Spending More, By Legislative Type

Row pct. Column pct.	Oppose	Support	Total
Inclusive*			
Fail	3 (50.0%) (42.9%)	3 (50.0%) (18.8 %)	6 (100%) (26.1%)
Pass	4 (23.5%) (57.1%)	13 (76.5%) (81.3%)	17 (100%) (73.9%)
Total	7 (30.4%) (100%)	16 (69.6%) (100%)	23 (100%) (100%)
Exclusive**			
Fail	18 (47.4%) (78.3%)	20 (52.6%) (62.5%)	38 (100%) (69.1%)
Pass	5 (29.4%) (21.7%)	12 (70.6%) (37.5%)	17 (100%) (30.9%)
Total	23 (41.8%) (100%)	32 (58.2%) (100%)	55 (100%) (100%)

* Pearson's R = .253, p > .10
** Pearson's R = .168, p> .10

of the 23 exclusive measures with a majority of funds spent opposing the measures were approved by voters, compared with 4 of the 7 inclusive measure with the same funding context. The relationship is further corroborated by a review of the symmetric measures for this relationship, which were not significant. The lack of statistical significance suggests that the substance of measures is every bit as important as those who fund them and how contributions are allocated.

These findings help us to better understand the subtleties of campaign spending. Oppositional spending is not generally effective except when it opposes exclusive measures that deny mass-level citizens access to proposed benefits. Where inclusive measures are before voters, the distribution of benefits seems to outweigh the effect of campaign finance. We may conclude from this observation that the public's preference for inclusive measures is a stronger indication of a measure's potential for success than the incidence of oppositional spending; however this conclusion should be continued and developed further in the multivariate analysis below.

Findings: Multivariate Analysis

Together, the variables considered above add detail to our understanding of what contributes to ballot issue outcomes. This understanding can be increased further by a consideration of the cumulative impact the variables have on voting behavior. The test for a cumulative effect employed a logistic regression equation. Logistic regression is useful in estimating the effect of these variables on a dichotomous dependent measure, like the PASSFAIL variable employed here.

Table 5.4 shows the impact that the three main variables discussed above (FUNDSOUR, SPENDMORE, and TYPE) had on a measure's electoral success. To begin, the model was highly significant (p<.001). Both FUNDSOUR and LEGTYPE were significant at the p<.05 level. That these variables were significant but SPENDMORE was not suggests that the substantive type of a measure and the kind of support it receives (from citizens or organizations) have a stronger impact than whether more money was spent for or against the measure. The inclusion of the three independent variables in this equation increased the prediction of a measure's approval by voters. This increased predictive power was determined by comparing the modal value's frequency, which for this equation was a 56.4 percent failure rate, to the correct prediction percentage generated by the model. Here, the overall prediction was 71.79 percent, or 16 points higher than we would expect without the addition of these independent variables.

This model supported the findings discussed earlier with bivariate correlation. From this analysis, we can confirm that the source of spending (individual or organizational) and the type of legislation (inclusive or exclusive) have an impact on the electorate's ultimate voting decisions. It was not surprising to find that SPENDMORE was not significant, since our discussion of it above pointed to some weaknesses in the variable's explanatory power. Again, this was the case because the aggregate spending for or against a measure only impacted exclusive measures, not inclusive measures.

Table 5.4   Logistic Regression Estimates and (Standard Errors) for General Campaign Spending and Legislative Type Variables

	Equation One
Constant	2.2084**
	(1.75)
LEGTYPE	1.9878***
	(.5926)
SPENDMORE	-.7955
	(.549)
FUNDSOUR	-.7557**
	(.35)
Log Likelihood	86.599
X²	20.246***
Correctly Predicted	71.79%
Number of Cases	78

** p < .05, *** p < .01

When we compared the independent variables in this equation, the substantive type variable seemed to enhance prediction more than the campaign finance variables. The significance of TYPE was .0008, while the significance of FUNSOUR was .0308 and SPENDMORE.1473. This comparison stands in contrast to much of the literature's claim that money dominates direct democracy. Furthermore, when we include campaign finance variables with a greater level of specificity, the results show an even greater role for the substance of a measure. When we replace the general funding source variable FUNDSOUR with more detailed funding variables FUNDOPP (funding for opposing committees) and FUNDSUPP (funding for supporting committees), we see that the relative strength of the TYPE variable becomes greater. Table 5.5 shows that the addition of the more detailed funding variables increased the prediction of voting outcomes by 3.65 points. However, while the model was more successful in predicting values for the dependent variable, campaign spend-

Table 5.5   Logistic Regression Estimates and (Standard Errors)
for Committee-Level Campaign Spending and Legislative
Type Variables

	Equation One
Constant	4.088** (1.7828)
LEGTYPE	1.3198* (.7492)
FUNDSUPP	-.2187 (.4171)
FUNDOPP	-.7345 (.4771)
FUNDSOUR	-.8513 (.5875)
Log Likelihood	62.69
X²	14.902***
Correctly Predicted	77.19%
Number of Cases	78

* p < .10, ** p < .05, *** p < .01

ing variables were not significant. The only variable significant in this equation was TYPE (p < .1). This suggests that TYPE is an important variable in ballot issue politics.

Conclusion

The analysis in this chapter suggests that differences in the types of contributions which ballot-issue committees receive is important to the electorate's choices. While voters may not always be aware of who the contributors are, as such an awareness would take a fair amount of work on their part, there is a clear relationship between funding source and electoral outcomes. While further research is necessary to reveal this relationship more clearly, this observation points to a public less easily manipulated by big money interests than some researchers have suggested.

The current research has shown that voters can be quite sophisticated when making choices to support or reject ballot issues. While this does not always happen, the public's treatment of the different sources of campaign finance, as well as the differences in the access to inclusive benefits, points to their capacity to handle complex information. The key to improving direct democracy, then, may be found in improving the means for disseminating relevant voter information to citizens before they make their decisions. If we accept the fact that voters are sophisticated enough to differentiate among funding sources and ballot types, then as a community we ought to make greater efforts to improve access to voter information. Fortunately, efforts of this kind have been made more possible with the introduction of the Internet as a means of sharing public information.

It seems quite reasonable, after a review of the data considered here, to conclude that voters do care where the money comes from. Continuing research, however, must be undertaken to corroborate what has been learned here. While the present research may have increased the level of detail offered by aggregate studies of direct democracy, this research must be expanded before any definite conclusions can be offered. For instance, at the aggregate level, it will be important to test the subject matter of ballot issues to further unpack the relationship between campaign spending and ballot issue outcomes. Although case studies have done an excellent job of increasing our understanding of the role of campaign spending in ballot issue campaigns, there is the potential for detailed case studies to focus on the more controversial ballot issues or on one substantive type of measure, ignoring the more general contributions of initiative and referendum voting. This unbalanced approach is a likely cause of the existing literature's failure to identify the role of citizens in supporting, rather than blocking, proposed ballot issues, as well as its premature conclusions regarding the role of campaign finance generally.

Additionally, it will be necessary to further disaggregate contributions data. In this research we identified some important differences in the way organizational and individual contributions affect ballot elections, but it is necessary to continue this research by breaking down organizational contributions further in order to analyze the different types of organizations participating and their relative impact on outcomes.

The current research has shown that individual citizens do play an influential role in ballot issue politics, that differences in the substance of measures attract different types of campaign funding, and that the public is likely to respond to these differences when considering their support for a ballot issue. Hopefully, the research has demonstrated the value of increasing our analytical focus on these and other related phenomena. The analysis should be done using both aggregate data and rigorous case studies to increase our understanding of what motivates voting decisions in ballot issue elections. This will allow us to more completely evaluate the nature of direct democracy and its significance as a lawmaking institution in contemporary American politics.

References

Berg, Larry, and Craig Holman. 1989. The initiative process and its declining agenda-setting value. *Law and Policy* 11: 451–66).

Broder, David. 2000. *Democracy derailed: Initiative campaigns and the power of money*. Orlando, FL: Harcourt, Inc.

California Commission on Campaign Financing. 1992. *Democracy by initiative*. Los Angeles: Center for Responsive Government.

Cronin, Thomas. 1989. *Direct democracy: The politics of initiative, referendum, and recall*. Cambridge: Harvard University Press.

Hero, Rodney E., and Caroline J. Tolbert. 1996. A racial/ethnic interpretation of politics and policy in the states of the U.S. *American Journal of Political Science* 40: 851–71.

Magleby, David. 1984. *Direct legislation: Voting on ballot propositions in the United States*. Baltimore: Johns Hopkins University Press.

_____. 1994. Direct legislation in the American states. In *Referendums around the world*, edited by David Butler and Austin Ranney. Washington, DC: American Enterprise Institute.

Smith, Daniel A., and Robert J. Herrington. 2000. The process of direct democracy: Colorado's 1996 Parental Rights Amendment. *Social Science Journal* 37 no. 2: 179–94.

Zisk, Betty. 1987. *Money, media, and the grass roots: State ballot issues and the electoral process*. Newbury Park, CA: Sage Publications.

CHAPTER 6

The Initiative to Party: The Role of Political Parties in State Ballot Initiatives

Dan Smith, University of Florida-Gainesville

In several of the twenty-four, mostly western states, that permit the initiative, political parties have become more involved in ballot contests than scholars generally have acknowledged. While several scholars and journalists have noted the self-promotional use of the initiative process by California Governor Pete Wilson and other prominent elected officials and candidates running for office (Mahtesian 1998, 38–39; Schrag 1998, 225–29; Tolbert and Hero 1998, 224; Chavez 1998, 34–38), state party organizations have also turned to the initiative to achieve their goals. State (as well as national) Republican and Democratic parties have contributed substantial amounts of money as well as in-kind support to select ballot campaigns. Yet little is known about why party officials and their organizations participate in the initiative process. Indeed, any involvement of political parties in the initiative process seems counterintuitive. Drawing on interviews with party officials and analyzing comparative campaign finance data from California and Colorado, two states with historically high levels of initiative use (Tolbert, Lowenstein, and Donovan 1998; Magleby 1994, 226), this chapter explores the complex and often covert relationship between ballot measures and political parties.

The Relationship between Parties and the Initiative Process

Since its introduction in South Dakota in 1898, its defenders portray direct democracy as a "pure" and unmediated procedure (Wilcox 1912, 3–10). Proponents of the referendum, initiative, and recall—the three components of direct democracy—intended the reforms to allow citizens to recapture control over government officials and the system of representative government. In particular, the so-called citizen initiative was intended to grant individuals and groups rebuffed by partisan state legislatures the right to petition their government for redress. Today, the initiative continues to be widely regarded as a safety-valve mechanism, "a safeguard against the concentration of political power in the hands of a few" (Schmidt 1989, 25–26). In addition, the initiative process—in theory at least—is understood to be egalitarian. It allows "narrow-based, well-organized," as well as "broad, diffuse" groups (Donovan et al. 1998, 82), the possibility to enact statutes or constitutional amendments, bypassing their state legislatures. Hence, participation by political parties in ballot campaigns belies the popular notion that the initiative is an extra-legislative process controlled by nonpartisan, civil society groups.

A century ago, one of the main targets of direct democracy—second only to the handful of special interests that were unduly swaying elected officials— were the parties and the party bosses who controlled state legislatures (Munro 1912, 16–17; Hall 1921, 121–22; Cronin 1989, 50–57). As direct democracy advocate Nathan Cree wrote in 1892, the reforms were largely intended "to break the crushing and stifling power of our great party machines and to give freer play to the political ideas, aspirations, opinions, and feelings of the people. The reforms would tend to relieve us from the dominance of partisan passions and to have an elevating and educative influence upon voters" (cited in Cronin 1989, 46–48). Furthermore, according to a political scientist in 1900, "the selfish and the dishonest who would use the government to enrich themselves personally and the class which they represent, the 'Boss' and his men who are the curse of the system in America—all these are manifestations which cause reflective people to pause and tremble for the future of representative government" (Oberholtzer 1900, 392–93). At that time, the involvement of political parties in the initiative process ran counter to the idea that direct democracy would be an unmediated, populist process necessarily of, by, and for the people. The mechanisms of direct democracy introduced by populist and then progressive reformers at the turn of the century, according to Mc-

Cuan et al. (1998), intentionally "subverted the traditional electioneering function of the party and provided the opportunity for private (i.e., nonparty) organizations to offer advice and conduct campaigns" (60). Indeed, when the
initiative process was first being advanced, the role of parties was "strictly limited, more or less by design" (McCuan et al. 1998, 60).

The systemic electoral reforms adopted by voters in over a dozen states during the Progressive Era—most notably the direct primary and the initiative
process—had the simultaneous effect of weakening political parties and fos-
tering the growth of the interest group system (McSeveney 1994). William S.
U'ren, the leader of the People's Power League in Oregon, commented in the
early 1900s that "[p]arty political organizations [were] in failing health" and
"the absolute power...to decide many questions at one election and each separately on its own merits [appeared] to be fatal to the perfection of party dis-
cipline and organization" (cited in Barnett 1915, 186). As political parties declined in stature, special interests, known then as the "people's lobby"
(Clemens 1997), gained strength, filling the institutional void left by parties.
But during the 1910s, dozens of statewide citizen-led initiatives were placed
on the ballot that targeted not only party bosses but also vested special interests. Like many prominent statesmen of his time, Woodrow Wilson, an ar-
dent foe of direct democracy during the formative years of the mechanism,
would later change his mind, stating in 1911, "It takes power from the [party]
boss and places it in the hands of the people" (quoted in Cronin 1989, 38).
For a brief time, it appeared as though special interests and party machines
would indeed cede some of their power to "the people" via the initiative.

Today, public opinion regarding ballot measures tends to reflect the populist sentiment of old. Surveys continue to find that a majority of citizens
"ought to be able to vote on important issues and policies instead of having
their representatives voting for them" (Cronin 1989, 79). "Distrust of parties
and legislatures," Magleby contends (1984), "makes direct legislation an attractive alternative" (16). Recent polls have found that nearly two-thirds of
those surveyed support statewide ballot initiative elections (Citrin 1996,
270–73). In general, citizens like being able to vote on ballot measures
(DiCamillo and Field 1997; Dubois and Feeney 1992), although at times they
have expressed their concerns about how the process actually functions (Magleby 1984; Hagen and Lascher 1998). In response to this positive public opinion, several state legislatures during the last decade have considered adopting
the initiative (Vincent 1996, 6). In addition, over the past thirty years the gov-
ernors of Alabama, Connecticut, Delaware, Georgia, Hawaii, Kentucky, Minnesota, New Jersey, New York, Pennsylvania, Rhode Island, and Texas have

spoken out in favor of the initiative process (Cronin 1989, 51). Cherished by many Americans as a symbol of democratic participation, citizen involvement, and direct popular rule, the initiative process continues to be viewed by proponents as a check on the system of (un)representative government and unsavory partisan politics (Smith 1998a, 15–16).

For nearly a century, then, political parties have felt the sting of direct democracy. Parties, of course, have always been much less "relevant" in campaigns for ballot measures than they have been in races for political office (McCuan et al. 1998, 60–61). Nearly all ballot measures are sponsored and funded by groups falling beyond the reach of political parties (California Commission 1992, 68–69). Magleby (1984) explains how "parties are excluded from participation in drafting the measures and therefore may not play much of a role in interpreting them to the voters" (189). Not only have parties been omitted from initiative politics, but scholars have noted how they also have been weakened institutionally by the process. While state party organizations have not faded from the scene, they certainly are not the institutional strongholds they once were (Hedge 1997; Bibby and Holbrook 1996). The flourishing of direct democracy, no doubt, has impinged state party strength. Over forty years ago, Kelley (1956) commented on how "the popularity of direct legislation in the state [California] both reflects and increases the weakness of its parties" (63). More recently, Magleby (1984) has observed: "While direct legislation has not removed special-interest groups from active participation in legislative politics, it (along with other reforms of direct democracy) has made the political party a far less potent force in state politics" (199).

Overall, with its growing presence in the states that permit it, the initiative process has displaced some of the power once commanded by state legislatures. Direct legislation, in the form of initiated statutes and constitutional amendments, now influences the political agenda of not only the states permitting direct democracy but the nation as a whole (Magleby 1994, 218). The legislative agendas in the state capitols are influenced by issues that are placed, or even threatened to be placed, on the ballot (Gerber 1996; 1998). Direct democracy, Rosenthal (1998) laments, "has been growing in strength at the expense of representative processes," and as a result, "state government is no longer conducted with the consent of the governed" (4). However, according to Rosenthal (1998), state government "is conducted with significant participation by the governed, and by those who claim to speak for the public's interest, according to a more populist plan" (4–5).

So why does it seem that parties have not become more involved in the initiative process? Scholars generally concur that partisan organizations are not engaged in the initiative process because they have little to gain politically from their participation. Magleby (1984) contends that "[t]here are good reasons for political parties to avoid stands on ballot measures, as the success or defeat of an initiative rarely translates into any payoff to the electoral fortunes of the party candidates in the election" (174). Voters, Magleby suggests, tend to support or oppose propositions independent of their partisan leanings. Gerber and Lupia (1995) contend that "partisan cues are usually absent in direct legislation elections" (290). Other scholars claim that the participation of parties may be limited to the "type" of ballot measure on the ballot. A fourfold typology offered by Donovan et al. (1998), which classifies initiatives by their policy outcomes, finds that "majoritarian" ballot measures might encourage party participation. With "majoritarian" initiatives—those ballot contests in which the groups promoting and opposing a ballot measure tend to be "large and diffuse"—Donovan et al. (1998) suggest that "candidates and political parties dominat[e] the campaign discourse" (93). In their study of California initiatives, they find that proponents of these measures often "welcome the adoption of their issue by other groups, political parities, or politicians" (94). They cite two specific examples in California where outside groups, including parties, became heavily involved in initiative campaigns dealing with social and moral questions: Proposition 187, the 1994 antiimmigration measures; and Proposition 209, the 1996 antiaffirmative action measure. Other such "majoritarian" initiatives susceptible to party involvement include measures dealing with broad-based tax cuts, political reform, and crime. Bones and Benedict (1975), in their historical study of direct legislation in Washington, find that "Washington parties take stands on few propositions," but they suggest that some initiatives—specifically those dealing with "welfare, taxes, and government reform"—are somewhat more likely to have partisan cues and support (350). Consistent with these findings, Bowler and Donovan (1998) claim that in governance-related ballot measures, such as term limits for elected officials, partisan voters are able to "respond to their party's interest over the course of an initiative campaign" (140). The policy-driven matrices offered by Donovan et al. (1998) and Campbell (1997), while somewhat problematic in terms of how they define group support or opposition (for criticisms, see Smith and Herrington 1999; Smith 1998c), do provide insight into where we might expect to see party involvement in the initiative process.

There is growing evidence, though subtle, that some state parties are becoming more than bit players in majoritarian as well as other types of initiatives. There are signs that the initiative landscape, with regard to political parties, is changing. That parties are not visibly involved in most initiative campaigns does not mean they are absent from ballot measures process. State party organizations, and even the Democratic National Committee (DNC) and the National Republican Committee (RNC), are not sitting idly by as ballot measures become more prominent features of state policy making. From a rational actor perspective, this engagement by party organizations seems perfectly logical. As ballot measures become more important vehicles for policy change, it is rational that party organizations will try to selectively use the initiative process as a way to advance their political agendas as well as their candidates for public office. Strategic and financial participation in ballot measure campaigns by parties also has the potential of offsetting their depreciated influence in the policy-making arena. As one astute journalist has recently observed, "[o]rganized money moves inexorably toward where the action is, and these days, that place is the ballot as often as it is the statehouse" (Mahtesian 1998, 42). Although the initiative process continues to be used primarily by citizen- and special-interest groups as a means to circumvent partisan state legislatures, party organizations—while not terribly fond of it—clearly appreciate the power of direct democracy.

Why Parties are Taking the Initiative

In California and Colorado, as well as in several other states, party organizations are becoming selective players, albeit usually silent, in the initiative process. Even though they are still undoubtedly less relevant players than special interests and even citizen groups, state (and national) political parties are likely to continue to encroach on the initiative process when it is to their strategic advantage. Why, then, are parties encroaching on the turf of direct democracy? What is the rationale behind political parties' excursion into initiative politics? What kinds of political gains are to be made by siding one way or the other on an initiative? And, perhaps most important, is their involvement successful?

There appear to be at least three motivating factors, which are not mutually exclusive, for parties becoming involved in the initiative process. First, a party may become involved if a ballot measure has a chance of promoting voter turnout for the party's own candidates for elected office. Second, a party may become engaged in initiative politics if a proposed measure can serve as a wedge issue against the other party. Third, a party may choose to support or oppose a proposition if there is a high level of ideological compatibility between the party's platform and the proposed measure. Recent developments in California and Colorado indicate that party officials consider all three of these reasons when determining whether to become directly or indirectly involved in a particular initiative campaign.

Increasing Voter Turnout

There is a common perception among journalists and scholars that ballot initiatives stimulate voter interest, and in turn, increase turnout on Election Day. An article in *Congress Daily,* an outlet of the *National Journal,* declared in 1998 that "high-profile initiatives on statewide ballots could dramatically affect voter turnout in some House and Senate races this fall and potentially influence who wins" (Turnout could hinge on initiatives 1998). Schmidt (1989), a vocal advocate of direct democracy, contends: "Increased citizen participation through ballot measure campaigns has a 'spillover effect' on candidate campaigns: those who turn out specifically to vote on the Initiatives usually vote for candidates as well, thereby raising overall voter participation" (27). Schmidt further claims that in the late 1970s and early 1980s, voter turnout was highest in states that allowed ballot measures. Despite the popular view, scholars have all but debunked the old canard that voter turnout increases when initiatives are on the ballot. Drawing on data from the California Polls and the findings of Everson (1981), Magleby (1984) concludes that the impact of initiatives on turnout is negligible. "In sum," Magleby writes, "over the last twenty years, turnout generally has been the same whether or not states had the initiative process" (98).

Although citizen-initiated measures on the ballot do not appear to increase voter turnout, students of the initiative process have observed how candidates as well as elected officials try to use ballot measures to propel their own campaigns. This is different from the common practice of elected officials who endorse ballot measures to help mobilize voter turnout for the particular initiative (Karp 1998; Lupia 1994). In their research on the race/ethnicity context of ballot measures, Tolbert and Hero (1998) find that initiatives can shape races for political office. However, they also suggest that there may be severe political costs for candidates who link themselves to initiatives, as was the case with Kathleen Brown and her vocal opposition to Proposition 187 in 1994 (224).

In California, perhaps more so than in other states, embracing and demagoguing hot-button ballot issues by a candidate to showcase his or her credentials has been around for some time (Schrag 1998, 226). Schrag describes how Secretary of State Jerry Brown cosponsored a campaign finance ballot measure in 1974 and Attorney General John Van De Kamp cosponsored three ballot initiatives in 1990. Both men tried to use initiatives to energize their campaigns for governor. More recently, the most blatant and well-documented use of the initiative by a candidate to bolster voter turnout has been that of Pete Wilson. Beginning in 1990 with Proposition 115, a tough-on-crime measure, the California governor actively latched himself to numerous majoritarian ballot measures in an effort to promote his own candidacy (Schrag 1998, 225–26). For example, when he was running for reelection in 1994, Wilson actively supported two measures that were popular among the party faithful: Proposition 184, a harsh three-strikes measure, and Proposition 187, a punitive anti-illegal immigration measure (Schrag 1998, 227–31). Wilson spent $2 million of his campaign funds on advertisements for Proposition 187 and became the initiative's "point man" (Chavez 1998, 37).

It should be emphasized that in his repeated quests for political office, Wilson has not exploited the initiative solely for personal gains. During his eight-year tenure, the California governor promoted propitious ballot measures to advance the cause of the Republican Party more generally. Prohibited from running for governor for a third term in 1998, Wilson actively backed two California ballot measures that year that the Republican party thought would promote voter turnout for the GOP slate of candidates. During the June primary, Wilson contributed not only his name but also over $1 million from his personal campaign fund to help place Proposition 226, dubbed "Paycheck Protection," on the ballot (California Secretary of State 1998b). Up until Election Day, Republican support for the initiative was consistently strong, never dipping below 57 percent approval (Magleby and Patterson 1998, 22). Four months later, during the general election, Wilson sponsored Proposition 8, a measure to provide accountability in the public schools. According to a high-ranking official of the California GOP, "for all intents and purposes, [Wilson] is the leader of the GOP, so when the governor came to the party and said, 'I'd like you to kick in some money for the Prop. 8 campaign,' the party responded approvingly" (California Republican Party 1998).

In Colorado, three-term Governor Roy Romer has actively campaigned for several ballot measures during his tenure in office to help turn out the vote for the Democratic Party. As de facto head of the state Democrats for the past twelve years (and head of the DNC in 1997–1998), Romer publicly endorsed and opposed measures dealing with the funding of public education, abortion, and tax and spending limitations (Smith 1996). The Colorado Democratic chairman from 1992–1994, lawyer Howard Gelt (1998), indicated that while the party worked closely with Romer on several initiatives in the early 1990s, there was not "any overt involvement" of parties in the initiative process, since the coordination between the party and the public officials is "incredibly covert." In 1992 and 1994, according to Gelt (1998), the Democratic Party's coordinated campaign committee met regularly with organized labor interests and the groups supporting and opposing the initiatives to talk strategy, arrange literature drops, send out direct mailings with slate cards and sample ballots, and plot TV advertising. In 1992, Romer was not up for re-election. Nevertheless, the party, in an effort to get out the vote, worked closely with the governor in opposition to Amendment 2, the anti-gay rights measure, and in support of Romer's own sales tax increase for education, Amendment 6 (Gelt 1998).

Going beyond the endorsements by prominent party members, the party organizations in California and Colorado often take their own public stances on ballot measures. Parties endorse initiatives in an effort to stimulate partisan voter anxiety or excitement about the measures, which they hope will translate into increased across-the-board support for the party. According to a California GOP official, "get-out-the-vote" (GOTV) was one of the main reasons why the party supported Proposition 187 in 1994. "It was a calculated effort on our part to back the measure," according to the party officer, "because the measure was very popular and seemed like it was going to pass" (California Republican Party 1998). Governor Wilson supported the measure because it was a "good" initiative and it would "help him and the party" (California Republican Party 1998). In 1998, the state Republican Party, headquartered in Burbank, voted in its September party convention to support or oppose each of the eight initiatives on the 1998 general election ballot. The California Democratic Party (1998) also took a formal position on all of the measures, except for Proposition 5, the Indian gaming measure (for reasons to be discussed below).

In Colorado, the state Democratic Party did not officially endorse or oppose any of the eight statewide measures in 1998. According to its bylaws, the party may take a public stance on an issue with the approval of either the central committee or the chair. Party chairman, Phil Perington, was not about to "stick his neck out" on any of the issues and did not recommend any party endorsements (Perington 1998). However, when Perington was in Washington, D.C., during the fall, the topic of supporting or opposing issues came up in a meeting of the party's coordinating committee. In Perington's absence, the committee, against party rules and defying Perington's will, decided on its own to send out an absentee ballot mailing with the party taking a position against Amendments 11 and 12, the two antiabortion measures (Perington

1998). In contrast, the state Republican Party, which has bylaws similar to those of the Democrats with regard to taking positions on initiatives, supported or opposed all of the statewide measures, as well as the three statewide referendums. According to Steve Curtis (1998), chairman of the Colorado GOP, "[i]t's the responsibility of the parties to come out and advocate issues.... [S]itting on the fence doesn't excite people." The party wins, Curtis contends, "when we turn the base out." The party came out strong against Referendum B, a statutory measure placed on the ballot by the legislature to retain excess taxes to spend on education and transportation needs. The party placed NO ON B yard signs and bumper stickers in its office for activists to pick up, and Curtis spoke out in favor of the referendum, which was defeated by a two-to-one margin on Election Day.

Not only do the two major parties in California and Colorado publicly endorse or oppose measures; they also contribute money to issue groups in their effort to get out the vote. In California, the two major parties routinely count as contributions to issue groups any money they spend on their direct mailings to party members that support or oppose ballot propositions. For example, in the 1998 primary election, the state GOP, in late contributions alone, reported in-kind contributions of $1,100 to the issue committees supporting Proposition 219, Proposition 221, Proposition 222, Proposition 227, and to the one opposing Proposition 220. In addition, the party made an in-kind contribution of $3,300 to the issue committee opposing Proposition 224 and contributed $14,740 to the opponents of Proposition 223 and $29,740 to the proponents of Proposition 226 (California Secretary of State 1998b). More substantially, Governor Wilson and the California Republican Party were the top two contributors to Proposition 8 in the 1998 general election, Governor Wilson's public education "reform" swan song (California Secretary of State 1998b). Wilson contributed $499,485 and the California Republican Party anted up $175,878 after Wilson came to the party and said: "I'd like you to kick in some money" for the campaign (California Republican Party 1998). On the flip side, the Democratic State Central Committee of California, based in Sacramento, reported making in-kind and monetary contributions to issue committees in both the primary and general elections. A few weeks before the primary election, the state Democratic Party contributed $13,046 to the group opposed to Proposition 226. The state organization also spent $21,000 in the 1998 general election opposing Proposition 8 and over $25,000 opposing Proposition 9, a measure that would recapture costs from the utility industry (California Secretary of State 1998a).

In 1998, a small controversy engulfed the Colorado Democratic Party following the November election over the role played by the DNC in two statewide issue campaigns. On 27 October 1998, the DNC, cochaired by out-going Colorado Governor Roy Romer, funneled $60,000 to the issue committee supporting Referendum B, which would allow the state to spend surplus taxes on roads and schools, and $20,000 to the opponents of Amendment 17, which would give tax credits for private education. Even though the state Democratic Party took no official stance on the two measures, during the campaign Romer pushed for Referendum B and fought against Amendment 17 in an effort to indirectly bolster turnout of registered Democrats. State party chairman Perington disagreed with Romer's strategy, commenting after the election that he "would rather have seen that money go to a get-out-the-vote effort," since "it would have helped with a lot of candidates" (Young 1998).

Ballot Measures as "Wedge" Issues

In California, but not in Colorado, there is evidence that the Republican Party has tried to use ballot measures to split its opponent's base of support. While these so-called wedge initiatives tend to receive extensive media coverage, the parties in both states have not used them often. In fact, party officials in Colorado could not recall any recent initiatives that served as wedge issues in races for political office (Bain 1998; Curtis 1998; Gelt 1998; Perington 1998). This is primarily due to Colorado's strict campaign finance laws passed in 1996 that limit party contributions and expenditures and to the relatively weak party identification in the state. (Over one-third of the electorate in 1998 was registered as "Unaffiliated" [Sanko 1998]). What remains the best example of a political party trying to exploit a majoritarian ballot initiative to split the opposition is the GOP's adoption of Proposition 209, the 1996 California Civil Rights Initiative.

The resounding passage of Proposition 209 created shock waves that continue to reverberate across the country even today. Chavez's (1998) extended case study of the measure that called for the dismantling of affirmative action programs in the state details how the Republican Party provided essential funding to Ward Connerly's organization in an effort to split Democratic support for President Bill Clinton in his reelection bid (252). Disavowing his long-standing support for affirmative action, Governor Wilson and the California GOP helped save the floundering campaign for Proposition 209. Wilson and the GOP envisioned the measure severing moderate Democratic supporters from President Clinton and turning them to Bob Dole's camp. Schrag (1998) relates that Wilson, in a teleconference call with Newt Gingrich, claimed that Proposition 209 was "a partisan issue...that works strongly to our advantage [and] has every bit the potential to make a critical difference" to defeat Clinton and elect Dole (226). For his part, Clinton did his best to shy away from the measure, only discussing the substance of the measure when prodded by the media. Clinton's chief political strategist, Harold Ickes, strongly advised the president not to discuss affirmative action, since it was a "hot button issue" which might disaffect white ethnic supporters in California (Shrag 1998, 223–24). While the relationship with the state GOP was never cozy, Connerly and his fellow backers of Proposition 209 received heavy levels of direct funding from the state Republican Party and indirect support from the RNC. The California Republican party contributed $997,034 to the Yes campaign on Proposition 209, and the Senate Republican Majority Committee contributed an additional $90,000 (California Secretary of State 1996). The RNC, independent of Connerly's group, made "independent expenditures," producing its own television ads championing Proposition 209 (Chavez 1998, 252).

While examples are few and far between, state parties, as well as the RNC and DNC, may continue to exploit wedge initiatives for their partisan advantage. The two national parties have made significant transfer payments to supposedly nonpartisan "educational" committees, which have then passed the contributions on to issue groups that promote or oppose state-level ballot measures. While these payments are extremely difficult to trace—since they are not required to be reported to the state election commissions or the Federal Elections Commission—there is evidence that the RNC in 1996 transferred more than $4.5 million to Grover Norquist's "nonpartisan" organization, Americans for Tax Reform (ATR), for the explicit purpose of being spent to promote certain ballot measures (Smith 1998b; Levin 1997). Norquist passed on a substantial amount of the RNC money to groups in California, Colorado, and Oregon that sponsored conservative ballot measures, including antitax, right-to-work, and "paycheck protection" ballot measures. For example, in 1996 ATR contributed $509,500 to Bill Sizemore's group, Oregon Taxpayers United (OTU), which comprised nearly 58 percent of the total contributions OTU received that year (Smith 1998c). In 1998, ATR funneled $441,000 to the conservative group, Campaign Reform Initiative (CRI), the primary issue group backing Proposition 226 (California Secretary of State 1998b). This practice of using "nonpartisan" "educational" organizations as flow-through entities to influence elections is starting to be used by some offshoots of state parties (to be discussed in the following section).

Ideological Compatibility

In Colorado, more so than in California, the Republican and Democratic state parties, as well as "educational" committees set up by former party officials, have become directly and indirectly involved in ballot initiatives for ideological reasons. In the most recent election in Colorado, the state Republican Party and two "educational" committees were engaged in several ideological majoritarian measures. Somewhat surprisingly, though, the state parties in California have also become involved in measures with broad support and narrow opposition ("entrepreneurial/populist") and even ones with narrow support and opposition ("interest-group"), which was not expected by Donovan et al. (1998, 83–89).

Prior to coming under the leadership of Curtis in 1997, the Colorado Republican party tended to stay out of ballot initiative politics. Don Bain (1998), the GOP chairman from 1994 through 1996, maintains that "the party should not get involved in issues at either the legislative or issue level." He claims that during the 1994 and 1996 elections, the Republican Party was not involved with any initiatives, even though Amendment 15, a campaign finance measure, "directly impacted the party." For Bain, a lawyer, "the party is mechanical, not philosophical," even though the state party has been tempted to support paycheck protection and affirmative action measures. Bain argues that if the party becomes involved in the process, it "brings out opposing special interests that galvanize against the issue or candidates." Therefore, says Bain, "the party should basically stay out of ballot issues."

In the 1998 general election, much to Bain's disapproval, the Colorado Republican party actively supported three highly controversial majoritarian initiatives. The party backed Amendment 11, a ban on "late-term" abortions; Amendment 12, a requirement that minors obtain "parental consent" to have an abortion; and Amendment 17, a $2,500 "tax credit" (school voucher) for parents with children attending nondenominational or sectarian private schools (Curtis 1998). The decision for the state Republicans to become involved in the ballot issues was made by party chairman, Steve Curtis. Prior to the November election, the proponents of the antiabortion and school choice measures approached Curtis to solicit the party's help. Obliging, the party provided substantial in-kind contributions to the two groups supporting the measures. On the two antiabortion measures, the GOP provided technical advice and strategy to the proponents. Key Republican party officials sat in on meetings with the initiative supporters, held phone conferences, discussed the concept and related issues, and advanced "general themes" for the ad campaign leading up to the election. On Amendment 17, Curtis provided a party donor list to the tax credit proponents, led by Steve Schuck, a Colorado Springs real estate developer and former chairman of the Independence Institute. According to Curtis (1998), even if the party had supplementary funds to contribute to the two issue committees, he would not have given them, since the people who give money to the party expect it to support the party or to support GOP candidates.

Why did the Colorado GOP actively support the three measures in 1998? According to Curtis (1998), the Republican Party, while traditionally not involved with groups backing or opposing ballot measures, decided to "cross the line" and participate because the three initiatives had strong ideological "consistency with the party's platform." Ballot initiatives, Curtis believes, "should fall within the camp of one or the other party," and parties, which "haven't stuck to their guns" on the issues, should take an active stance on them. Initiatives provide "a real opportunity to advance the party's cause," Curtis asserts. Striking the populist chord heard a century ago, Curtis claims that legislative "change through parties is a slow and tedious process," so parties "need to take the bull by the horns." The initiative process, for Curtis, provides a much more expedient mechanism to change policy than the legislative process. Curtis, a moral conservative, contends that even with Republican majorities in the state House and Senate, there is "no way an abortion bill will make it to [newly elected Republican Governor] Owens' desk and get signed."

Conversely, while officials in the state Democratic Party were personally opposed to the three conservative measures on the ballot in 1998, the party took no official stance on the measures (Perington 1998). However, Howard Gelt, a former chair of the Democratic Party, was indirectly involved in promoting and opposing ballot measures through an extra-party "educational" committee he established in the spring of 1998. For Gelt (1998), there is a symbiotic relationship between ballot issues and candidates, as initiatives tend to shape the issues that are central to candidates' campaigns for political office. "Ballot measures," in 1998, according to Gelt, were "driving candidates," because "candidates are captive of issues." Republican candidates lined up in support of the antiabortion measures and the school tax credit issue, whereas Democrats bidding for office opposed the measures. Major contributors to issue committees and candidates for political office were also largely synonymous during the election, according to Gelt. "You can take every initiative and cross-cut it with the principle supporters of the candidate campaigns," Gelt claims.

To help forge the link between candidates and ballot issues, and to avoid the contribution and expenditure limitations placed on state parties, Gelt set up his "nonpartisan" "educational" committee to independently inform voters about the candidates' stances on the various ballot issues. Interestingly, former Republican Party chair Don Bain also set up an "educational" committee to challenge Gelt's committee. Gelt formed the "nonpartisan" Save Colorado First committee; Bain formed the "nonpartisan" Centennial Spirit committee. Both committees skirted the fine line of overtly supporting Democrat and Republican candidates, respectively. During the fall campaign, the two groups raised and spent over $1 million, although the committees were not required by state law to disclose their contributions or expenditures (Bain 1998; Gelt 1998). Gelt, for example, met regularly with Fufi Mendez, who along with Planned Parenthood, led the opposition to the two antiabortion measures (Gelt 1998). In fact, Gelt served as the cochair of Mendez's finance committee opposing the abortion initiatives. In its commercials, the Save Colorado First committee painted GOP gubernatorial candidate Bill Owens as antichoice and provouchers. Similarly, Centennial Spirit, under the direction of Bain, painted Democratic candidates for statewide office and their stances on ballot measures in a negative light (Abbott 1998). The two committees' informational commercials on the candidates were, according to Gelt (1998), "absolutely correlated on what was on people's minds"—that is, the explosive initiatives on the ballot.

Steve Curtis, Don Bain, and Howard Gelt all viewed the three socially divisive measures on the 1998 ballot in ideological, rather than functional terms. In contrast to the Proposition 187 and Proposition 209 campaigns in California, in which the California Republican party financially backed the measures to promote GOP turnout and divide the traditional Democratic base respectively, the three conservative ballot measures in Colorado did not have apparent GOTV or wedge effects. In fact, the opposite may have been the case. GOP support for the antiabortion and school voucher initiatives may have had a backlash effect. It may have mobilized Democratic, Independent, and even moderate Republicans to come out to vote against the initiatives and, in turn, against Republican candidates. Evidence of this was Republican Bill Owens' razor-thin margin of victory over Democrat Gail Schoettler, despite the sizable number of registered Republicans in the state (Brown 1998). Nevertheless, party chairmen in Colorado, more so than in California, have turned to the initiative process to promote the underlying ideologies of the two parties.

In 1998 in California, the two parties, for ideological as well as monetary reasons, took positions on a range of ballot measures that Donovan et al. (1998) describe as "entrepreneurial/populist" and "interest-group" (84). California Republican and Democratic Party officials found that by endorsing ballot initiatives that were consistent with their parties' ideologies, they were actually able to *raise* funds for their parties. Usually when a party sponsors a measure, money flows in only one direction—from the party to the issue committee. But as the two parties in California recently experienced, by endorsing measures opposed by narrow special interests, they actually "netted money from proposition campaigns" (California Republican Party 1998). In 1998, the Republican state party sent out over 13 million pieces of direct mail. Before several of the mailings, party officials approached the issue committees, explained to them what the party's official position was regarding their ballot measures, and asked them, "Would you like to buy some support...at cut rates...in our mailing?" The committees opposing the regulation of electric utilities (Proposition 9) and the tobacco tax for early childhood programs (Proposition 10) both placed ads in the Republican mailers, and donated money to the party to offset the cost of mailing. According to a state GOP official, this was "a relatively new practice" for the party (California Republican Party 1998).

More notably, the state Democratic Party found that by not taking an official stance on a measure, it could raise funds for the organization. At its ballot endorsement meeting in August, the Democratic Party endorsed all eight issues for the 1998 general election, *except* for Proposition 5, the Indian gaming measure. Attending the meeting were "tons of Indians and union" members, voicing their respective support and opposition to Proposition 5 (California Democratic Party 1998). However, the chairman of the party, former state Senator Art Torres, refused to allow a vote on the measure by the 300-member executive board because it was potentially a divisive issue for two core constituents of the party. Because the party did not vote to endorse or oppose the measure, the nonvote was largely viewed as a "victory by the Indians," which led several Indian tribes to contribute money to the state party (California Democratic Party 1998). The party also officially opposed Proposition 9, the measure sponsored by progressive groups to recapture costs on electricity suppliers, and Proposition 8, Governor Wilson's public education reform measure. In return, the party received substantial contributions from several utility companies and the teachers union (California Secretary of State 1998a).

Conclusion

This chapter examines the role political parties play in the initiative process and the reasons for their involvement. Contrary to the expectations of several scholars, state (and even national) party organizations have become entangled in the complex web of direct democracy. It is clear from the evidence presented here that parties are not as impotent or as irrelevant in the initiative process as they might seem upon first glance. While Magleby's (1984) concern that political parties are institutionally weakened by the initiative process because single-issue groups are able to frame and advance ballot measures without having to compromise or build coalitions (189) remains valid, parties today are turning to the initiative to regain their strength. It is unquestionable that "major policy conflicts can take place outside of the legislature" via the initiative process; however, it is less certain that initiatives are "beyond party politics," as Donovan and Bowler maintain (1998, 3). In both direct and indirect ways, parties are utilizing the initiative process to increase the turnout of their electoral base on Election Day, to drive a wedge into their opposition's constituency, and to promote the ideological points of their platforms. The reasons for party involvement in the initiative process are not mutually exclusive, nor are they necessarily predictable. What is certain is that more comparative research needs to be conducted on the complex relationship between party organizations and the array of issue groups that participate in the initiative process.

References

Abbott, Karen. 1998. Nonprofit organization says Owens would be quicker to solve traffic congestion. *Rocky Mountain News,* 23 October, 29A.

Bain, Don. 1998. Telephone interview with the author, 2 November.

Barnett, James. 1915. *The operation of the initiative, referendum, and recall in Oregon.* New York: MacMillan Co.

Bibby, John, and Thomas Holbrook. 1996. Parties and elections. In *Politics in the American States,* edited by Virginia Gray and Herbert Jacob, 6th ed., 78–121.Washington, DC.: CQ Press.

Bones, Hugh, and Robert Benedict. 1975. Perspectives on direct legislation, *The Western Political Quarterly* 28: 330–51.

Bowler, Shaun, and Todd Donovan. 1998. *Demanding choices.* Ann Arbor: University of Michigan Press.

Brown, Fred. 1998. Unaffiliateds lean a little to the left. *Denver Post,* 11 November, 11B.

California Commission on Campaign Financing. 1992. *Democracy by initiative.* Los Angeles: Center for Responsive Government.

California Democratic Party. (Anonymous party official.) 1998. Telephone interview with author. Sacramento, CA, 8 December.

California Republican Party. (Anonymous party official.) 1998. Telephone interview with author. Burbank, CA, 1 December.

California Secretary of State. 1996. Yes on Prop. 209. Available at: <http://www.ss.ca.gov/prd/ bmc96/prop209.htm>

_____. 1998a. Late contributions and independent expenditures, 1998 General Election. Available at: <http://www.vote98.ss.ca.gov/lcrV98>

_____. 1998b. Late contributions and independent expenditures, 1998 Primary Election. Available at: <http://www.ss.ca.gov/prd/bmprimary98>

Campbell, Ann. 1997. The citizens initiative and entrepreneurial politics: Direct democracy in Colorado, 1966–1994. Paper presented at the annual meeting of the Western Political Science Association, Tucson, AZ. March.

Citrin, Jack. 1996. Who's the boss? Direct democracy and popular control of government. In *Broken contract? Changing relationships between Americans and their government,* edited by Stephen Craig. Boulder, CO: Westview Press.

Chavez, Lydia. 1998. *The color bind: California's battle to end affirmative action.* Berkeley: University of California Press.

Clemens, Elisabeth. 1997. *The people's lobby.* Chicago: University of Chicago Press.

Cronin, Thomas. 1989. *Direct democracy: The politics of initiative, referendum, and recall.* Cambridge: Harvard University Press.

Curtis, Steve. 1998. Telephone interview with the author, 1 December.

DiCamillo, Mark, and Mervin Field. 1997. Voters recognize many negatives about ballot proposition elections, but still think they are a good thing. The Field Institute, release #1854, 3 November.

Donovan, Todd, and Shaun Bowler. 1998. An overview of direct democracy in the American states. In *Citizens as Legislators,* edited by Shaun Bowler, Todd Donovan, and Caroline Tolbert. Columbus: Ohio State University Press.

Donovan, Todd, Shaun Bowler, David McCuan, and Ken Fernandez. 1998. Contending players and strategies: Opposition advantages in initiative campaigns. In *Citizens as Legislators,* edited by Shaun Bowler, Todd Donovan, and Caroline Tolbert. Columbus: Ohio State University Press.

DuBois, Philip, and Floyd Feeney. 1992. *Improving the California initiative process: Options for change.* University of California: California Policy Center Report.

Everson, D. 1981. The effects of initiatives on voter turnout: A comparative state analysis. *Western Political Quarterly* 34: 415–25.

Gelt, Howard. 1998. Telephone interview with the author. Denver, CO, 30 November.

Gerber, Elisabeth. 1996. Legislative response to the threat of popular initiatives. *American Journal of Political Science* 40: 99–128.

————. 1998. Pressuring legislatures through the use of initiatives: Two forms of indirect influence. In *Citizens as Legislators,* edited by Shaun Bowler, Todd Donovan, and Caroline Tolbert. Columbus: Ohio State University Press.

Gerber, Elisabeth, and Arthur Lupia. 1995. Campaign competition and policy responsiveness in direct political behavior. *Political Behavior* 17: 287–306.

Hagen, Michael, and Edward Lascher. 1998. Public opinion about ballot initiatives. Paper presented at the annual meeting of the American Political Science Association, Boston, MA, September.

Hall, Arnold. 1921. *Popular government.* New York: MacMillan Co.

Hedge, David. 1997. *Governance and the changing American states.* Boulder: Westview Press.

Karp, Jeffrey. 1998. The influence of elite endorsements in initiative campaigns. In *Citizens as Legislators,* edited by Shaun Bowler, Todd Donovan, and Caroline Tolbert. Columbus: Ohio State University Press.

Kelley, Stanley. 1956. *Professional public relations and political power.* Baltimore: The Johns Hopkins University Press.

Lascher, Edward, Michael Hagen, and Steven Rochlin. 1996. Gun behind the door? Ballot initiatives, state policies and public opinion. *Journal of Politics* 58: 760–75.

Levin, Carl. 1997. Incomplete hearings from the Senate campaign finance investigation. Congressional Record, 105th Congress, 1st Session, 10 November. Available at:
<http://www.senate.gov/~levin/floor/111097a.htm>

Lowenstein, Daniel. 1982. Campaign spending and ballot propositions: Recent experience, public choice theory, and the First Amendment. *UCLA Law Review* 86: 505–641.

Lupia, Arthur. 1994. Shortcuts versus encyclopedias: Information and voting behavior in California insurance reform elections. *American Political Science Review* 88: 63–76.

Magleby, David. 1984. *Direct legislation: Voting on ballot propositions in the United States.* Baltimore: The Johns Hopkins University Press.

_____. 1994. Direct legislation in the American states. In *Referendums around the world,* edited by David Butler and Austin Ranney. Washington, DC: American Enterprise Institute.

Magleby, David, and Kelly Patterson. 1998. The art of persuasion: Consultants and the rise of direct democracy. Paper presented at the annual meeting of the American Political Science Association, Boston, MA, September.

Mahtesian, Charles. 1998. Grassroots charade. *Governing,* November, 38–42.

McCuan, David. Shaun Bowler, Todd Donovan, and Ken Fernandez. 1998. California's political warriors: Campaign professionals and the initiative process. In *Citizens as Legislators,* edited by Shaun Bowler, Todd Donovan, and Caroline Tolbert. Columbus: Ohio State University Press.

McSeveney, Samuel. 1994. The fourth party system and progressivism. In *Parties and politics in American history,* edited by Sandy Maisel and William Shade. New York: Garland Publishing.

Munro, William, ed. 1912. *The initiative, referendum, and recall.* New York: Appleton and Co.

Oberholtzer, Ellis. 1900. *The referendum in America.* New York: Charles Scribner's Sons.

Perington, Phil. 1998. Telephone interview with the author. Denver, CO, 8 December.

Rosenthal, Alan. 1998. *The decline of representative democracy.* Washington, DC: CQ Press, 1998.

Sanko, John. 1998. Independents swell voter rolls. *Rocky Mountain News,* 4 August, 8A.

Schmidt, David. 1989. *Citizen lawmakers: The ballot initiative revolution.* Philadelphia: Temple University Press.

Schrag, Peter. 1998. *Paradise lost: California's experience, America's future.* New York: New Press.

Smith, Daniel. 1996 Populist entrepreneur: Douglas Bruce and the tax and government limitation movement in Colorado, 1986–1992. *Great Plains Research* 6: 269–94.

—————. 1998a. *Tax crusaders and the politics of direct democracy.* New York: Routledge.

—————. 1998b. Unmasking the tax crusaders. *State Government News* 41: 18–21.

—————. 1998c. The legacy of Howard Jarvis and Proposition 13 1996 tax limitation initiatives in the American states. Paper presented at the annual meeting of the Western Political Science Association, Los Angeles, March.

—————. 1999. Reevaluating the causes of Proposition 13. *Social Science History* 23: 2.

Smith, Daniel, and Robert Herrington. 1999. The process of direct democracy: Colorado's 1996 Parental Rights Amendment. *Social Science Journal* 37: 2.

Tolbert, Caroline, Daniel H. Lowenstein, and Todd Donovan. 1998. Election law and rules for using initiatives. In *Citizens as Legislators*, edited by Shaun Bowler, Todd Donovan, and Caroline Tolbert. Columbus: Ohio State University Press.

Tolbert, Caroline, and Rodney Hero. 1998. Race/ethnicity and direct democracy: The contextual basis of support for anti-immigrant and official English measures. In *Citizens as Legislators*, edited by Shaun Bowler, Todd Donovan, and Caroline Tolbert. Columbus: Ohio State University Press.

Turnout could hinge on initiatives. 1998. *Congress Daily,* 6 October.

Vincent, Barbara. 1996. Expanding the process. *The Initiative Press & Seminars,* 6 February.

Wilcox, Delos. 1912. *Government by all the people.* New York: MacMillan Co.

Young, Ricky. 1998. DNC donation to state issues criticized. *Denver Post,* 11 December, B1.

PART II

Ethnic Minorities
and Direct Democracy

CHAPTER 7

The Three Strikes Initiative: The Impact of Racial and Ethnic Composition on Voting Patterns and Attitudes Toward Crime

Linda Lopez, American Political Science Association (APSA)

Many research strategies have been developed by urban scholars to understand racial and ethnic coalition formation; however, very little scholarly attention has been given to coalition formation around certain initiative issues. Given increases in initiatives on the California ballot dealing specifically with minority communities, voting on these public policy issues would offer some indication about whether there is cooperation among racial and ethnic groups. As a consequence, an alternate way to understand coalition formation is to analyze ethnic and racial group voting patterns concerning particular issues. Los Angeles is an excellent site to evaluate electoral coalitions at the local level, given its multiracial and multiethnic composition.

In 1994, two initiative measures were placed on the California ballot that directly affected minority communities: Proposition 187, the Save Our State initiative restricting the services provided to illegal immigrants; and Proposition 184, the Three Strikes You're Out Initiative, invoking harsher punishment for third-time convicted criminals. I focus on Proposition 184 as one way to understand whether certain demographic, social, and political characteristics of groups in Los Angeles affect political outcomes in communities.

Criminal punishment is one of the most important public policy issues at the federal, state, and local level. In many states, and in Congress as well, anticrime legislation has been the central element of concern as constituents become more fearful of crime (see Appendix 7A). In 1994, public anger over crime found political justification in the enactment of stricter sentencing laws and the passage of the "three strikes and you're out" initiative in California.[1] Other states have followed California's lead by adopting similar laws.[2]

In November 1994, California voters approved the three-strikes initiative by 72 percent.[3] The initiative's overwhelming approval is symbolic of the public's fear of crime, manifested by its high level of support for tougher sentences for criminals and its mistrust in the ability of the criminal justice system to effectively deal with problems of crime. Prior to the passage of proposition 184, a *Los Angeles Times* national poll[4] found strong support for the measure: 58 percent favored the three-strikes initiative regardless of the costs; 21 percent favored it depending on the costs: and 17 percent opposed it. Politicians have capitalized on the crime fear by proposing quick-fix responses to crime and have embraced tough criminal sentencing proposals to reduce crime. Governor Pete Wilson's reelection gubernatorial campaign is one example of the use of a tough crime platform in courting voters to the polls.

In contrast to the immigration initiative, which is an ethnically based issue, affecting immigrant groups and Latinos more directly, the crime initiative is different in that tougher sentencing laws disproportionately affect minority communities as a whole.[5] A shared-discrimination theory is useful in understanding why African-American and Latino communities might vote similarly on issues dealing with tougher sentencing laws. Both communities may feel that their groups are disproportionately represented in the criminal justice system since the system is racially and ethnically biased.

---

1. This law received initial passage in the state legislature in March 1994 (AB 971) and was signed by Governor Pete Wilson. The law mandates a sentence of 25 years to life for felons found guilty of a third serious crime. In addition, it doubles sentences for people convicted of a second felony, requires that sentences be served consecutively, and requires that crimes committed in other states be counted. It also limits time off for good behavior earned during prison and narrows the latitude of prosecutors in ignoring prior crimes when negotiating plea agreements.

2. Other states which have approved some form of the "three strike's" law include Alaska, Connecticut, Delaware, Georgia, Massachusetts, Missouri, New Jersey, New York, North Carolina, Ohio, Oklahoma, Rhode Island, Virginia, Washington, Wisconsin. In total, variants of the law have been introduced in over thirty states; see Larry Rohter, In wave of anti-crime fervor, states rush to adopt laws, *New York Times*, 10 May 1994, A1.

3. Statement of the vote, Elections Division, Sacramento, 8 November 1994, 111.

4. The *Los Angeles Times* poll taken in January of 1,516 adults nationwide.

5. Comparative incarceration rates in California prisons indicate population characteristics as follows: 29.5% White; 32.14% Black; 34% Hispanic; 5.1% other. See <www.cdc.state.ca.us/factsht.htm>.

Consequently, these minority communities, on the basis of shared policy concerns, are more likely to oppose longer jail sentences. Alternatively, a self-interest model might suggest the following: The issue of tougher sentencing laws might prompt a response by minority voters in these communities to support these measures based on a shared interest among voting minorities as well as white voters that something must be done to rid their communities of crime. These theoretical concerns are relevant in gauging possible differences in the level of racial and ethnic support for tougher sentencing laws.

The vote on this initiative provides the basis to conduct analyses on expected group differences as well as to determine possible electoral cooperation among Anglos, Asians, Latinos, and African-Americans. Furthermore, it provides a basis for determining whether certain variables underscore cleavages that may serve to undermine ethnic and racial electoral cooperation. Depending on the issues, changes may occur in the nature of the coalition. In other words, issues may serve to provoke electoral cleavages and alignments that may shift significantly. Given the changing nature of issues from one election year to another, it seems logical to focus on one election year to understand voting preferences during one period in time and to conduct and in-depth analysis of voting behavior patterns of each racial and ethnic group.

The study of this initiative is relevant for public-policy concerns affecting minority communities in Los Angeles specifically. The salience of race and ethnicity in California is illustrated by the increase of initiatives placed on the ballot by ideologically conservative organizations to restrict the rights of minority groups. The passage of Proposition 187 and the passage of the Civil Rights Initiative restricting affirmative action point to a trend in the use of the initiative process to restrict minority political rights. Even though the initiative process was originally conceived to allow citizens to take political matters into their own hands and to make public policy, it has increasingly become countermajoritarian. Citizen-based initiatives are often placed on the ballot by individuals with special interests who wish to determine public-policy outcomes. Minorities are disproportionately affected because they frequently do not have the voting numbers to defeat measures that produce negative consequences for their communities. For example, the voting-age population of Latinos is low compared to their overall population because of several formal barriers such as noncitizenship, a lack of proficiency in the English language, and low voter registration levels. Cooperative electoral arrangements between ethnic and racial minorities become increasingly important for minorities in the struggle to secure their political rights. Nevertheless, the level of cross-racial coopera-tion may be contingent on the issue and how the issue affects each group. Class interests may prevail in the electoral choices minority groups make rather than ideology. As a result, fragile coalitions are likely if there is no durable alliance that can bring these groups together to seek a collective goal.

This research, as well as political analysis, extends the voting behavior lit-erature and the racial voting literature by focusing on the importance of how issues set the context for structuring minority political preferences at the group level rather than the individual level. Theories of political behavior have tended to focus on the political preferences of individual actors within communities; however, this research departs from this tradition by focusing on group political activity and the importance of demographic, social, and economic characteristics in shaping voter outcomes in these areas. Accord-ing to general theories of voting behavior and racial voting literature, there is evidence that certain demographic, political, social, and economic vari-ables affect voting patterns at the national and city levels. These factors, in-cluding class, race and ethnicity, age, gender, and partisanship are used to understand minority political choices on issues and the degree to which these factors affect intergroup cooperation and/or intergroup conflict. I argue that issues set the context in local politics for the degree of intergroup coopera-tion and that several variables may produce cleavages that mitigate the prospects for multiracial electoral coalitions. The empirical analysis assesses crime by utilizing group-level data in precincts, as well as survey data. The strength of this approach is to extend traditional analysis by using a multi-variate analysis that focuses on individual-level data through the utilization of polls and, more importantly, by using a group-level political analysis of aggregate data in these precincts. Despite the importance of survey data in gaining information about bivariate relationships and the impact of certain variables on political choices at the individual level, a multivariate analysis that includes aggregate data provides a broader and richer understanding of group processes and political outcomes. This is significant in that political choices are often expressed in group terms and not as isolated individual choices in the political arena.

The chapter draws on national and local voting literature to understand how race and ethnicity, age, gender, party identification, and socioeconomic status might be used to assess political behavior in Los Angeles—and specif-ically, how demographic, social, and political factors influence political out-comes in communities and the importance of group political activity in a city which is becoming transformed in its political structure and demographics.

Party Identification

The social-psychological approach to analyzing voting behavior was first elaborated in the study by Campbell, Converse, and Stokes (1960),[6] in which party identification was the most immediate determinant of the vote. According to these authors, party identification can be viewed as the psychological commitment or attachment to a political party that normally predisposes voters to evaluate the party and its candidates in a favorable light. Nie, Verba, and Petrocick (1979) challenged this major finding by suggesting that changes in voting behavior occurred as a result of the emerging importance of specific issues in the 1960s and the introduction of a new electorate in the voting population.

Socioeconomic Status

Despite the research which emphasizes party identification with voting behavior, several empirical studies have also examined the effects of socioeconomic status on political participation. The results of these studies suggest a strong positive correlation between socioeconomic status (SES) and political participation(Alford and Freidland 1975; Lipset 1960; Milbrath and Goel 1977)—that is, the higher one's social status the higher the rate of one's political participation. This finding was observed with whatever measure was employed to reflect socioeconomic status—occupation, education attainment, or family income.[7] The socioeconomic model was introduced by Verba and Nie (1972) to understand political behavior. According to this model,

> The social status of an individual—his job, education, and income— determines to a large extent how much he participates. It does this through the intervening effects of a variety of civic attitudes conducive to participation: attitudes such as a sense of efficacy, of psychological involvement in politics, and a feeling of obligation to participate. (12)

Their data confirmed that "citizens of higher social and economic status participate more in politics" (13). Additional support for the socioeconomic status model was found by Milbrath and Goel (1977), who concluded that

---

6. For additional results from the Michigan studies, see Campbell et al. 1966.

7. See Milbrath and Goel (1977, 114-28) for a review of these studies.

"higher class persons are more likely to participate in politics than lower-class persons" (92).

In another study, Wolfinger and Rosentone (1980) examined the effect of demographic characteristics on turnout using census data for November 1972 and 1974. The independent variables they analyzed included age, education, occupation, race, sex, region, marital status, and employment on the dependent variable voter turnout. The probit analysis used suggests a very strong relationship between rates of voting and years of education. The second relevant finding was that turnout increases with income, even though there is some variation between occupation and turnout rates. Finally, education has the most powerful independent influence on turnout.

Race and Ethnicity

Like socioeconomic status, or, more broadly, social class, race and ethnicity have also been the subject of empirical and theoretical interest for social scientists. Huckfeldt and Kohfeld (1989) examine the decline of class and the emergence of race in American politics after World War II. Their main thesis is

> The politics of race often proves to be incompatible with the politics of class in American political life. More precisely, race frequently serves as a wedge that disrupts lower-class coalitions, thereby driving out class in political arrangements. Working-class and lower-middle class whites are frequently ruptured along racial lines. (xi)

In a similar argument Key (1949) and Schattschneider (1960) point to racial conflict between partners of lower-class coalitions leading to the demise of class-based politics.

Carmines and Stimson (1989) examine the origins and development of new issues that have transformed the political system. In particular, their research focuses exclusively on how racial issues fundamentally affected the party system. Race became central in structuring belief systems among the electorate and had a profound impact on American politics. According to the authors, political evolution occurred around the issue of race: "[T]he issue was capable of altering the political environment.... [I]t had a long cycle, and led to fundamental and permanent change in the party system" (11). The major political parties took different political stances, and issues of race moved to the center of public discourse, creating mass partisan polarization in the electorate.

The literature on the determinants of voting behavior (party, socioeconomic status, and race and ethnicity determinants) is limited. On the one hand, there is very little incorporation of other racial or ethnic groups in voting research. While there is extensive research on the variations of voting between black and whites, there has been very little research conducted on voting issues concerning Latinos and Asians. One might easily find other voting determinants to explain voting preferences of these groups at the local level. For example, a study focusing exclusively on the voting behavior of Latinos might yield alternative explanations for their voting preferences. Thus, it may be that traditional voting determinants such as party identification, socioeconomic status, or race may not entirely explain variations in voting within the Latino voting population. A closer analysis of group voting in communities or neighborhoods with high concentrations of Asians or Latinos might point to factors such as generation status, residential location, or language as possible explanations for variations in group voting. Nationally based studies avoid this more in-depth analysis by overlooking the role of internal divisions within groups that might affect group preferences. This monolithic view of minority voting patterns inhibits a full understanding of voting by failing to capture the heterogeneity that might affect voting decisions. For example, socioeconomic status might be a factor that divides blacks concerning certain issues. That is, higher-status blacks might have a different voting preference for housing issues than lower-status blacks. These variations, if found, might yield a more accurate analysis of voting patterns than traditional voting-behavior studies suggest. The failure to capture variations within groups is also prevalent in theories explaining racial and ethnic political coalition formation.

The electoral coalition literature on minority group political participation has focused on cooperative arrangements across groups at the local level. More specifically, research on political coalitions has treated racial and ethnic categories as monolithic, without considering how internal group differences effect political coalition formation, particularly relating to electoral activity. Research on Los Angeles voting behavior (Sonenshein 1993; Hahn, Klingman, and Pachon 1976; Halley, Acock, and Greene 1976) suggests a bi-racial model in which blacks and whites ally as coalition partners. One study identified cleavages in bi-racial coalition building along factors such as class (Hahn, Klingman, and Pachon 1976), and racial identification (Halley, Acock, and Greene 1976). Yet, factors contributing to variances in internal group voting have been overlooked.

The emphasis on cross-racial comparison is illustrated in research focusing exclusively on cooperative political arrangements between blacks and white liberals. Carmichael and Hamilton's study was one of the first to examine the prospects of white and black political partnerships. Stokely Carmichael and Charles Hamilton (1967), in *Black Power the Politics of Liberation in America*, developed a theoretical framework to understand why blacks and liberal whites were unable to form strong durable coalitions. They suggest that self-interest drives the relationship between the two resulting in divisiveness. According to their normative theory of self-interest, blacks must resolve four fundamental issues before eliciting the support of whites.

In contrast to Carmichael and Hamilton's interest based perspective, other approaches to the study of coalition formation center around shared ideology as the mechanism to induce cooperative political arrangements. The study of Browning, Marshall, and Tabb (1984) of ten northern California cities examined racial and ethnic coalition formation and its impact on policy responsiveness from 1960 through 1979. The theory of incorporation posits that groups' interests must be advanced in the dominant coalition in order for minorities to gain certain benefits for their communities. Incorporation is measured as the extent to which racial and ethnic minorities are represented in the governing coalition. According to Browning, Marshall, and Tabb (1984), electoral activity is the best strategy to achieve minority incorporation. Their findings suggest that electoral coalitions including white liberal ideologues and blacks, as well as some Latinos, increase the level of minority incorporation.[8]

A more extensive analysis of biracial coalition politics in Los Angeles is developed by Sonenshein (1993). His research suggests the importance of biracial coalitions in producing minority incorporation in Los Angeles from 1969 through 1992. His theory posits three fundamental requirements for coalition formation: 1) The primary basis for political coalitions between blacks and whites is ideological. Minority mobilization and liberal ideology are the cornerstones of any interracial coalition pursuing minority incorporation. 2) The existence of white liberal support for racial liberalism is insufficient to guarantee the creation of successful interracial coalitions. The prospects for interracial coalitions are deeply influenced by interest alliance or conflict. 3) Fi-

---

8. According to Browning, Marshall, and Tabb (1990), minority incorporation is measured as "the extent to which the group interests are effectively represented in policy-making." The level of incorporation is a function of whether blacks and Hispanics are represented in coalitions that dominate policy making; mere representation in the coalition is insufficient to guarantee any share of political influence over government. The key to control city government and to make it responsive is to influence policy making through active participation in the decision making process.

nally, interracial leadership ties arise out of factional divisions within the black and white communities. These factional ties underlie elite links based on trust and equal political status (20).

While the electoral coalition literature advances some degree of Black-Latino coalition formation in local politics (Browning, Marshall, and Tabb 1984; Sonenshein 1993; Arian, Goldberg, Mollenkopf, and Rogowsky 1990; Swain 1993; Tate 1993; Henry and Munoz 1991; Jackson 1991, Hahn, Kling-man, and Pachon 1976) to elect mayors, these coalitions are fragile. Other explanations are developed by scholars to understand the fragility of these coalitions and, in particular, group conflict theory. Instead of focusing on the shared economic, political, and social position of blacks and Latinos, some scholars (McClain and Karnig 1990; Oliver and Johnson 1984; Sonenshein 1993; Jennings 1992) argue that competition over scarce resources makes it unlikely that these two groups will form cooperative political arrangements. Group conflict theory posits that racial and ethnic groups exhibit feelings of mistrust on the basis of competition over scarce resources and not solely on the basis of prejudice (Bobo 1988). These scarce resources may include jobs, as well as adequate housing and government services. Despite a shared economic position by blacks and Latinos, these scholars conclude that a coalition is unlikely because the two populations may not have a common idea of what interests are important.

Johnson and Oliver (1989) point to group conflict theory as a source of interethnic conflict between blacks and Latinos in Los Angeles. Their findings suggest racial polarization between the two groups over jobs and housing, as well as differences in political and cultural attitudes. However, the theory of competition only helps explain how group differences rather than internal differences, along class and ideology, might generate strains. In contrast to the economic competitive framework, shared minority status may serve to promote durable multiracial coalitions.

Uhlaner (1989) examined the prospects of coalition among blacks, Latinos, and Asian-Americans in California by investigating levels of perceived prejudice experienced by each group. Shared perceptions and experience of discrimination are central to her analysis rather than shared interests as the basis for a coalition. Consequently, this commonality of shared discrimination may serve as the foundation to build cross-racial coalitions. Nevertheless, Uhlaner suggests that cooperation is not imminent based on shared discrimination. Similar structural positions may instead generate competition as each group feels that the other group threatens its own group interests. Finally, leaders become increasingly important in organizing groups around common interests.

Another related focus of scholars has been the relationship between racial and ethnic electoral mobilization and its impact on the election of minority mayors or white liberal mayors who represent the interests of minority groups. Studies of minority mayors in major urban centers such as New York (Arian, Goldberg, Mollenkopf, and Rogowsky 1990; Mollenkopf 1990), Chicago (Starks and Preston 1990), Los Angeles (Sonenshein 1993; Hahn, Klingman, and Pachon 1976; Halley, Acock, and Greene 1976), San Francisco, (DeLeon 1992), and Atlanta (Stone 1989) generally examine voting behavior relating to the election of a candidate. The point of reference becomes how minority groups mobilize to elect leaders who will provide benefits to minority communities. As a result, candidate-centered politics becomes the focus of research rather than how issues structure electoral coalitions.

Analysis of issue voting patterns rather than strict analysis of mayoral voting patterns becomes increasingly important in assessing likely coalition partners. In California, the analysis of initiatives as issues of public policy provides an alternate manner in analyzing voting behavior among minority groups. Even though issues are contingent on time and may change, a political trend has emerged since 1994: Matters of public policy that may negatively affect minority communities have been increasingly placed on the ballot. Evidence of this trend in deciding public policy issues by resorting to the initiative process was illustrated by the placement of the Civil Rights Initiative on the 1996 California ballot. Research that investigates voting behavior in the electorate might help in assessing coalition prospects.

The "Los Angeles Literature"

Research on Los Angeles politics has focused exclusively on biracial models and individual level analysis of political outcomes without investigating the relative importance of group political outcomes. That is, demographic and social characteristics of each racial and ethnic group in Los Angeles may in fact affect the political outcomes in certain neighborhoods in Los Angeles. A proper understanding of the political ethos of cities must incorporate separate analyses of how factors such as race, class, ethnicity, age, gender, partisanship, and generation status determine group political outcomes and of how group differences within the context of these characteristics might either prevent group cohesion or bring these groups closer in making political choices about issues that affect their communities. This study explores group-level political processes rather than individual-level voting patterns because individuals are rarely isolated from their communities in making decisions about politics. The group becomes the focus of this research rather than individuals' political patterns in order to assess how changes in social and economic factors impact politics in Los Angeles.

Earlier research (Hahn and Almy 1971; Hahn, Klingman, and Pachon 1976; Halley, Acock, and Greene 1976) on Los Angeles voting behavior points to key factors dividing racial and ethnic communities. Hahn's, Klingman's and Pachon's research suggests a number of cleavages in the Los Angeles electorate. For example, the findings suggest little evidence for an electoral coalition between blacks and other minorities in the authors' analysis of the 1969 and 1973 mayoral election. Socioeconomic factors serve to undermine these prospects. In analyzing black voting patterns, Hahn, Klingman, and Pachon (1976) argue that "the data did not corroborate the view that electoral choices of middle or upper-middle class black areas would diverge from working class black areas" (515). By contrast, the Chicano vote divided along class lines. According to their findings, "[W]hen education and income increased in predominately Chicano areas, the vote for Bradley and Pines declined" (515). Moreover, support for Bradley came from low-income rather than high-status Latinos. Consequently, when socioeconomic status increased, the vote for the black candidate decreased. In other research conducted by Hahn and Almy (1971), they concluded that higher socioeconomic areas of Los Angeles were more predictive of the vote than racial identity. The findings were inconsistent with other research conducted on the 1969 Los Angeles mayoral election, in which Jeffries and Ransford (1980) and Acock and Halley (1975) found racial identification as most predictive of voter preferences.

Additional research on whether class or racial identification affects voter preferences pointed to racial identification as more important than class. Halley, Acock and Greene's (1976) research investigated socioeconomic status and racial identification in the 1973 mayoral election and found the overriding importance of racial identity in structuring voting decisions. The importance of class and racial factors in Los Angeles voting analysis is clear but is insufficient in capturing political outcomes at the local level. It is simply not enough to place race or class as the only meaningful variables in understanding group political outcomes, because other factors may indeed become significant, depending on the saliency of policies.

Along with socioeconomic and racial identification, political ideology is an additional factor in understanding political coalitions in Los Angeles. In fact, Sonenshein (1993) suggests that ideology was the glue that united blacks and white liberals (especially Jewish voters) in a political coalition over a twenty-year period in Los Angeles. Liberal ideology was a significant factor in building strong and durable alliances. For example, blacks are strongly Democratic in partisanship and generally liberal in ideology (Nie, Verba, and Petrocick 1979, 255–56). Even though there is evidence of a division between middle-class blacks and lower-class blacks, African-Americans are more liberal ideologically at every income level than their white counterparts (Gilliam and Whitby 1989). On a number of issues, the black middle class is more liberal than poor blacks (Welch and Combs 1985). This suggests that blacks are ideologically more liberal; however, depending on the issues involved, there may be variations in their level of support.

In contrast to the black community's strong partisanship with the Democratic Party and liberal ideology, the Latino community is more heterogeneous. There is some evidence of conservative trends within the Latino community. For example, the 1993 mayoral election showed that 70 percent of Latinos voted for Woo, a Democratic candidate, while 30 percent voted for Republican Richard Riordan. A *Los Angeles Times* exit poll conducted on the California vote for Proposition 187 also illustrates Latino cleavages, with 77 percent of registered voters voting no and 23 percent voting yes. Besides variances along political ideology that affect levels of participation, immigrant status may affect how these groups vote. Foreign-born immigrants may have differing political needs than native-born Mexican Americans and may structure voting preferences accordingly. Moreover, a class bias may prevent middle-class Mexicans from having commonalities with recent immigrants who are generally of lower-class status. Immigrant status becomes increasingly important in voting analysis of immigration issues and in assessing whether there are cleavages concerning this factor within the Latino electorate.

The emphasis of this study is to focus on issue cooperation by comparing demographic and social characteristics of areas that affect voter preferences in these geographic locations. I expect several variables to affect voting preferences: socioeconomic status (education and income), party preference or affiliation (Democrat or Republican), race and ethnic composition, immigrant status (distribution of citizens versus noncitizens), and generation status (first-generation and all others).

Research Questions

Are there distinctive factors that affect the prospects for multiracial coalition formation in Los Angeles? If so, how do these factors affect the prospects for electoral coalition formation across groups around certain issues (such as

Table 7.1   Independent and Dependent Variables

INDEPENDENT	Measurement
Income	median family income
Education	median years of education
Race	%white, %black, %Asian, %non-
Ethnicity	%Hispanic (Mexican-American)
Party Identification	%Democrat, %Republican
Gender	%female, %male
DEPENDENT	**Measurement**
Vote on Crime	% for or against crime

crime)? I test these research questions by focusing on racial and ethnic voting patterns concerning the crime initiative (Proposition 184 or the "Three Strikes You're Out" initiative).

Conceptualizing the Variables

The variables utilized in the study are put into operation based on the theoretical concern to understand group processes and to aggregate political behavior. Because the unit of analysis in this study is the precinct, I am interested in capturing the characteristics of an area rather than the characteristics of an individual that have been traditionally analyzed by political scientists. In conceptualizing the variables outlined below, we need to consider how the geographic location, in this case the precinct, provides a context where the impact of compositional factors can be examined that can help explain the political ethos and socioeconomic processes of groups. The understanding of the political ethos of a community may also generate preliminary explanations for potential political coalitions. As such, the characteristics of the precinct and census tract data provide a useful unit of analysis to understand the political outcomes of these communities.

Class can be measured by as a function of socioeconomic status and has been measured previously in several ways. Consistent with Hahn, Klingman, and Pachon (1976), I will measure class using income and education. Median family income[9] can be utilized as an indicator of average income and median years of education as an average indicator of education level in a community. Educational attainment[10] is classified by the U.S. Census Bureau according to the highest level of school completed or the highest degree received. The median income and median education are employed for the precinct because they are less sensitive to extreme values, such as the mean that can skew data findings.

The conceptualizing of race and ethnicity measurements follows Census definitions. Even though there are several ethnicities under the general heading for the Hispanic category, I am specifically interested in the voting-behavior patterns

---

9. The Census Bureau asks questions related to income to respondents and defines median family income based on "the income distribution into two equal parts, one having incomes above the median and the other having incomes below the median." For households and families, the median income is based on the distribution of the total numbers of units, including those with no income. The median for persons is based on persons with income.

10. Educational attainment is measured by respondent's answer to item #12 on the Census questionnaire. "How much school has the person completed? Fill one circle for the highest level completed or degree received. If currently enrolled, mark the level of previous grade attended or highest degree received:

No school completed
Nursery School
Kindergarten
1st, 2nd, 3rd, or 4th
5th, 6th, 7th or 8th
9th grade
10th grade
11th grade
12th grade, no diploma
HIGH SCHOOL GRADUATE—high school DIPLOMA or the equivalent (For example, GED)
Some College but no degree
Associate degree in college—Occupational program
Associate Degree in college—Academic Program
Bachelor's Degree (For example: BA AB BS)
Master's Degree (For example: MA, MS, MEng., MEd, MSW, MBA)
Professional Social Degree (For example: MD, DDS, DVM, LLb, JD)
Doctorate Degree (For example: Ph.D., EdD)."

of Mexican Americans. To target this group, I will utilize the response to the Spanish/Hispanic origin question on item #7; persons of Hispanic origin are those that classified themselves as "Mexican," "Puerto Rican," or "Cuban," and those who indicated "Other Spanish/Hispanic" origin. Ethnicity is relevant to Mexican Americans rather than racial classification. The "other race" category is offered as an option (item # 4) for Spanish/Hispanic origin groups (such as Mexican, Cuban, or Puerto Rican) and leads to much confusion in self-reporting because Hispanics might identify as racially white or black. Consequently, the Hispanic origin question is utilized as a better indicator. Concerning other racial groups in this study, African-American is measured as the percentage of native-born blacks. Anglos will be targeted by the response to the race question (whether the person is non-Hispanic white). Anglo is measured as the percentage of whites. Finally, Asian[11] is measured as the percentage of native-born Asians.

I have chosen to measure partisanship as the percentage of Democrats and Republicans in a precinct. Election returns of precincts in Los Angeles will provide a raw breakdown of Democratic and Republican voters.

Dependent Variables

The dependent variable is measured as a continuous variable, with precincts voting from 0 to 100 percent for or against the measure.

Hypotheses

The first hypothesis is that all racial and ethnic groups in these census tracts will favor tougher sentencing laws on the guiding theory that all groups have a self-interest in eradicating crime in their neighborhoods. Similarly, women and older voters in these geographic locations may be prompted to vote in favor of the law, based on the view that they are more prone to be victims of crime and vote accordingly. I hypothesize that Republican areas will be more likely to favor tougher sentencing laws for criminals, based on their conservative ideology, and a tougher stance on crime-related issues. In terms of education and income, I hypothesize a relationship between these variables and the level of support for tougher sentencing laws, but the direction of this relationship is not finite. These hypotheses have been developed based on the theory that each initiative or issue has the possibility of altering coalition for-

---

11. The Census describes "Asian" as including "Chinese, Filipino, Japanese, Asian Indian, Korean, Vietnamese and Other Asian."

mation. Additionally, the variables introduced are necessary to determine the relationship between area characteristics and race and ethnicity, partisanship, class, age, gender, and foreign born status. I expect voting outcomes to vary, depending on each variable.

Race and Ethnicity

Latinos: Census tracts with high percentages of Latinos will be characterized by higher percentages voting for the crime initiative after controlling for other variables.

Anglos: Census tracts with high percentages of Anglos will be characterized by higher percentages voting for the crime initiative after controlling for other variables.

Asians: Census tracts with high percentages of Asians will be characterized by higher percentages voting for the crime initiative after controlling for other variables.

African-Americans: Census tracts with high percentages of African-Americans will be characterized by higher percentages voting for the crime initiative after controlling for other variables.

Partisanship

Census tracts with high percentages of Republicans will be characterized by higher percentages voting for the crime initiative after controlling for other variables.

Gender

Census tracts with high percentages of women will be characterized by higher percentages voting for the crime initiative after controlling for other variables.

Age

Census tracts with older voters will be characterized by higher percentages voting for the crime initiative after controlling for other variables.

Income

Census tracts with higher median incomes will be characterized by higher percentages voting for the crime initiative after controlling for other variables.

Education

Census tracts with higher education will be characterized by higher percentages voting for the crime initiative after controlling for other variables.

Research Methodology

The unit of analysis for this study is the precinct because it provides a way to assess the manner in which a variety of social and demographic characteristics may impact voter outcomes in an area. The two principle sources of data employed in the analysis are precinct voting returns in Los Angeles for the initiatives and census tract data from the 1990 United States Census. To compare electoral and socioeconomic data, precinct maps for Los Angeles are superimposed upon the housing census maps of numbered blocks.

The approach for this study is to utilize aggregate data of communities as the unit for investigation to understand relationships between community level variables and the behavior of electorates (Matthews and Prothro 1966, 101-175; Crain and Rosenthal 1967, 970-984). Rather than focusing on explanations about individual voting behavior using aggregate data, valuable political analysis can be derived from analyzing electorates in precincts. These units are small enough to proxy communities and ascertain how voters in each precinct vote as a body that is increasingly relevant for multiracial electoral coalitions and pan-ethnic movements. These areas have political significance insofar as they make it possible to identify how areas with large Latino populations are likely to vote or whether the socioeconomic status of an area affects political outcomes. Another important reason to consider the census tract the primary unit of analysis is that rights and interests are often affirmed in group terms through mobilization efforts, whether they be symbolic, grassroots, or electoral. For example, the political struggle of minority groups in seeking equal opportunity and citizenship rights has been shaped by their shared history of discrimination. Consequently, political activity and the development of electoral politics at the local level are assumed to ensure that policies ameliorate the status of minority groups. However, researchers must also recognize the complex dynamics of the interactions of internal class cleavages, ethnic diversity, and political orientations within each minority community to understand how political choices are made. Hence, I argue for the utilization of census tracts as proxies of communities to investigate minority electoral politics.

Table 7.2   Trend of Voter Awareness and Initial Disposition on Prop. 184

	Likely Voters	Registered Voters		
	Late October	Late October	September	July
Have seen/heard	93%	92%	90%	86%
Support Yes	56%	57%	59%	49%
Oppose No	25%	25%	21%	19%

Data Gathering Methodology

Data for this research was collected from the Los Angles City Clerk's Office, Election Divisions, which maintains files of voting turnout on statewide initiatives. From these data, a special data set was created using voter turnout data on the two statewide initiatives from 6,104 precincts in the city of Los Angeles. These data were aggregated to the census tract level to permit an analysis of voting patterns in the electorate. Prior research on Los Angeles voting behavior suggests that "cities generally contain relatively clear residential divisions by social status as well as by ethnicity and race" (Hahn and Almy 1971, 512). Survey polls assessed voter trends prior to the passage of the Three Strikes law.

Survey Polls

In examining the "three strikes" initiative, voter trends showed consistent support for it prior to its passage. Polls indicated over 90 percent approval among both likely voters and registered voters (see Table 7.2).

The nationwide survey taken in January 1994 (Table 7.3) indicated a high level of support for three strikes legislation across all racial and ethnic groups. Racial polarization occurs in the effect of discrimination as it relates to the law, thus supporting the theory that shared minority status affects attitudes toward the effects of the legislation. Latino (26 percent) and black respondents (43 percent) were more likely to view the law as increasing discrimination, as opposed to Anglo respondents (18 percent). Another poll taken to capture level of support for the measure indicated that 64 percent of the electorate was inclined, in July and October, to vote for the measure (Table 7.4). All polls showed consistent support for the measure in July and October, just prior to

Table 7.3   Racial and Ethnic Attitudes/Three Strikes Law

	Anglo	Black	Latino
Q. 70[a] (Attitude to Three Strikes Law)			
Favor 3 strikes	81%	67%	80%
Oppose	15%	28%	11%
D/K	4%	5%	9%
Q. 71[b] (Increase Spending to Build Prisons for Three Strikes Law)			
Still favor	74%	70%	76%
Oppose in that case	18%	27%	18%
D/K	8%	3%	6%
Q. 72[c] (Three Strikes Law Increases Discrimination Against Minorities)			
Cause Increases Discrimination	18%	43%	26%
Enforced Equally	71%	44%	60%
D/K	11%	13%	14%

Source: *Los Angeles Times* poll, January 1994.

a. "The U.S. Senate has passed a three strikes and you're out law, which requires any criminal convicted of three violent felonies to be imprisoned for life without the possibility of parole. Do you favor or oppose the passage of the three strikes and you're out law?"

b. "Because passing a three strikes and you're out law would swell the number of prisoners, many states would have to build new prisons. That would mean funds might have to be taken away from other programs or taxes might have to be raised. Would you favor the three strikes and you're out law even if it meant your state had to take money from other programs or had to take raise your taxes in order to build new prisons?"

c. "If anti-crime laws and prison sentences become stricter in this country, do you think that will cause increased discrimination against minority racial groups, or do you think those stricter laws and prisons sentences will be enforced equitably for all racial groups?"

Table 7.4   Voter Awareness and Support after Ballot Summaries Are Read

Prop. 184	July	October
Have seen/heard measure	86%	93%
Inclined to vote yes on measure	49%	56%
Vote yes after summaries are read	64%	64%
Vote no after summaries are read	24%	28%
Undecided after reading summaries	12%	8%

Source: Field Poll, 28 July 1994, No. 1726, pp. 2–3, and 3 November 1994, No. 1734.

the election in November. This research examines the hypothesis that there is heterogeneity along several variables, which is central in explaining city variations in the vote for Proposition 184. I utilize 1990 census data for Los Angeles to understand how social characteristics of a geographical unit (census tract) set the context for explaining social and political process moving beyond individual-level factors to explain voting patterns.

Analysis

Table 7.5 estimates the impact of several variables on the dependent variable. The Pearson's correlation against the dependent variable indicated that the percentage of Hispanics was the only variable that was not statistically significant. There was a strong negative relationship between the percentage of black voters and the percentage of votes for tougher sentencing laws for criminals. In addition, there was a strong positive relationship between the percentage of Republicans in Los Angeles census tracts and the percentage of those voting yes on Proposition 184, indicating that high percentages of Republicans were more likely to vote for the tougher sentencing laws. In terms of race and ethnicity factors, white voters in these census tracts were more likely to vote for the proposition, as indicated by the Pearson's correlation (.491). There was also a strong negative relationship between the percentage of black voters and the percentage of those supporting the policy. There was also a weak positive relationship between the percentage of Asian voters and the percentage of those voting yes on Proposition 184. The age variable also illustrates a positive relationship between the percentage of older voters and

Table 7.5   Pearson's Correlation between Selected Independent Variables and Support for Crime Initiative (Los Angeles), 1994

Independent Variables	Dependent Variables
	Crime (Proposition 184)
Percent Asian	.276**
Percent black	-.729**
Percent Hispanic	.004
Percent white	.491**
Percent female	-.381**
Percent Democrat	—
Percent Republican	.767**
Percent young	-.121**
Percent middle-age	.186**
Percent old-age	.19**
Median income	.26**
Median education	.131**

Note: *$p<.05$; **$p<.01$ (two-tailed),
N=760 (census tracts).

the percentage of those voting yes on tougher measures against crime. This indicates that as the percentage of older voters increased in census tracts, the higher the level of support for tougher sentencing laws. Finally, a positive relationship existed between education and income and those that voted for tougher sentencing laws.

In the initial examination of the Pearson's correlation, the correlation matrix illustrated some multicollinearity problems. Income and education were intercorrelated (.732) and thus education was dropped for purposes of con-

Table 7.6 Crime Initiative Regressed on Selected Independent Variables

	Model 1	Model 2
Percent Asian	-.128***	—
Percent Black	-.514***	-.343***
Percent White	-.409***	—
Percent Female	.019	—
Percent Republican	.885***	.714***
Median Income	-.197***	-.298***
Percent Old	.026	.029
Adjusted R²	.763***	.724

Note: *p<.05; ***p<.001

structing the regression model because income was more strongly correlated with the dependent variable. Similarly, the percentage of non-Hispanic whites and the percentage of Hispanics were also intercorrelated (-.612). The non-Hispanic white variable was more strongly correlated to the dependent variable and was utilized in the final regression model.

A series of ordinary least squares (OLS) regression equations were used to estimate the impact of the independent variables on the dependent variable and the level of support for the crime initiative. In this model, race and ethnicity, partisanship, age, gender and income, were the independent variables and the percentage vote for Proposition 184 was the dependent variable. In the first regression model, the percentage of females was not statistically significant, and neither was the percentage of old persons. For purposes of constructing the second regression model, the percentage of females was not introduced, while the percentage of old persons was included for theoretical reasons. After running the regression model without the female variable, the percentage of Asians and the percentage of non-Hispanic whites were not statistically significant in the final regression model (see Model 2). The final regression model (Model 2) in Table 7.6 highlights some notable findings.

The regression coefficients in Model 2 demonstrate that race, partisanship, and income are relevant in explaining the vote for the Three Strikes initiative. The data suggest that the percentage of blacks is the only racial variable affecting the level of support for tougher sentencing laws. There is a negative relationship between the percentage of blacks and the percentage of those who voted for the proposition, meaning that as the percentage of African-Americans increased in these census tracts, the less likely they were to support the tougher sentencing laws.

With reference to the partisanship variable, in particular, Republican census tracts, the data suggest a strong positive relationship between the percentage of Republicans and those that voted for the proposition. Partisanship is the most explanatory variable, based on the score of the regression coefficient (.714). The data suggest that as the percentage of Republicans increased in the census tracts, the higher level of support for tougher sentencing laws. Income also seems to affect the level of support for tougher sentencing measures. An inverse relationship exists between income and the percentage of yes voters for the proposition.

Discussion

The findings suggest that partisanship is the more explanatory variable in understanding the level of support for Proposition 184. The data suggest that geographic areas with high percentages of Republicans will have a tendency to support tougher sentencing laws. This supports the original hypothesis that Republican partisanship may mean that the ideological view to get tough on criminals has an impact on Republican voting preferences, specifically concerning measures that aim at providing longer jail sentences for criminals. Republican partisanship is a proxy for conservative ideology and the philosophical view among conservatives that harsher penalties should be given to criminals. As far as partisanship is concerned, Republican affiliation is highly relevant in understanding why communities in Republican areas vote for tougher sentencing laws.

Despite the importance of partisanship on voting behavior patterns concerning crime-related issues, race also has an effect, albeit secondary. African-American communities are less likely to support measures that call for stricter laws against criminals. This finding rejects the original hypothesis that African-Americans would be more likely to support tougher measures based on the self-interest theory that something must be done to eradicate crime in their neighborhoods. This preliminary result does provide support for the shared discrimination theory and has implications for intergroup coalition building.

Discrimination may serve as the foundation to bridge African-Americans and other racial groups—namely, Latinos—concerning issues related to crime. Both groups share minority status and may exhibit actual experience with discrimination in the criminal justice system or may perceive the criminal justice system to discriminate against them on the basis of their minority status. The experience of discrimination and the perception of being discriminated in the criminal justice system may be a critical factor in the formation of coalitions between Latinos and African-Americans. Coalition formation around issues may depend on the ability of minority groups to understand their minority status and become politically aware of how to politicize these issues in their neighborhoods. Communities of African-Americans and Latinos seeking to build strong coalitions around crime-related issues will need to concentrate on their shared discrimination experience as a foundation to join with each other in order to further their common interests.

References

Acock Alan C., and Robert M. Halley. 1975. Ethnic politics and racial issues reconsidered: Comments on earlier study. *Western Political Quarterly* 28: 737–38.

Aldrich, John H., and Forrest D. Nelson. 1984. *Linear probability: Logit and probit models.* Newbury Park, CA: Sage Publications.

Alford, Robert R., and Roger Friedland 1975. Political participation and public policy. In *Annual review of sociology,* edited by Alex Inkeles, James Coleman, and Neil Smelser, 429–79. Palo Alto, CA: Annual Reviews, Inc.

Allport, Gordon. 1954. *The nature of prejudice.* Reading, MA: Addison-Wesley.

Arian, Asher, Arthur S. Goldberg, John H. Mollenkopf, and Edward T. Rogowsky. 1990. *Changing New York City politics.* New York: Routledge.

Babbie, Earl. 1995. *The practice of social research.* 7th ed. Belmont, CA: Wadsworth Publishing Company.

Berry, William D. 1993. *Understanding regression assumptions.* Thousand Oaks, CA: Sage Publications.

Bobo, Lawrence. 1988. Group conflict, prejudice and the paradox of contemporary racial attitudes. In *Eliminating racism: Profiles in controversy,* edited by Phyllis A Katz and Dalmas A Taylor. New York: Plenum.

Bobo, Lawrence, and Franklin Gilliam. 1990. Race, sociopolitical participation, and black empowerment. *American Political Science Review* 84: 377–93.

Browning, Rufus B., Dale Marshall, and David Tabb. 1984. *Protest is not enough: The struggle of Blacks and Hispanics for equality in urban politics.* Berkeley: University of California Press.

————. 1990. *Racial politics in American cities.* White Plains, NY: Longman.

Cain, B., D. Kiewiet, and C. Uhlaner. 1991. The acquisition of partisanship by Latinos and Asian Americans. *American Journal of Political Science* 35: 390–422.

Campbell, Angus, Philip E. Converse, Warren E. Miller, and Donald Stokes. 1966. *Elections and the political order.* New York: John Wiley & Sons, Inc.

Campbell, Angus, Philip Converse, Warren E. Miller, and Donald Stokes. 1960. *The American voter, unabridged edition.* Chicago: University of Chicago Press.

Carmichael, Stokely, and Charles V. Hamilton. 1969. *Black power: The politics of liberation in America.* New York: Vintage Books.

Carmines, Edward G., and James A. Stimson. 1989. *Issue evolution: Race and the transformation of American politics.* Princeton: Princeton University Press.

Charles, Henry, and Carlos Munoz, Jr. 1991. Ideological and interest linkages in California rainbow politics. In *racial and ethnic politics in California,* edited by Byran O. Jackson and Michael Preston, 323–39. Berkeley: Institute of Governmental Studies.

Clark, William V. 1992. Residential preferences and residential choices in a multiethnic context. *Demography* 29: 451–66.

Crain, Robert L., and Donald B. Rosenthal. 1967. Community status as a dimension of local decision-making. *American Sociological Review,* 32: 970–84.

Davis, Mike. 1992. *City of quartz.* New York: Vintage Books.

De La Garza, Rodolfo, Louis DeSipio, Chris F. Garcia, John Garcia, and Angelo Falcon. 1992. *Latino voices: Mexican, Puerto Rican, and Cuban perspectives on American politics.* Boulder: Westview Press.

DeLeon, Richard. 1991. The progressive urban regime: Ethnic coalitions in San Francisco. In *Racial and ethnic politics in California,* edited by Byran

O. Jackson and Michael B. Preston, 157–92. Berkeley: Institute of Governmental Studies.

_____. 1992. *Left coast city: Progressive politics in San Francisco 1975–1991*. Kansas: University of Kansas Press.

Freedman, D. A., S. Klein, J. Sacks, C. Smith, and C. Everett. 1990. Ecological regression and voting rights. Working paper, technical report no. 248, 90–123, Department of Statistics, University of California-Berkeley.

Garcia, John A. 1993. Coalition formation within the Mexican origin community and Latino-African-American communities: Delineation of common threads. Paper presented for the Conference on Black-Latino Politics, sponsored by the African and African-American Studies Program, Yale University.

Gilliam, Franklin D., Jr., and Kenny J. Whitby. 1989. Race, class, and attitudes toward social welfare spending: An ethclass interpretation. *Social Science Quarterly* 70: 88–100.

Hahn, Harlan, and Sheldon Kamieniecki. 1987. *Referendum voting social status and policy preferences*. New York: Greenwood Press.

Hahn, Harlan, and Timothy Almy. 1971. Ethnic politics and racial issues: Voting in Los Angeles. *Western Political Quarterly* 24: 719–30.

Hahn, Harlan, David Klingman, and Harry Pachon. 1976. Cleavages, coalitions and the black candidate: The Los Angeles mayoralty elections of 1969 and 1973. *Western Political Quarterly* 29: 521–30.

Halley, Robert M., Alan C. Acock, and Thomas Greene. 1976. Ethnicity and social class: Voting in the Los Angeles municipal elections. *Western Political Quarterly* 29: 507–20.

Henry, Charles, and Carlos Munoz, Jr. 1991. Ideological and interest linkages in California rainbow politics. In *Racial and ethnic politics in California*, edited by Byran O. Jackson and Michael B. Preston, 323–38. Berkeley: Institute of Governmental Studies.

Hero, Rodney E. 1989. Multiracial coalitions in city elections involving minority candidates: Some evidence from Denver. *Urban Affairs Quarterly* 25: 342–51.

Hinckley, Barbara. 1981. *Coalitions and politics*. New York: Harcourt, Brace, Jovanovich.

Huckfeldt, Robert, and Carol W. Kohfeld. 1989. *Race and the decline of class in American politics*. Chicago, University of Illinois Press.

Jackson, Byran O. 1991. Racial and ethnic voting cleavages in Los Angeles politics. In *Racial and ethnic politics in California,* edited by Byran O. Jackson and Michael B. Preston, 93–215. Berkeley: Institute of Governmental Studies.

Jackson, Byran O., and Michael B. Preston. 1991. *Racial and ethnic politics in California.* Berkeley: Institute of Governmental Studies.

Jeffries, Vincent, and H. Edward Ransford. 1980. *Social stratification: A multiple hierarchy approach.* Boston: Allyn Bacon.

Johnson, James H., and Melvin L. Oliver. 1989. Inter-ethnic minority conflict in urban America: The effects of economic and social dislocations. *Urban Geography* 10: 449–63.

Key, V. O. 1949. *Southern politics: In state and nation.* New York: Alfred A. Knopf.

King, Gary. 1997. *A solution to the ecological inference problem: Reconstructing individual behavior from aggregate data.* Princeton: Princeton University Press.

Lewis-Beck, Michael S. 1980. *Applied regression.* Thousand Oaks, CA: Sage Publications.

Lipset, Seymour M. 1960. *Political man.* Garden City, NY: Doubleday and Company.

Matthews, Donald R., and James W. Prothro. 1966. *Negroes and the new southern politics.* New York: Harcourt, Brace, & World.

McClain, Paula D., and Albert K. Karnig. 1990. Black and Hispanic socioeconomic and political competition. *American Political Science Review* 84: 535–44.

Milbrath, Lester, and M. L. Goel. 1977. *Political participation: How and why do people get involved in politics?* 2nd ed. Chicago: Rand McNally College Publishing Co.

Mladenka, Kenneth. 1990. Blacks and Hispanics in urban politics. *American Political Science Review* 83, no. 1: 167–91.

Mollenkopf, John. 1990. New York: The great anomaly. In *Racial politics in American cities,* edited by Rufus Browning, Dale R. Marshall, and David Tabb, 75–87. New York: Longman.

Munoz, Carlos Jr., and Charles Henry. 1991. Coalition politics in San Antonio and Denver: The Cisneros and Pena mayoral campaigns. In *Racial politics in American cities,* edited by Byran O. Jackson and Michael B. Preston, 179–90. Berkeley: Institute for Governmental Studies.

Nie, Norman, Sidney Verba, and John R. Petrocick. 1979. *The changing American voter.* Cambridge, MA: Harvard University Press.

Oliver, Melvin L., and James H. Johnson, Jr. Interethnic conflict in an urban ghetto: The case of Blacks and Latinos in Los Angeles. *Research in Social Movements, Conflict, and Change* 6: 57–94.

Preston, Michael B., Lenneal J. Henderson, and Paul L. Puryear. 1987. *The new Black politics: The search for political power.* New York: Longman.

Ranney, Austin. 1962. The utility and limitations of aggregate data in the study of electoral behavior. In *Essays on the behavioral study of politics,* edited by Austin Ranney, 91-102. Urbana: University of Illinois Press.

Robinson, W. S. 1950. Ecological correlations and the behavior of individuals. *American Sociological Review* 15: 351–57.

Schattschneider, E. E. 1960. *The semi-sovereign people.* New York: Holt, Rinehart and Winston.

Schroeder, Larry D., David L. Sjoquist, and Paula E. Stephan. 1986. *Understanding regression analysis: An introduction guide.* Thousand Oaks, CA: Sage Publications.

Shively, W. Phillips. 1969. Ecological inference: The use of aggregate data to study individuals. *American Political Science Review* 63: 1183–90.

Sigelman, L., and Susan Welch. 1993. The contact hypothesis revisited: Interracial contact and positive racial attitudes." *Social Forces* 71: 781–95.

Sonenshein, Raphael J. 1990. Bi-racial coalitions in big cities: Why they succeed, why they fail. In *Racial politics in American cities,* edited by Rufus P. Browning, Dale Marshall Rogers, and David H. Tabb, 193–211. White Plains, NY: Longman.

_____. 1993. *Politics in black and white: Race, power in Los Angeles.* New Jersey: Princeton University Press.

Sonenshein, Raphael, and Nicholas Valentino. 1995. Minority politics at the crossroads: Voting patterns in the 1993 Los Angeles mayoral election. Paper delivered at the annual meeting of the Western Political Science Association.

Starks, Robert T., and Michael B. Preston. 1990. Harold Washington and the politics of reform: 1983–1987. In *Racial politics in American Cities,* edited by Rufus Browning, Dale Rogers Marshall, and David Tabb, 88–106. New York: Longman.

Stone, Clarence. 1989. *Regime politics: Governing Atlanta 1946–1988.* Kansas: University of Kansas Press.

Swain, Carol M. 1993. *Black faces, Black interests: The new Black voters in American elections.* Cambridge: Harvard University Press.

Tate, Katherine. 1993. *From protest to politics: The new Black voters in American elections.* New York: Russell Sage Foundation.

Tolbert, Caroline, and Rodney E. Hero. 1996. Race/ethnicity and direct democracy: An analysis of California's illegal immigration initiative. *Journal of Politics* 58: 807–18.

Uhlaner, Carole J. 1989. Perceived discrimination and prejudice and the coalition prospects of Blacks, Latinos and Asian Americans. In *Racial and ethnic politics in California,* edited by Bryan Jackson and Michael B. Preston, 339–71. Berkeley: Institute of Government Studies Press.

Verba, Sidney, and Norman Nie. 1972. *Participation in America: Political democracy and social equality.* New York: Harper & Row Publishers.

Villareal, E. Roberto, and Norma G. Hernandez. 1991. *Latinos and political coalitions: Political empowerment for the 1990s.* New York: Greenwood Press.

Vincent Jeffries, and Edward E. Ransford. 1972. Ideology, social structure and the Yorty-Bradley mayoralty election. *Social Problems* 19: 368–69.

Welch, Susan, and Lee Sigelman. 1993. The politics of Hispanic Americans: Insights from national surveys, 1980-88. *Social Science Quarterly* 74: 76–94.

Welch, Susan, and Lorn Foster. 1992. The impact of economic conditions on the voting behavior of Blacks. *The Western Political Quarterly* 45: 221–36.

Welch, Susan, and Michael W. Combs. 1985. Intra-Racial differences in attitudes of Blacks: Class cleavages or consensus? *Phylon* 66: 91–97.

Wolfinger, Raymond E., and Steven J. Rosenstone. 1980. *Who votes?* New Haven: Yale University Press.

Zaller, J. Information, values and opinion. 1991. *American Political Science Review* 85: 1215–37.

Zaller, J., and S. Feldman. 1992. A simple theory of the survey response: Answering questions versus revealing preferences. *American Journal of Political Science* 36: 579–616.

Appendix 7A

The Jones Three-Strikes Law

The text is almost identical to the text of Proposition 184 passed on November 1994. Since the proposition has passed, it supersedes the Jones Law but has little partial effect on the penal code. The initiative can only be repealed by initiative or by two-thirds of the state legislature.

Bill NUMBER: AB 971   CHAPTERED 03/07/94
BILL TEXT

CHAPTER 12
FILED WITH THE SECRETARY OF STATE MARCH 7, 1994
APPROVED BY GOVERNOR MARCH 7, 1994
PASSED THE ASSEMBLY MARCH 3, 1994
PASSED THE SENATE JANUARY 31, 1994
AMENDED IN ASSEMBLY JANUARY 26, 1994
AMENDED IN ASSEMBLY JANUARY 13, 1994
AMENDED IN ASSEMBLY JANUARY 3, 1994
AMENDED IN ASSEMBLY APRIL 12, 1993
INTRODUCED BY Assembly Members Jones and Costa
(Principal co-authors: Senators Wyman and Presley) (Co-authors: Assembly Members Aguiar, Allen, Alpert, Andal, Boland, Bowler, Bronshvag, Valerie Brown, Brulte, Bustamente, Conroy, Epple, Escutia, Ferguson, Goldsmith, Harvery, Haynes, Hoge, Horcher, Johnson, Morrow, Mountjoy, Nolan, O'Connell, Polanco, Pringle, Quackenbush, Richter, Seastrand, Takasugi, Umberg, Weggeland, and Woodruff)
(Co-authors: Senators Boatwright, Hurtt, and McCorquodale)

March 1, 1993
An act to amend Section 667 of the Penal Code, relating to sentencing, and declaring the urgency thereof, to take effect immediately.

Legislative Counsel's Digest

AB 971 Jones. Sentencing: prior felony conviction. (1) Existing law, added by initiative statute, provides, among other things, that any person who is convicted of a serious felony, as defined, and who has been previously convicted of a serious felony in California, or of any other offense committed in another jurisdiction which includes all of the elements of a serious felony, shall receive, in addition to the sentence imposed for the present felony, a 5-year enhancement for each prior felony conviction on charges brought and tried separately.

This bill would declare the intent of the Legislature to ensure longer prison sentences and greater punishments for this who commit a felony and have been previously convicted of a serious and/or violent felony offense.

This bill would, in addition, provide that in addition to any other enhancement or penalty provisions that may apply, (1) if a defendant has one prior felony conviction, as defined, the determinate term, or minimum term for an indeterminate term, shall be twice the term otherwise provided as punishment for the current conviction, (2) if a defendant has two or more prior convictions, the term for the current felony conviction shall be an indeterminate term or imprisonment in the state prison for life with a maximum term of the indeterminate term as the greatest of (a) 3 times the term otherwise provided as punishment for each current felony conviction subsequent to the 2 or more prior felony convictions, (b) imprisonment in the state prison for 25 years, or c) the term determined by the court for the underlying conviction, including any applicable enhancement or punishment provisions.

The bill would also provide, among other things, that the probation shall not be granted nor shall the execution or imposition of sentence be suspended if the defendant has a prior felony conviction.

2. The bill would declare that it is to take effect immediately as an urgency statute.

THE PEOPLE OF THE STATE OF CALIFORNIA DO ENACT AS FOLLOWS:
Section 1. Section 667 of the Penal Code is amended to read:
667. (a)(1) In compliance with subdivision (b) of Section 1385, any person convicted of a serious felony who has been convicted of a serious felony in this state or of any other offense committed in another jurisdiction which includes all of the elements of any serious felony, shall receive, in addition to the sentence imposed by the court for the present offense, a five-year en-

hancement for each such prior conviction on charges brought and tried separately. The term of the present offense and each enhancement shall run consecutively.

2. This subdivision shall not be applied when the punishment imposed under other provisions of law would result in a longer term of imprisonment. There is no requirement of prior incarceration or commitment for this subdivision to apply.

3. The Legislature may increase the length of the enhancement of sentence provided in this subdivision by a statute passed by majority vote of each house thereof.

4. As used in this subdivision, "serious felony" means a serious felony listed in subdivision (c) of Section 1192.7.

5. This subdivision shall not apply to a person convicted of selling, furnishing, administering, or giving, or offering to sell, furnish, administer, or give to a minor, any methamphetamine-related drug or any precursors of methamphetamine-related drug or any precursors of methamphetamine unless the prior conviction was for a serious felony described in subparagraph (24) of subdivision (c) of Section 1192.7.

b. It is the intent of the Legislature in enacting subdivisions (b) to (I), inclusive, to ensure longer prison sentences and greater punishment for those who commit a felony and have been previously convicted of serious and/or violent felony offenses.

c. Notwithstanding any other law, if a defendant has been convicted of a felony and it has been pled and proved that the defendant has one or more prior felony convictions as defined in subdivision (d), the court shall adhere to each of the following:

1. There shall not be an aggregate term limitation for purposes of consecutive sentencing for any subsequent felony conviction.

2. Probation for the current offense shall not be granted, nor shall execution or imposition of the sentence be suspended for any prior offense.

3. The length of time between the prior felony conviction and the current felony conviction shall not affect the imposition of sentence.

4. There shall not be a commitment to any other facility other than the state prison. Diversion shall not be granted nor shall the defendant be

eligible for commitment to the California Rehabilitation Center as provided in Article 2 (commencing with Section 3050) of Chapter Division 3 of the Welfare and Institutions Code.

5. The total amount of credits awarded pursuant to Article 2.5 (commencing with Section 2930) of Chapter 7 of Title of Part 3 shall not exceed one-fifth of the total term of imprisonment imposed and shall not accrue until the defendant is physically placed in the state prison.

6. If there is a current conviction for more than one felony count not committed on the same occasion, and not arising from the same set of operative facts, the court shall sentence the defendant consecutively on each count pursuant to subdivision (e).

7. If there is a current conviction for more than one serious or violent felony as described in paragraph (6), the court shall impose the sentence for each conviction consecutive to the sentence for any other conviction for which the defendant may be consecutively sentenced in the manner prescribed by law.

8. Any sentence imposed pursuant to subdivision (e) will be imposed consecutive to any other sentence which the defendant is already serving, unless otherwise provided by law.

(d) Notwithstanding any other law and for the purpose of subdivisions (b) to (I), inclusive, a prior conviction of a felony shall be defined as:

1. Any offense defined in subdivision (c) of Section 667.5 as a violent felony or any offense defined in subdivision (c) of Section 1192.7 as a serious felony in this state. The determination of whether a prior conviction is a prior felony conviction for purposes of subdivisions (b) (I), inclusive, shall be made upon the date of that prior conviction and is not affected by the sentence imposed unless the sentence automatically, upon the initial sentencing, converts the felony to a misdemeanor. None of the following dispositions shall affect the determination that a prior conviction is a prior felony for purposes of subdivisions (b) to (I), inclusive:

A. The suspension of imposition of judgment or sentence.

B. The stay of execution of sentence.

    C. The commitment to the State Department of Health Services as a mentally disordered sex offender following a conviction of a felony.

    D. The commitment to the California Rehabilitation Center or any other facility whose function is rehabilitative diversion from the state prison.

2. A conviction in another jurisdiction for an offense that, if committed in California, is punishable by imprisonment in the state prison. A prior conviction of a particular felony shall include a conviction in another jurisdiction for an offense that includes all of the elements of the particular felony as defined in subdivision (c) of Section 667.5 or subdivision (c) of Section 1192.7.

3. A prior juvenile adjudication shall constitute a prior felony conviction for purposes of sentence enhancement if:
    A. The juvenile was 16 years of age or older at the time he or she committed the prior offense.
    B. The prior offense is listed in subdivision (b) of Section 707 of the welfare and Institutions Code or described in paragraph (1) or (2) as a felony.
    C. The juvenile was found to be a fit and proper subject to be dealt with under the juvenile court law.
    D. The juvenile was adjudged a ward of the juvenile court within the meaning of Section 602 of the Welfare and Institutions Code because the person committed an offense listed in subdivision (b) of Section 707 of the Welfare and Institutions Code.
    E. For purposes of subdivisions (b) to (I), inclusive, and in addition to any other enhancement or punishment provisions which may apply, the following shall apply where a defendant has a prior felony conviction.
        (1)If a defendant has one prior felony conviction that has been pled and proved, the determinate term or minimum term for an indeterminate term shall be twice the term otherwise provided as punishment for the current felony conviction.
        (2)(A) If defendant has two or more prior felony convictions as defined in subdivision (d) that have been pled and proved, the term for the current felony conviction shall be indeterminate term of life imprisonment with a maximum term of the indeterminate sentence calculated as the greater of:

  i. Three tines the term otherwise provided as a punishment for each current felony conviction subsequent for each current felony conviction subsequent to the two or more prior felony convictions.

  ii. Imprisonment in the state prison for 25 years

  iii. The term determined by the court pursuant to Section 1170 for the underlying conviction, including any enhancement applicable under Chapter 4.5 (commencing with the Section 1170) of the title 7 of Part 2, or any pending prescribed by Section 190 or 3046.

B. The indeterminate term described in subparagraph (A) shall be served consecutive to any other term of imprisonment for which a consecutive term may be imposed by law. Any other term imposed subsequent to any indeterminate term described in subparagraph (A) shall not be merged therein but shall commence at the time the person would otherwise have been released from prison.

 (f) (1) Notwithstanding any other law, subdivisions (b) to (I), inclusive, shall be applied in every case in which defendant has prior felony conviction as defined by subdivision (d). The prosecuting attorney shall plead and prove each prior felony conviction except as provided in paragraph (2).

  (2) The prosecuting attorney may move to dismiss or strike a prior felony conviction allegation in the furtherance of justice pursuant to Section 1385, or if there is insufficient evidence to prove the prior conviction. If upon the satisfaction of the court that there is insufficient evidence to prove the prior felony conviction, the court may dismiss or strike the allegation.

 (g) Prior felony convictions shall not be used in plea bargaining as defined in subdivision (b) of Section 1192.7. The prosecution shall plea and prove that all known prior felony convictions shall not enter into any agreement to strike or seek the dismissal of any prior felony conviction allegation except as provided in paragraph (2) of subdivision (f).

 h. All references to existing statutes in subdivisions (c) to (g), inclusive are statutes as they existed on June 30, 1993.

 i. If any provision of subdivisions (b) to (h), inclusive, or the application thereof to any person or circumstance is held invalid, that invalidity shall not affect other provisions or applications of those subdivisions which can be given effect without the invalid provision or application, and to this end the provisions of those subdivisions are severable.

j. The provisions of this section shall not be amended by the Legislature except by statute passed in each house by roll call vote entered in the journal, two-thirds of the membership concurring, or by statute that becomes effective only when approved by the electors.

SEC 2. This act is an urgency statute necessary for the immediate preservation of the public peace, health, or safety within the meaning of Article IV of the Constitution and shall go into immediate effect. The fact constituting the necessity are:

In order to ensure longer prison sentences and greater punishment for those who commit a felony and have been previously convicted of serious or violent felony offenses, and to protect the public from the imminent threat posed by those repeat felony offenders, it is necessary that this act take effect immediately.

CHAPTER 8

Race, Capitalism and the Media: A Study of Proposition 209 Editorials

Catherine Nelson, Sonoma State University

In November 1996, California voters passed Proposition 209, which banned racial, ethnic, and gender "preferences" and discrimination in the awarding of state jobs, contracts, and access to higher education. There was also a provision (Clause C) that allows for gender distinctions in employment where reasonably necessary. One of the principle elements of the public debate over the proposition was its effect on the ability of women and minorities to have access to economic opportunity in the form of education and government employment and contracts. Because of this debate, Proposition 209 was at the nexus of conflicting opinions regarding the fundamental economic assumptions about equal opportunity, individual merit, and the government's role in a free market, that underlie policies designed to assist those historically denied access to social and economic resources in this county. A prime location for the contestation of economic principles during the Proposition 209 debate was the news media. Some of the most open and clear differences in this regard were apparent in newspaper editorials about the proposition.

Because race was such a central element of the economic aspects of the Proposition 209 debate, both mainstream and ethnic/racial newspapers addressed it in their editorials. This paper analyzes California mainstream and ethnic/racial newspaper editorials written about the proposition, with the purpose of investigating whether or not both types of newspapers' editorials were based upon a common economic frame consisting of the basic principles of capitalism, equal opportunity, individual merit, and a free market. Previous work in this area demonstrates that race and capitalism are inextricably intertwined, that the mainstream and alternative presses approach reporting in different ways (which affect how reporting is done) and that media reporting on race and inequality covers whites and persons of color differently concerning economic matters. This analysis goes beyond previous studies in that it extends the investigation of race and capitalism in the media to a comparison of the economic assumptions that the mainstream and ethnic/racial media use as the basis for their positions on government policies designed to address the status of racial groups in this country. The goal, based upon the evidence that the mainstream and alternative media are likely to approach this debate differently, is to discover the degree to which the fundamental elements of capitalist doctrine are contested in the different media.

Race and Capitalism

Green (1981) argues that "free market ideology has a significance that extends far beyond the influence of its most visible adherents, for it helps set the tone for and define the boundaries of the popular discussion of public policy" (212). This is particularly true of the affirmative action debate. Underlying that debate on both sides are assumptions about the free market, individual merit, and the role of government in the economy, which are not only tied directly to capitalism but have consequences for the racial hierarchy of power in the United States. Newspaper editorials, in reflecting these assumptions, provide the public with a way to interpret the claims of participants in the public dialogue about affirmative action. Thus, it is important to begin this discussion with a brief review of capitalist ideology, its connection to racial stratification, and the literature that explores the connection between race and economics in the media. This will establish the framework for the analysis of economic assumptions contained in mainstream and ethnic/racial newspaper editorials about Proposition 209.

The economic ideas informing political debate in the United States can be directly tied to Adam Smith. The basis of Smith's economic system is individual self-interest and the competition that results from similarly motivated individuals acting in the same manner. (Heilbronner 1986, 55). In general conditions of scarcity, individuals, based upon their self-interest, compete with each other to produce goods to satisfy the never-ending desire of consumers. The marketplace is free, in that anyone can enter the competition to produce goods to sell for profit. Whoever produces the product consumers desire most will receive the most profit. And, given this equal opportunity to compete, whoever is the strongest competitor will receive the most reward—that is, profit. And this is just (Tarcher 1996, 29). By their very success, the strongest competitors have demonstrated that they are the most qualified to receive a reward. In addition, they are also contributing to the common good by increasing the amount and variety of goods available and by providing employment for those engaged in producing the goods. In effect, capitalism lifts up the most qualified as it lifts up society as a whole.

There remains, of course, the problem of how to explain the poor. Tarcher (1996) argues that in free market ideology lesser rewards for the poor are considered just as well. As he puts it, in capitalist thought "[i]t is only just to assume that the poor or unsuccessful are suffering the consequences of their own unwillingness or inability to compete, produce, and contribute to the common good" (29). While the chance to become successful was made equal by the free market (Hartz 1955, 219–20), a guarantee of results was not.

Government should not intervene to assure equality of results because the market can only function properly to combat scarcity and lift up society as a whole if it is free. There should be no government interference in the choice of producers as to what to produce or how to produce it or in the choice of consumers as to what to purchase. Individual choices about what to purchase determine what is produced, and any government interference restricts that freedom. This is a negative type of freedom—that is, freedom from government interference (Tarcher 1996, 29). For Adam Smith, the consequences of government interference were grave. The natural liberty humans enjoy means that they are should be left alone to pursue their self-interest in their own way. Government action carried the threat of taking away from those who had earned and giving to those who had not. As Hartz (1955) comments, state action was considered "the root of inequity, it took away from one man and gave to another" (216). The worst thing of all was that the person to whom something had been given had not earned it.

Individualism had a further significance: It allowed the blurring of class lines. Equality of opportunity in the capitalist marketplace meant that everyone had an equal opportunity to compete to improve his or her lot in life. There were no rigid class lines. This "classlessness" as Hartz calls it, was, in effect, competition among those who did not have access to the same economic rewards as those who did have. Rather than acting against the upper class according to a common interest of having been excluded from access to economic reward, the lower class, in capitalist ideology, was "smashed into a million bits, so that its fierce acquisitive passion, instead of being expended against property, would be expended against itself in the quest for property" (Hartz 1955, 223).

The crucial piece of the puzzle missing from free market ideology is that the equal access to opportunity it promotes has never been based on reality. Historically, opportunity in the United States has been associated with race: Those who are white have had more access to resources and more economic success. The link between race and capitalism is theorized by several authors. Roediger (1999) argues that "whiteness" and the superiority and advantage attached to it were created by the working class in the early nineteenth century as a way to distinguish itself from slaves and adapt to the rigors and new ethos of an industrial economy. "Whiteness," in effect, acted as a "wage," a type of pleasure embodied in status and privilege that made up for alienating class relationships (13).

Almaguer (1994) argues that social, economic, and political structures in nineteenth century California, undergirded by white supremacy, capitalism, and patriarchy, molded the "class- and gender-specific experiences of both the white and nonwhite populations" (209). According to Almaguer, central to the doctrine of white supremacy were the ideas of manifest destiny and "free labor ideology." Manifest destiny was "the task of bringing civilization and Christianity to uncivilized heathens" (12). Free labor ideology included the right to private property, economic individualism, and the belief that free labor creates value. The specific connection to race was that European-American men believed they were entitled to privileged economic mobility over existing nonwhite populations. As Almaguer argues,

> Who gained access to land, owned business, became skilled workers, and more generally, was subjectively placed in either a "free" wage labor market or an "unfree" labor system was fundamentally determined on the basis of race. Access to every level of the capitalist system of production introduced in nineteenth-century California was largely determined by this status. (13–14)

In the same vein as Roediger's idea of "whiteness" as a wage, Harris (1995) and Lipsitz (1998) both argue that "whiteness" is a type of "property" that gives its owners advantage legally, politically, and economically. Harris (1995) argues that rights in property are conflated with race. The oppression of blacks and Native Americans in the United States "was based upon a radicalized conception of property that was implemented with force" and sanctioned by law (277). Examples are the codification of slavery, which began as early as the late 1600s, and its embodiment in the Constitution in the representation provision for the House of Representatives. Everything, from voting privileges to access to job opportunities, was based upon race. And, according to Harris, as the law restricted nonwhites' access to these opportunities and rights, "whiteness" itself was protected and enhanced (285–90).

Lipsitz (1998) also constructs "whiteness" as a type of property that has a cash value acquired through discriminatory markets, such as unequal educations for children of different races, private networks for access to employment opportunities, and the intergenerational transfer of wealth (vii). In an observation particularly relevant for this study, Lipsitz comments that California was the "Mississippi of the 1990's," because of the passage of Propositions 187 and 209 that restrict state efforts to provide access to state services and other resource opportunities for persons of color (xviii). In effect, politicians cultivated distrust of the poor, immigrants, and racial minorities in an effort to hide the fact that their policies were destroying the economic and social infrastructure of the state (xix).

Thus, if capitalist ideology is located in actual historical circumstance, it is evident that it has been associated with white privilege, as embodied in both economic practice and statutory law. Also, political divisions along racial lines have facilitated white privilege at the expense of persons of color. Opportunity and ability to succeed are ideologically justified on the basis of individual merit and a free market, but racial stratification indicates that those who have the opportunity to succeed and do succeed are more likely to be white. If government acts to affect who has access to opportunity and success through such programs as affirmative action, white privilege, either implicitly or explicitly, is a part of the underlying economic framework affecting the political debate. This study seeks to illuminate the racial dimensions of capitalist ideology in mainstream and ethnic newspaper editorials about Proposition 209 in order to assess the status and legitimacy of race as a central element of the debate over the economic consequences of affirmative action.

The Mainstream and Alternative Media

The difference between the mainstream and alternative media is crucial for this study, because the audience a newspaper is trying to reach affects how it will frame an issue. In this case, a central question is whether or not the economic ideology in editorials about Proposition 209 will be based upon whether the newspaper is targeting a "general" audience or a specific racial or ethnic one. As the literature review will demonstrate, because mainstream and ethnic newspapers have different audiences, what is perceived as news and how it is presented are distinctly different in each case.

As Hindman (1998) argues, the factors that differentiate the mainstream press from the alternative press are rooted in the audience each serves. In her study of an inner-city neighborhood newspaper caught between mainstream and alternative journalism, Hindman found that the mainstream press, because of the historical commercial necessity of serving a heterogeneous audience, developed an "objective" standard of reporting that insured balanced, factual stories, and the reporter's distance from the stories it told. Sources tend to be official, and reporters' beats bureaucratic. With no "bias" in the reporting, readers are left to make up their own minds about the meaning of the story. Hindman argues, however, that there is a bias in this style of reporting in the defining of what constitutes "news" and how it is treated: Given the sources and types of stories selected, "the news and its presentation reflect the concerns of those with power" (178).

The alternative media, on the other hand, have as their main purpose the representation of disenfranchised groups. Hindman (1998) argues that the neighborhood press, as a form of alternative media, has as its focus the problems and issues of a specific neighborhood. In direct contrast to the mainstream press, the neighborhood press in its reporting will confront the powerful institutions of society. Reporters emphasize personal knowledge of the issues and activism in getting them addressed. The news is provided specifically from the perspective of the neighborhood, and the newspaper emphasizes "giving power, access, and group identity to city neighborhoods" (181). From this perspective, alternative newspapers engage in what to mainstream newspapers would be antithetical, advocacy journalism (180).

While Hindman (1998) is discussing the neighborhood press as a form of alternative media, her comments are nonetheless relevant for a study of the differences between the editorials about Proposition 209 in the mainstream and ethnic/racial press. She establishes that both forms of media have a particular bias, the mainstream media reporting the concerns of those in power and the alternative press reporting from the perspective of the disadvantaged. In addition, the sources, styles of reporting, and issues addressed communicate this bias to the respective press's audience. The question this suggests for the current study is whether or not these differences extend to the editorials of mainstream and alternative newspapers.

This point is supported by the argument of Brislin (1995) that the ethnic press has most often been considered a subset of the alternative press, in the same category as the labor and social-issues presses that have short life spans and accomplish little (3). He highlights the unique contribution of the ethnic press, as both an agent of assimilation and pluralism, in that it both preserves cultural identity and fosters adaptation to mainstream culture. Brislin (1995) argues that individual newspapers within a particular ethnic context can perform different aspects of this dual role. In discussing the role of the Japanese press in Hawaii, Brislin makes a distinction between the *Nippu JiJi*, a conservative newspaper encouraging "passive assimilation," and the *Hawaii Hochi*, an activist newspaper that "strove to preserve the key identity of its culture through instruction in language and the learning of traditions" (4). Brislin further argues that the "ethnic and foreign-language press have played a central role in establishing and maintaining a pluralistic society in Hawaii, assisting in preserving some cultural traditions and adapting others to the mainstream of American culture," so that pluralism replaces assimilation as the metaphor of choice when referring to groups becoming a distinct part of American culture (25). What Brislin's work suggests for this study is whether this distinction between assimilation and pluralism is reflected in the ideology of editorials about Proposition 209. If the assimilation thread is stronger, that could indicate an acceptance of more dominant capitalist economic assumptions displayed in the ideology of the mainstream press as they argue for or against Proposition 209.

Race and Inequality in the Media

The importance of the framing of race in the media for this study cannot be underestimated. What framing means is important in establishing that newspaper editorials are a legitimate site for the investigation of economic ideologies. The framing of race and inequality specifically is important, because the literature reveals that race is often framed in conjunction with economic terms, especially the inequality or lack of qualifications of persons of color, as contrasted with the more successful, qualified white population. The connection made in the media among race, ability, and economic success indicates that racial hierarchy is a fundamental element of the economic ideology the media presents to the public. This analysis builds upon the existing literature about the framing of race and inequality in order to investigate whether there are any common economic assumptions made in the mainstream and alternative media in the debate over Proposition 209, a policy that may restrict certain racial groups' access to the opportunities that capitalist ideology promises are available to everyone.

News frames, according to Entman (1997), are themes that are chosen, "highlighted and reinforced through repeated prominent display, vivid illustration, and emotion arousing vocabulary" (1). The themes in a news frame can convey a particular ideology, belief system, or what Gamson and Modigliani (1987) refer to as a "package," which provides the basis for the interpretation of relevant events (2). The media, through the advocacy of a particular position and the rationale for it, are part of the creation and re-creation of news frames linked to racial relationships (Gomes and Williams 1990, 62). In the case of this study, the frame is capitalism, and editorials are used as the basis of analysis because they are the articles in newspapers where the open advocacy of policies or positions legitimately take place.

In the context of economic inequality, the portrayal of race by the media directly addresses responsibility for economic circumstances. For example, Iyengar (1991) studied the impact of framing by television news on how people attribute responsibility for poverty and racial inequality. He found that the episodic framing of poverty—that is, poverty presented as a case study or event-oriented report, depicting public issues in terms of concrete circumstances (14)—increased attributions of individual responsibility (67). Thematic framing, the framing of public issues in a more general context, in the form of a takeout or backgrounder report directed at general outcomes or conditions (14), increased attributions of social responsibility.

Coverage of different types of poor people, however, may affect societal attributions, depending upon the characteristics of the specific poor person. As Iyengar found, "[N]ews coverage of black poverty in general, and episodic coverage of black poverty in particular, increases the degree to which viewers hold individual (read poor blacks) responsible for racial inequality" (1991, 67). Iyengar also found that gender, as well as race, can activate a more individualistic conception of responsibility for poverty. The effect is to blame the individuals (i.e., women) for their poverty rather than attribute responsibility to social causes. Single mothers are particularly at risk for what Iyengar calls the "blame the victim syndrome." In addition, race, gender, age, and marital status can combine to elicit a strong attribution of individual responsibility for poverty. That is, black, adult single mothers were particularly likely to be held responsible for their poverty (1991, 68).

Newspaper reporting about racial disparities in social and economic conditions can also "implicate some individuals and classes of persons in the generation of risks and others in differential exposure to these risks" (Gandy and Goshorn 1995, 135). This could affect public perceptions about which public policies geared toward assisting those at risk are justified, based upon the race of the at-risk population. For example, Gandy and Goshorn (1995) found that, in stories about racially comparative risk, framing is more likely to be in

terms of black loss. Indeed, lead paragraphs that emphasize the high probability of white success are accompanied by headlines that reflect the high probability of black loss. And the larger the proportion of blacks in the market, the
more likely papers were to use a lead focusing upon the probability of black
failure (145–46).

Later, Gandy et al. (1997) again addressed the question of the connection
between the media framing of risks and public perceptions about the role of
government in helping to alleviate those risks. In their study Gandy et al.
argue that the media is an important source of information used in forming
impressions about hardship in a society and of analyses that help construct
these impressions by providing information on who is responsible for the conditions that create the hardship (1997, 159). If individuals are viewed as being
responsible for their own situation, they are not seen as deserving of government assistance. In terms of racial equality, in order for programs designed to
eliminate racial disparities to be accepted, Gandy et al. argue that two conditions must be present. First, the inequality must be perceived as substantial,
and, second, it cannot be easily explained by individual responsibility (1997,
159). Given this framework, one of the main questions Gandy et al. (1997,
168) asked was: "What patterns are evident in the ways in which newspapers
frame stories about risk and racial disparity in exposure to hazards?"

They found that stories and headlines that involved a racial comparison
were most often framed in terms of disparity, rather than in terms of discrimination or bias. A majority of headlines reflected black loss or negative
outcomes for blacks. Lead paragraphs made specific reference to a high probability of black loss rather than the low probability of black success. Whites
were infrequently the subject of a comparison of risk, but when they were (in
lead paragraphs), the higher probability of gain was emphasized more frequently than the lower probability of loss (Gandy et. al 1997, 172). The importance of the authors' results for this study, given the framework of the
question they asked, is that blacks, in risk comparisons with whites, are more
likely to be the subject of racial disparity comparisons, and then on the losing side. The low incidence of discrimination and bias as the frame for loss
implies that the disparity is not readily explained in terms of government or
social responsibility. The implication is that public opinion, influenced by
these frames, would be less likely to support government action to alleviate
the disparity.

The portrayal of immigrants by the media is also an important for this
study, because it very closely connects specific ideas about the potential for
economic success and failure to different groups based upon race. Coutin and

Chock (1995) studied newspaper coverage of the Immigration Reform and Control Act of 1986 to investigate how journalists wrote about the possible eligibility for amnesty of different persons under this law, specifically "the assumptions about citizenship and alienage that lie behind the media's portrayal of amnesty applicants" (125). They argue that journalists used "legalizations narratives" that convey the geographical, social, and legal journeys immigrants take in the course of moving from an identity as aliens to an identity as "proto-citizens" (125).

Coutin and Chock found newspapers used two frames of crisis and opportunity. The first frame presented illegal immigrants as a threat to society because they were destructive, lawless, foreign, and unrooted. The second portrayed illegal immigrants as a boon because, in taking advantage of their new opportunities, they "reenacted the process that had created the nation" (1995, 127). They recognized the opportunities available in the United States and entered this country despite the dangers of being pursued. They struggled to exist, with the dream of someday achieving citizenship. When the 1986 Act was passed, their opportunity came, and they were grateful to the government for it (Coutin and Chock 1995, 127). Class and racial differences were minimized between eligible aliens and citizens but emphasized between citizens/amnesty applicants and ineligible illegal aliens (129). Gender was also used to illustrate the worthiness of those illegal immigrants eligible for amnesty: Coverage tended to focus upon married men, who were portrayed as more rooted and assimilable than their single counterparts, or upon single women, who were goal-oriented, industrious, and quite unlike "welfare mothers" who had children at public expense. Married women were an extension of married men (130). Clearly, this study provides evidence that distinctions are made in reporting about the "worthiness" of individuals and their potential to succeed, based upon race, gender, and formal eligibility for membership in U.S. society.

Thus, the media help to create and re-create racial attitudes, including those about race as it affects the attribution of responsibility for economic circumstances, as well as opinion about whether or not the government should act to assist those at economic risk and, if the government should act, which groups deserve public assistance. Indeed, as shown by studies of media coverage of affirmative action, these are the very themes that are central to the debate over affirmative action as it relates to economic opportunity generally and to Proposition 209 more specifically. For example, Entman (1997) found a similar racial and economic context in his study of media and the affirmative action debate. Entman discovered that the dominant theme in media coverage of public opinion about affirmative action was "high intensity emotional conflict of interest between mutually antagonistic whites and African Americans," with "angry opposition from whites, confronted by obstinate, self-interest support among blacks" (4, 6). Affirmative action policy was framed as a zero sum policy in which only one group could win, and one lose. The emphasis was upon blacks benefiting at the expense of whites (7-8). Entman argues that this "conflict frame" (1-2) emphasizes what he refers to as the "hegemonic American ideology: individualism, individual responsibility for one's status, and suspicion of government programs that might promote equality of outcomes" (11).

These same themes appear in the study of Gamson and Modigliani (1987) of media commentary about affirmative action. The authors found that over a twenty-year period there were three main issue packages surrounding the affirmative action debate. The first was Remedial Action, which addressed whether or not race-conscious programs should be used to remedy the historical effects of racial discrimination. The second was Delicate Balance, or how to create a balance between victims of discrimination without creating new ones through, for example, preferential treatment. The third package was No Preferential Treatment, which discouraged race-conscious policies because they always create preferential treatment and unfair advantage for some at the expense of others (145-146). When Gamson and Modigliani mention how race was referred to by the media, it was usually in terms of assistance to black minorities at white expense (152-163).

The studies of Entman (1997) and Gamson and Modigliani (1987) illustrate the prominence of capitalist economic ideology in media coverage of affirmative action and the underlying racial context for the debate over the policy. This study is grounded in these and other studies included here, in that it uses them to establish the signposts of capitalist economic ideology to look for in editorials about Proposition 209. It extends this research to a comparison of mainstream and ethnic newspaper editorials in order to gauge the similarities and differences in the acceptance of capitalist norms by these media and any challenges to those norms that may be present.

Data and Methods

In this study, an editorial is defined as "an unsigned institutional opinion on an issue or event" (Hynds 1990, 303). Eleven of the editorials are from the five largest mainstream newspapers in California, the *Los Angeles Times* (4), the *Orange County Register* (3), the *San Francisco Chronicle* (1), the *Sacra-*

mento Bee (1), and the *San Diego Union Tribune* (1). Editorials from the *Los Angeles Times, San Francisco Chronicle,* and the *San Diego Union Tribune* were downloaded from the Lexis Nexis database. Editorials from the *Orange County Register* were downloaded from the Proquest database. Editorials from the *Sacramento Bee* were acquired directly from its offices. Seven of the editorials are from four ethnic newspapers indexed in the Ethnic Newswatch database, identified as California newspapers and targeted to a specific group: *Asian-Week,* Asian (2), the *Los Angeles Sentinel,* African-American (2), the *Sun Reporter,* African-American (1), and *La Opinion,* Latino (2).[1] Only those editorials that directly argued for or against Proposition 209 were chosen.

With a limited number of editorials to analyze, the method used must be rigorous enough to produce legitimate results from a small sample, and qualitative in nature in order to bring to light the ideological assumptions made in newspaper editorials. For this reason, framing analysis was chosen. Gamson and Modigliani (1987) explain that every policy issue has a culture, an ongoing changeable discourse that provides meaning and a basis for the interpretation of relevant events. The discourse might consist of "metaphors, catchphrases, visual images, moral appeals, and other symbolic devices" (2). These elements of the discourse can be viewed as an interpretive package. In addition, any give policy issue will have competing packages. General audience media are one forum for public discourse on policy issues. They are both producers of issue cultures and also sites where the various packages surrounding an issue culture are contested (2-3).

Each package has what Gamson and Modigliani (1987) call a core frame, a centralizing organizing idea for making sense of relevant events and establishing a connection between them (143). A frame implies a range of positions so that there can be disagreement, or more than one package, among those who share a common frame. Each package has its own symbols that suggest the frame and its accompanying issue positions in shorthand, making it possible to reveal the entire package with "a deft metaphor, catchphrase, or other symbolic device" (3). As an example, it is expected in this study that the core frame of all the editorials will be capitalism, or free-market ideology. The issue would be affirmative action, and the issue culture would include packages both for and against affirmative action that would take different positions

---

1. Translation of *La Opinion* editorials provided by Elizabeth C. Martinez, Ph.D., Associate Professor of Modern Languages, and Jose Castro, student, both of Sonora State University.

on individual responsibility for social circumstances, the role of government in addressing those circumstances, and how race affects both.

Questions

The questions asked in this study are based upon the themes revealed in the earlier discussion of free market ideology, the difference between the mainstream and the alternative media, and race and inequality in the media. The first question addresses the central place of a free-market frame in American political discourse, as reflected in California's newspapers: Will the editorials in both the mainstream and ethnic/racial newspapers share basic free market ideology as a frame, including the elements of opportunity, individual merit, and limited government? The second question addresses the expected "antiaffirmative action/pro-209" package: Will the antiaffirmative action/pro-209 package in editorials emphasize individual responsibility for social circumstances and a reduced role for government in addressing those circumstances, and deemphasize race as a factor in access to opportunity? The third question addresses the expected "proaffirmative action/anti-209" package: Will the proaffirmative action/anti-209 package in editorials emphasize social responsibility for individual circumstances and a government role in addressing those circumstances, and emphasize race as a factor in access to opportunity? The fourth question addresses the differences between the mainstream and the ethnic/racial media: Will there be differences between the mainstream and the ethnic/racial press in terms of an appeal to a specific audience and an argument for that audience to act based upon its identity? In all four questions, the role of race in the answers will be given primary attention.

Results

The editorials were analyzed according to the mainstream or the ethnic/racial newspaper category and their position on Proposition 209. There were two mainstream newspapers with editorials supporting the proposition, the *Orange County Register* and the *San Diego Union Tribune*. There were no ethnic/racial newspapers supporting the proposition. Three mainstream newspapers took an editorial position against Proposition 209, the *Los Angeles Times*, the *San Francisco Chronicle*, and the *Sacramento Bee*. All four ethnic/racial newspapers also took an editorial position against the proposition.

Mainstream Newspapers
Supporting Proposition 209

The *Orange County Register* and the *San Diego Union Tribune* both had editorials which reflect the free market frame, and both praised Proposition 209 for bringing California state policy more into line with that philosophy. Both based their positions on the fundamental assumption that the best market is a free market, which is one without government interference. Such an arrangement provides the best opportunity for everyone to compete and, most important, for the freedom and ability to make an individual choice about what occupation to compete in. This freedom is the standard for justice and fairness. The *San Diego Union Tribune* (1996) set up equal opportunity as the "American ideal" and individual merit through open competition as the only fair way to apportion reward (18 October, B8). Any government action that gives preference to one group over another, to the detriment of individual merit as a standard, is "favoritism" (18 October, B8). The *Orange County Register* (1996) calls free markets "unpredictable, because of individuals choosing occupations based upon reasons of culture, happenstance, personal preference or idiosyncrasies" (8 March, B.08). The way for individuals who aspire toward jobs to achieve success is not through government action but hard work "so they can realize their dreams" (8 March, B.08). The *Register* (1996) also favorably quotes students of color who want to make it on their own merits rather than as the beneficiaries of special government action (8 March, B.08). The implications of these arguments are that individual merit is the best basis for judging one's worth and that the market is the best judge precisely because it is based upon freedom rather than arbitrary government regulation.

With regard to their specific pro-Proposition 209 stance, The *San Diego Union-Tribune* and the *Orange County Register* displayed what can be called the "individualist package" within the issue culture of affirmative action. This package is characterized by a commitment to the free-market principles of individual merit and equal opportunity, opposition to affirmative action as governmental interference with the free market, and at least superficial deference to the presence of discrimination in society. The *Union-Tribune* (1996) builds its argument upon the position that government action in the form of affirmative action, ostensibly designed to redress racial discrimination in the market place, is actually dangerous to the equal opportunity to compete based upon individual merit. It argues that "preferential treatment based on skin color or national origin is the antithesis of equal opportunity" (18 October,

B8). Affirmative action is really a "racial spoils system," dangerous because "once government tries to impose equality of outcome, instead of equality of opportunity, the crucial goal of advancement based upon individual merit is hopelessly sacrificed" (18 October, B8). Nonetheless, the *Union-Tribune* (1996) does recognize the existence of "economic disparities that separate Americans along racial and ethnic lines" and the need for the government to act to remedy those differences. However, rather than race-based remedies which can cause division, remedies need to be based upon something more suitable to a free market—that is, economic need. This can provide the "disadvantaged of all races and ethnic groups the tools needed to advance economically" (18 October, B8).

The *Orange County Register* (1996) also uses themes reflective of the individualist package in its reasoning for supporting Proposition 209, particularly resistance to government interference in the market to redress racial discrimination. It does pay deference to the presence of racial discrimination in society, but only with a slight nod. The *Register* acknowledges that it would be "Pollyannaish" to claim that "old-fashioned discrimination" had been eliminated and argues that a moral society should act to root out discrimination based upon race, sex, or ethnicity (8 March, B.08). However (*the Register* claims), we have approached that ideal, so the argument that deviations between racial ratios in the workforce and such ratios in the larger community are the "fruit of discrimination" is a terrain staked out by "self-professed liberals and other affirmative actions enthusiasts with their yen for a society sprung from a government planner's tidy dreams" (8 March, B.08). And the clause in the proposition that allows qualifications based upon sex when "reasonably necessary" is only to make sure that "common sense doesn't get trampled." For example, male prison guards should not conduct body searches on female inmates (25 August, G.01). The *Register*'s commitment to individual merit is also clear in its argument that affirmative action actually hurts minorities by implying that they did not win their position based upon individual merit, the gold standard of success in a free market system. Rather, minorities get jobs they may not be qualified for as a result of a system that "implies that they didn't win their degree on merit" (23 September, B.0).

Neither the *San Diego Union-Tribune* nor the *Orange County Register* makes a claim to be serving a specific audience. Rather, the implication is that they are addressing the larger public. One can infer from the *Union-Tribune*'s appeal to unity in its argument against Proposition 209 that it wants to address, if not create, a community that encompasses all racial and ethnic groups. For example, its editorial (1996) refers to equal opportunity as an "American" ideal, and its suggestion for need-based remedies for economic disparities is based upon a desire to expand such policies "for all disadvantaged Americans" (18 October, B8). The *Register* (1996) makes a similar appeal for unity, arguing that "racial preferences" divide communities along lines of color and ethnicity (23 September B.0). The clear implication from both newspapers is that the entire public shares an interest in preserving access to opportunity based upon individual merit. This mirrors the free-market ideology that makes no connection between economic success and race.

Mainstream Newspapers Opposing Proposition 209

The editorials in the *Sacramento Bee*, the *San Francisco Chronicle*, and the *Los Angeles Times* all reflected the free-market frame and took positions criticizing Proposition 209 as, to one extent or another, too drastic. All three newspapers emphasized the importance of equal opportunity and couched individual merit in terms of qualified individuals being assisted by affirmative action. There was also an implicit agreement that the best market was the one as free from government interference as possible: While government programs like affirmative action may be necessary, they should be limited, temporary, or subject to periodic public review.

Interestingly, the *Sacramento Bee* (1996) does not specifically mention equal opportunity, but it does refer to "long-term entitlements" as "antithetical to American ideals" (3 September, B6), implying that mandated advantage, as compared to advantage gained through competition based upon merit, is in contradiction with the same ideals of fairness and justice referred to in the pro-209 editorials. The *San Francisco Chronicle* (1996) specifically refers to affirmative action as being a "bridge to more equal opportunity," emphasizing that the goal should be the opportunity to compete, not government-guaranteed results. In addition, it refers to affirmative action as a way to bring disenfranchised groups into the "economic mainstream" (6 October, Editorial, 8). The editorials in the *Los Angeles Times* (1996) also reflect the equal-opportunity aspect of the free-market frame. The larger goal of equal opportunity to compete is established in references to how Proposition 209 "jeopardizes opportunity" (21 July, M, 4); affirmative action "opens the door to broader competition" (13 October, M, 4); and "affirmative action is an effective civil rights tool available to open the doors of opportunity" (1 November, Metro, B, 8).

All three newspapers also display a commitment to individual merit and a free-market system, although their willingness to tolerate government action to regulate what they argue are the negative effects of a free-market system is higher than the newspapers opposing Proposition 209. The commitment to individual merit is implicit in the argument that affirmative action is designed only to help qualified individuals. The *Sacramento Bee* (1996) makes the observation that most people might agree to "narrow preferences, other qualifications being equal." A problem would arise, however, if formulas were used that provided members of favored groups a "large advantage over more qualified candidates from other groups"(3 September, B6). The *San Francisco Chronicle* (1996) also highlights a commitment to individual merit by using arguments related to qualifications. It suggests that affirmative action is not about "hiring unqualified women and minorities over qualified white males" (6 October, Editorial, 8). The *Los Angeles Times* (1996) makes similar statements about the connection between qualified individuals and affirmative action. For example, it argues: "Without affirmative action, qualified women and minorities lose" (21 July, M, 4). Another *Times* editorial makes the point that the facts do not bear out the myth that Proposition 209 "promotes the admission of unqualified minorities" (28 October, Metro, B, 4). Finally, in a statement that combines the opportunity and merit arguments, the *Times* suggests: "Affirmative action, when properly implemented, merely opens opportunity to a broader range of qualified people" (1 November, Metro, B, 8).

The *Sacramento Bee*, the *San Francisco Chronicle*, and the *Los Angeles Times* all include the last element of the free-market frame, the danger of government interference in the marketplace, because it would jeopardize the freedom of choice the market guarantees. Again, this commitment is displayed in terms of the temporary nature of affirmative action plans or the notion that they need to be reviewed periodically. These caveats are reflective of these newspapers' greater tolerance of government action to remedy the inequities of the marketplace. The *Bee* (1996) argues that there are flaws and injustices in California's affirmative action programs and that "[t]he question is how long and in what form race-based affirmative action programs should be maintained" (3 September, B6). It suggests that such programs should be "sunsetted," "periodically—and publicly—reviewed," or "eliminated" when they have lost public support (3 September, B6). The *Chronicle* (1996) argues that affirmative action is "not a permanent solution" but, as previously suggested, a "bridge" to a more equal opportunity society (6 October, Editorial, 8). The *Times* (1996) also makes reference to problems with affirmative action plans and the necessity of fixing programs that are unfair or outdated. In one editorial, the *Times* argues that "some affirmative action programs have been executed improperly or unfairly" (21 July, M, 4) and that abuse and mismanagement of affirmative action programs should be fixed (13 October, M, 4). In addition, the *Times* also makes the argument that "a state review of public affirmative action programs…could help correct overly broad or out-dated efforts" (13 October, M, 4). Finally, the *Times* points out that affirmative action is not the only possible government remedy for discrimination, stating that it is "not a cure all, but it has helped tremendously"(1 November, Metro, B, 8).

With regard to their specific anti-209 positions, the *Sacramento Bee,* the *San Francisco Chronicle,* and the *Los Angeles Times* reflect what can be called the "diversity package" within the issue culture of affirmative action. This package is characterized by a commitment to equal opportunity and individual merit (as discussed above), approval of government action to rectify the very real racial disparities created by the free market, and a commitment to diversity in the marketplace as a worthy goal in and of itself. The newspapers participated in this package in differing degrees. For example, the *Bee* (1996) implicitly recognized the existence of racial and gender disparities in public programs when it refused to endorse Proposition 209 on the basis that its "inflexible provisions against any race or gender consideration…are too sweeping and categorical, and their consequences too unpredictable" (3 September, B6). However, it only reluctantly endorsed affirmative action programs, labeling them "racial preferences" and warning of the difficulty in deciding whom the preferences should go to in a state as diverse as California, particularly when trying to address the "historic disadvantages" suffered by recent immigrants whose disadvantages were not experienced in this country (3 September, B6). The Bee does, however, implicitly support diversity as a goal in asserting the need for race-based considerations when the legitimacy and fairness of a public enterprise, such as the Los Angeles Police Department or the judicial system, depend upon the community's sense that the enterprise contains representatives of the community that share its culture and background (3 September, B6).

The *Chronicle* (1996) is more explicit in its recognition of racial and gender disparities, arguing that "diversity is not even close to reality in the upper echelons" and that "biases against women and minorities are very real." The *Chronicle* (1996) is also explicit about the one group that historically has had power, in referring to the fact that "white males still control most hiring decisions" (6 October, Editorial, 8). It warns that if affirmative action is eliminated, there would be a risk of returning to the days when there was a tendency to "hire in one's image," referring to white males hiring those who are most like them (6 October, Editorial, 8). The *Chronicle* (1996) also displays less reluctance than the *Bee* to endorse affirmative action as a means to achieve diversity as a legitimate goal, tying that goal to the diversity of the state. It argues that Proposition 209 "would prevent public agencies from mainlining affirmative action practices designed to change their ethnic and gender makeup to better reflect the diversity of the community and state" (6 October, Editorial, 8).

The *Los Angeles Times* (1996) has perhaps most explicitly adhered to the diversity package. The *Times* builds an extensive case to justify its argument that there are racial and gender economic disparities and calls diversity an asset that Proposition 209 would turn into a liability. One editorial refers to the "continuing, documented instances of Americans being excluded because they are women or denied jobs or housing because of the color of their skin" and points out that "women are the victims of gender discrimination, not men, and that Blacks, Latinos, Asian Americans, and Native Americans are the victims of racial discrimination, not whites" (13 October, M, 4). The same editorial (13 October, M, 4) goes so far as to argue that the proposition would be more supportable without its "audacious pretense that 'preferences' for women and minorities are at the root of discrimination in California. Where is this parallel world in which powerful women and minorities run the government and corporations and turn away qualified white men?" The *Times* (1996) also asserts that Proposition 209 "wouldn't touch most preferences, that it targets only women and minorities" (28 October, Metro, B, 4).

As for diversity as a legitimate goal unto itself, the *Times* (1996) argues that affirmative action is valued by businesses because it helps them use diverse employees to reach a diverse market—"in short, affirmative action helps the bottom line" (1 November, Metro, B, 8). In addition, the *Times* uses the argument that women and minorities own a significant number of private businesses in California and deserve a larger share of public contracts, which affirmative action can help them achieve (1 November, Metro, B, 8). The *Times* also uses the argument that affirmative action encourages diversity in the work force and education (13 October, M, 4) and speaks approvingly of Los Angeles' Richard Riordan's comment that he opposes Proposition 209 because it "takes one of our greatest assents, our diversity, and tries to turn it into a liability" (21 July, M, 4).

Neither the *Sacramento Bee*, the *San Francisco Chronicle*, nor the *Los Angeles Times* makes a claim to address a specific community in their editorials. Much like the *San Diego Union-Tribune* and the *Orange County Register*, they frame their arguments in more universal terms. However, that universality is not based upon an appeal to the same kind of unity as that of the *Union-Tribune* and the *Register*. Rather, in strongly emphasizing diversity as a legitimate goal of government policy, these newspapers explicitly reach out to women and persons of color in a way that the newspapers that support Proposition 209 do not.

Ethnic Newspapers Opposing Proposition 209

The only major theme clearly from the free market frame emphasized by *AsianWeek*, the *Sun Reporter*, the *Los Angeles Sentinel*, and *La Opinion* is equal opportunity; individual merit is not explicitly mentioned. In the context of ethnic newspapers' greater attention to the existence of discrimination based upon race and gender, the positive role of government in rectifying that discrimination, and the necessity for political action on the part of particular ethnic/racial communities in making sure that government does act, silence about individual merit could occur because it is perceived as a code word for white advantage and success. One could argue that implicit in the emphasis upon equal opportunity is the acceptance of individual competition for reward once access to opportunity is secured. However, the silence about individual merit and the stronger emphasis upon discrimination based upon racial groupings and upon government and community action make it appear that an alternative frame to free-market ideology and its focus upon individual merit is emerging. The new frame could be called the "economic empowerment" frame because of a strong emphasis upon the existence of racial and gender discrimination in a white-dominated environment, and a commitment to equal opportunity and government and community action to achieve it. The package shown in ethnic newspapers could be called the "race and gender action" package, because of the emphasis upon action by specific ethnic, racial, and gender groups in rectifying discrimination.

The theme of equal opportunity is explicit in the editorials of *AsianWeek* (1996). Affirmative action is defined as "in spirit and most often in practice... access to equal opportunity" (19 April, v. 17, no. 34, 4). The editorials, in a reflection of the audience of the paper, also connect opportunity to disadvantage: "The key word is access—meaning opportunity, the opening of doors to those who have been shut out in the past" (24 October, v. 18, no. 9, 4). *AsianWeek* is clear, however, on the point that affirmative action is about access to opportunity only: "Results are never guaranteed" (24 October, v. 18, no. 9, 4). This does imply that government programs should only go so far. The *Sun Reporter* (1996) raises the issue of opportunities in referring to the history of affirmative action, arguing that the only reason the original policy was established was that "there was a great need to open up jobs, educational opportunities, and other social activities that are a part of public policy" (19 September, v. 52, no. 37, 7). The *Los Angeles Sentinel* (1996) also highlights equal opportunity, interestingly enough in one editorial in the context of an argument for changing the minds of white women about the proposition, from support of 209 to opposition to it. The specific reference is to professions that have "opened up to white women" because of affirmative action, including "doctors, lawyers, airline pilots even astronauts" (31 October, v. 62, no. 31, A6). In another editorial in the *Sentinel,* equal opportunity is referred to in terms of the consequences of Proposition 209 on avenues of inclusion for "minorities and women into contracting, employment and educational opportunities" (8 August, v. 62, no. 19, A6). And reference is made to the point that no matter how "watered down," without affirmative action "the majority of African Americans would be denied access to opportunity" (8 August, v. 62, no. 19, A6). The *Sun Reporter* and the *Sentinel* thus follow *AsianWeek* in connecting opportunity to disadvantage.

La Opinion (1996) follows the other three ethnic newspapers in connecting opportunity to disadvantage. In one editorial, affirmative action is described as procuring "equal opportunity for all" and as a way for minorities to have access to education, which is the "best method for a society to avoid unequal opportunities, and to achieve a good social-economic balance" (29 October, v. 71, no. 43, 7A). *La Opinion*'s editorials also follow those of the *Sentinel* in pointing out the consequences of Proposition 209 for opportunity for minorities, arguing that approval of the proposition would "interrupt the ready process of access for minorities to the benefits of this society" (12 August, v. 70, no. 331, 11A).

The connection of opportunity to disadvantage is the fundamental basis of the "economic empowerment" frame. All four ethnic newspapers, like their mainstream counterparts, the *Los Angeles Times* and the *San Francisco Chronicle,* who oppose Proposition 209, pay explicit attention to the existence of disadvantage in the form of racial discrimination. *AsianWeek* (1996) argues that discrimination still exists. One editorial states, "We still live in a race- and gender-conscious society. True, discrimination is not as blatant as in years past, but it remains pervasive" (24 October, v. 18, no. 9, 4). And reference is made to the large number of racial and sexual harassment cases filed each year with the Equal Employment Opportunity Commission as evidence that "inequalities still exist in our society" (24 October, v. 18, no. 9, 4). In pointing out discrimination in the Asian-Pacific American community, *AsianWeek* also asks whether or not "affirmative action has outlived its usefulness, and has now, in fact, held back Asian Pacific Americans.... [H]ave we really...reached a level playing field? We don't think so" (24 October, v. 18, no. 9, 4). It is interesting to note that *AsianWeek* makes the point that racism is not as blatant as in the past, which indicates that progress has been made, but not enough.

The *Sun Reporter* and the *Los Angeles Sentinel* also have hard-hitting analyses of discrimination and put them in terms of the communities to which they are designed to appeal. In regard to those who have been discriminated against in their exclusion from opportunities for education and employment, the *Sun Reporter* (1996) asserts: "Even the most unlearned black people, and all women of any race, know that they and some of the other ethnic members of the population had long been subjected to all of the discriminations that affirmative action has attempted to bring to an end" (19 September, v. 52, no. 37, 7). *The Reporter* also refers to the racism that "stains the fringe" of Proposition 209, warning that when a former KKK leader like David Duke and a black man like Ward Connerly agree on a racial issue, "something is awry" (19 September, v. 52, no. 37, 7). The *Los Angeles Sentinel* (1996) puts the existence of racial discrimination in terms of what groups have access to power and opportunity at the expense of those who do not. In an argument against the passage of Proposition 209, one *Sentinel* editorial argues that the proposition will legally close avenues now available for the inclusion of minorities and women "in favor of those who are now members of the 'in' group," who "will not want to share any of these opportunities, and this amendment will help preclude any inroads to such opportunities" (8 August, v. 62, no. 19, A6). Reference is also made to the "abuse or misuse" of affirmative action by the "same Establishment that is now trying to dismantle all programs which take race, sex, and ethnicity into consideration" (8 August, v. 62, no. 19, A6).

La Opinion (1996) also strongly stresses the existence of racial discrimination against its target community, but it also emphasizes that other ethnic groups, minorities more generally, as well as women, are the victims of discrimination. *La Opinion* documents the racial discrimination of Latinos in economic terms, referring to the group's rates of high unemployment, low income, and low participation in higher education. The same editorial also indicates that Latina women with a university education average less income than white women with similar education (29 October, v. 71, no. 43, 7A). Other comments are made about the low unemployment rate for African-Americans and the disparity between the income of women and that of men (29 October, v. 71, no. 43, 7A). *La Opinion* also follows the *Sentinel* in situating racial discrimination in the context of who has access to opportunity and who does not, with access, advantage, and privilege available to whites. *La Opinion* considers affirmative action a way to counteract the "privileges of white minorities [*sic*]" (12 August, v. 70, no. 331, 11A) and compares the income and education rates of minorities and women with those of whites (29 October, v. 71, no. 43, 7A). Indeed, women suffer disadvantages "even in the white majority" in comparison to men (12 August, v. 70, no. 331, 11A).

Unlike the newspapers in the diversity package, the four ethnic newspapers do not stress that the role of government should be limited or that policies such as affirmative action should be temporary. Rather, government is seen as one of two main vehicles for rectifying discrimination against racial groups and women. *AsianWeek* (1996) refers to affirmative action, a government policy, as "one of the most effective tools in countering racism" (19 April, v. 17, no. 34, 4) and argues that "because discrimination remains a fact of life, the government...has adopted affirmative action programs to those who have been disadvantaged"(24 October, v. 18, no. 9, 4). In addition, the Equal Employment Opportunity Commission is cited as a central government agency in dealing with racial and sexual harassment complaints (24 October, v. 18, no. 9, 4).

The *Sun Reporter* and *the Sentinel* also approve of government action to rectify racial discrimination, although the government is criticized in both newspapers' editorials for falling short of the goals of affirmative action programs. The *Reporter* (1996) refers to the help necessary from the federal government that has accompanied "every step forward that blacks have achieved," but it also mentions that the "same federal government always turned its back when blacks complained about the disenfranchisement that was practiced against them" (19 September, v. 72, no. 37, 7). Also, according to the *Reporter,* affirmative action has had limited success: "There is no doubt that affirmative action has made possible some improvements for those who suffered from the ill effects of discrimination based on race and gender" (19 September, v. 72, no. 37, 7), The *Sentinel* (1996) also gives affirmative action mixed reviews, arguing that, on the one hand, it is necessary to preserve what inclusion minorities and women have achieved in employment and educational opportunities. On the other hand: "No matter how bad affirmative action programs may be, they have improved significantly over time. They have also been watered down by the judicial system to be no more than outreach, recruitment, goals, timetables and good faith efforts" (8 August, v. 62, no. 19, A6). In an indication of the different orientation of the ethnic and mainstream newspapers concerning the affirmative action issue, these are the types of programs that newspapers such as the *Los Angeles Times* and *Sacramento Bee* would support.

La Opinion (1996) also supports government action to remedy racial discrimination, describing the Civil Rights Act of 1964 as a legal response to the inequality suffered by women and minorities and affirmative action as a "crucial component of laws against discrimination" (12 August, v. 70, no. 331, 11A). The argument is also made that the approval of Proposition 209 would "eliminate a legal basis for affirmative action programs" (29 October, v. 71, no. 43, 7A), a clear indication that government action in the form of law has a role in rectifying discrimination. Also, as in the other three ethnic/racial newspapers, *La Opinion* does not view affirmative action as a temporary remedy. Rather, such programs should be examined in terms of their effectiveness against racial discrimination with the intent of improving them (12 August, v. 70, no. 331, 11A). Proposition 209 is also criticized on the basis that "affirmative action programs cannot be eliminated when they have not fulfilled their objectives" (12 August, v. 70, no. 331, 11A). There is not the explicit criticism of government failure in *La Opinion* that is apparent in the *Los Angeles Sentinel* and the *Sun Reporter*; however, the clear implication is that government has not yet done enough to remedy racial discrimination.

The second major vehicle for rectifying discrimination against racial groups and women, and a fundamental aspect of the "economic empowerment" frame, is group action. The distinctive community nature of that action, in terms of specific racial, ethnic, and gender groups, is the key feature of the "race and gender action" package. All four ethnic newspapers strongly highlight the need for their communities to act in order to save affirmative action. Proposition 209 is an indication that government, though necessary, cannot alone be trusted to act. *AsianWeek* (1996) refers to the civil rights movement as the proper context for the debate over affirmative action and Proposition 209. By doing so, the newspaper underscores the need for action by racial minorities, especially blacks, to force the government to remedy racial discrimination in the first place (19 April, v. 17, no. 34, 4). In addition, Asian-Pacific Americans are highlighted as "being relegated to the sidelines in American society until the civil rights movement of the 1960s" (24 October, v. 18, no. 9, 4). In addition, reference is made to the unfulfilled dream of Martin Luther King, Jr., in the context of Asian-Pacific Americans needing "to be in the real world" and "rejecting misrepresented cures to discrimination" (24 October, v. 18, no. 9, 4).

The *Sun Reporter* and the *Los Angeles Sentinel* place heavy emphasis upon community action on the part of the black community, which indicates the specific community emphasis of these two papers. The *Reporter* (1996) credits the black community with achieving historic legal gains, including the fact that the government "turned its back when blacks complained about the disfranchisement that was practiced against them, until the great peaceful civil rights activities occurred in the 1950s and 1960s." The civil rights movement, headed by Reverend Martin Luther King, Jr., is also given credit in the *Reporter* for progress in the women's movement, "a movement which in time recognized that all women were victims of discrimination in the job market.... It was not until the civil rights demonstrations that many institutions of higher learning stopped discriminating against the admission of women,...the great privately endowed colleges and universities" (19 September, v. 52, no. 37, 7). The editorial ends with a warning about future action: "Proposition 209 is only a crude attempt to restore a period of injustice, which, we should not forget, brings social unrest" (19 September, v. 52, no. 37, 7). The *Sentinel* credits a bus tour of California organized by NOW, the Feminist Majority, and Jesse Jackson of the Rainbow/PUSH Action Network with beginning to turn public opinion against Proposition 209. One editorial argues that changing the minds of white women, the greatest beneficiaries of affirmative action, about Proposition 209 is the key to success. Another editorial makes an appeal to the black community to understand that it is directly responsible for acting on its own behalf and that relying upon other groups for assistance is not the best road to empowerment:

> If we as African Americans don't see the need to salvage what little we have to protect our Civil Rights, who else will fight our battle? Sure, we can ride on the coat-tails of the white women who have benefited from our struggle, but is that the answer to our challenge? If we don't see the need to fight for our Civil Rights, then we have conceded our right to equal opportunity in this society. Either we stand up and have our vote count on Nov. 5, or we can perish economically! (8 August, v. 62, no. 19, A6)

La Opinion (1996) also appeals for action based upon group identity, urging Latinos to vote against Proposition 209 (12 August, v. 70, no. 331, 11A; 29 October, v. 71, no. 43, 7A). That the appeal is made in Spanish indicates that the newspaper uses this crucial aspect of community identity for many Latinos as a mechanism to foster group action.

Summary and Conclusion

This study has found that there are two frames in the issue culture surrounding affirmative action. First is the more traditionally "American" free-market frame, with its emphasis upon individual merit, equal opportunity, and government noninterference in the market. Within the free-market frame are two packages. The first is the individualistic package, represented in the *San Diego Union Tribune* and the *Orange County Register*, which stresses equal opportunity and individual merit, opposition to affirmative action as government interference in the economy, and limited acknowledgment that racial discrimination and gender discrimination are problems. The second package is the diversity package, represented in the *Sacramento Bee*, the *San Francisco Chronicle*, and the *Los Angeles Times*. It is characterized by a commitment to equal opportunity and individual merit, specific acknowledgment that racial discrimination and gender discrimination are real problems, approval of government action in the form of affirmative action to rectify those forms of discrimination, and the promotion of diversity as a legitimate goal in and of itself.

The second frame, which emerges in ethnic newspapers, is the "economic empowerment frame." It is characterized by silence about individual merit, a commitment to equal opportunity, a recognition that racial discrimination and gender discrimination are real and pervasive, an emphasis upon government action to rectify those forms of discrimination, and an emphasis upon community action to make sure that the government acts. The package within this frame, as shown in *AsianWeek*, the *Sun Reporter*, the *Los Angeles Sentinel*, and *La Opinion*, is the "race and gender action" package, which is characterized by a commitment to action by specific racial, ethnic, and gender groups to rectify discrimination.

The significance of these results is profound. The emergence of an alternative to the free-market frame in the form of an economic-empowerment frame indicates that there are competing frames, as well as competing packages within each frame. This points to the undermining of the view that "American" economic ideology is monolithic and dominated by a commitment to equal opportunity because it is the best way to guarantee the continuance of individual merit as the standard for economic success. That individual merit disappears from the economic empowerment frame altogether may indicate that the words "individual merit" are rejected since they are code words for white success and advantage. The emphasis upon diversity in a package in three major mainstream newspapers indicates that the racial, ethnic, and gender concerns at the core of the economic-empowerment frame are having an impact upon the dominant free-market frame. This impact, in combination with the call to community action by all four ethnic newspapers, indicates that racial, ethnic, and gender concerns, and the challenge to white advantage that they represent, are at the forefront of the ongoing redefinition of economic frames in this country. On the cutting edge of the rearticulation of economic frames in the contemporary media, the ethnic newspapers in this study redefine their mission—from assimilation based upon integration with existing dominant norms that privilege whites to a pluralism that includes acceptance based upon acknowledgment of a unique racial or ethnic identity and of legitimacy based upon the active creation of that identity through political action.

References

Almaguer, Tomas. 1994. *Racial fault lines: The historical origins of white supremacy in California*. Berkeley: University of California Press.

Brislin, Tom. 1995. Weep into silence/cries of rage: Bitter divisions in Hawaii's Japanese press. *Journalism and Mass Communications Monographs*. Monograph no. 154.

Coutin, Susan Bibler, and Phyllis Pease Chock. 1995. 'Your friend, the illegal': Definition and paradox in newspaper accounts of U.S. immigration reform. *Identities* 2, nos. 1-2: 123–48.

Entman, Robert M. 1997. Manufacturing discord: Media in the affirmative action debate. *Harvard International Journal of Press/Politics* 2, no. 4: 1–16.

Gamson, William A., and Andre Modigliani. 1987. The changing culture of affirmative action. *Research in Political Sociology* 3: 137–77.

_____. 1989. Media discourse and public opinion on nuclear power: A constructionist approach. *American Journal of Sociology* 95, no. 1: 1–37.

Gandy, Oscar H., Jr., and Kent Goshorn. 1995. Race, risk and responsibility: Editorial constraint in the framing of inequality. *Journal of Communication* 45, no. 2: 133–51.

Gandy, Oscar H., Katharina Kopp, Tanya Hands, Karen Frazer, and David Phillips. 1997. Race and risk: Factors affecting the framing of stories about inequality, discrimination, and just plain bad luck. *Public Opinion Quarterly* 61: 158–82.

Gomes, Ralph C.; Williams, Linda Faye. 1990. Race and crime: The role of the media in perpetuating racism and classism in America. *Urban League Review* 14, no. 1: 57–69.

Green, Philip. 1981. *The pursuit of inequality*. New York: Pantheon Books.

Harris, Cheryl I. 1995. Whiteness as property. In *Critical race theory: The key writings that formed the movement*, edited by Kimberle Crenshaw,

Neil Gotanda, Gary Peller, and Kendall Thomas, 276–91. New York: The New Press.

Hartz, Louis. 1955. *The liberal tradition in America: An interpretation of American political thought since the Revolution.* New York: Harcourt, Brace and Company.

Heilbroner, Robert L. 1986. *The worldly philosophers: The lives, times, and ideas of the great economic thinkers.* 6th ed. New York: Simon & Schuster.

Hindman, Elizabeth Blanks. 1998. 'Spectacles of the poor': Conventions of alternative news. *Journal and Mass Communication Quarterly* 75, no. 1: 177–93.

Hynds, Ernest C. 1990. Changes in editorials: A study of three newspapers, 1955–1985. *Journalism Quarterly* 67, no. 2: 302–12.

Iyengar, Shanto. 1991. *Is anyone responsible?: How television frames political issues.* Chicago: University of Chicago Press.

Lipsitz, George. 1998. *The possessive investment in whiteness: How white people profit from identity politics.* Philadelphia: Temple University Press.

Roediger, David R. 1999. *The wages of whiteness: Race and the making of the American working class.* Rev. Ed. New York: Verso.

Tarcher, Martin. 1996. *Escape from avarice.* Novato, CA: Chandler & Sharp.

Editorials Consulted

AsianWeek:
    "Double Vision," 19 April 1996, v. 17, no. 34, 4.
    "No on 209," 24 October 1996, v. 18, no. 9, 4.

La Opinion:
    "La CCRI deber ser rechazada," 12 August 1996, v. 70, no. 331, 11A.
    "No a la Proposicion 209," 29 October 1996, v. 71, no. 43, 7A.

Los Angeles Sentinel:
    "No! On Prop. 209," 8 August 1996, v. 62, no. 19, A6.
    "Stop Prop. 209," 31 October 1996, v. 62, no. 31, A6.

Los Angeles Times:
    "Some Official Clarity on a Misleading Proposition," 21 July 1996, Opinion, Part M, 4.

"Affirmative Action Still Is Needed: No on Prop. 209," 13 October 1996, Opinion, Part M. 4.

"Public Education Myths Fuel the Push for Prop. 209," 28 October 1996, Metro, part B, 4.

"Prop. 209 is a Fraud and Business Knows It," 1 November 1996, Metro, part B, 8.

Orange County Register:
  "Search for Racial Reason," 8 March 1996, B.08.
  "Hokum vs. CCRI," 25 August 1996, G.01.
  "Backfire in Society," 23 September 1996, B.0.

Sacramento Bee:
  "The Sledgehammer Remedy," 3 September 1996, B6.

San Diego Union-Tribune:
  "Avoiding discrimination Prop. 209 would provide equal opportunity," 18 October 1996, Opinion, B8.

San Francisco Chronicle:
  "Keeping Affirmative Action: Vote No on Prop. 209," 6 October 1996, Editorial, 8.

Sun Reporter:
  "One More Critic of 209," 19 September 1996, v. 52, no. 37, 7.

PART III

*The Ignored Initiative:
Direct Democracy
at the Local Level*

CHAPTER 9

Referenda Wars in Cincinnati: The Battle Over Strong Mayors and Sports Stadiums

Clyde Brown, Miami University
and
David M. Paul, The Ohio State University-Newark

Between August 1995 and May 1999 Cincinnati area citizens faced four major referendum battles. The first involved a change in the city's charter from a council-manager form of government to a strong-mayor form (a referendum that failed). The second proposed that Hamilton County, which includes Cincinnati, increase the local sales tax to fund the construction of two sports stadiums for the local professional football and baseball teams (a referendum that passed). The third attempted to establish a Hamilton County Charter to limit public funds for the construction of a new baseball stadium to one location (a referendum that failed). The fourth created a "stronger" mayor system by amending the city charter (a referendum that passed). The local corporate community and county Republican Party establishment led the charge for strong mayors and sports stadiums in Cincinnati.

These were highly visible direct democracy elections compressed into a short time period that involved a relatively small set of elite political actors. It is not the merits or demerits of the four issues, but rather the politics, i.e., the strategy and tactics, of the campaigns that interests us. More specifically, they collectively provide an opportunity to investigate (1) the factors which affect municipal referendum outcomes, (2) the role of organized interests and political elites in the campaigns, and (3) the impact of "political learning" across the elections.

Referendum politics (Magleby 1984; Zisk 1987) generally lacks the electoral "cues" that party-based or candidate-centered elections have because it is typically nonpartisan.[1] The major engines of electoral politics, local party organizations, are usually not involved extensively in referendum issues. Media, paid and free, become the principal means by which affected groups communicate with the public. Accordingly, it is important for the competing camps to "prime" (by assuring heavy news coverage and paid advertising) and "define" the issue (both the nature of the problem and the preferred solution) in the voting public's mind in as favorable a light as possible to achieve "interpretive dominance" (Ansolabehere, Behr, and Iyengar 1993; Rochefort and Cobb 1994; Stuckey and Antczak 1995). This process puts a premium on having the resources to communicate a succinct message that strikes a responsive chord with voters.

Additionally, Lowi (1964) has warned policy analysts not to expect political relationships to be the same across all policy types. Along these lines Wilson (1973) developed a useful typology that classifies policy issues in terms of their perceived costs and perceived benefits. (For an alternative conceptualization in the context of direct elections, see Donovan et al. 1998.) According to Wilson, "majoritarian politics," characterized by distributed costs and distributed benefits, leaves little room for special-interest-group influence since so many actors are involved. "Entrepreneurial politics" involves an effort to impose costs narrowly while benefiting the broader public; the affected interest is likely to oppose the proposed policy. "Client politics" is the classic interest-group situation: A special interest stands to receive concentrated benefits while the broader public will be stuck with the costs of the policy initiative. To the extent that there is a political contest over the policy question, it will be asymmetric, with one side being politically organized while the other is not. "Interest group politics" has the potential of a more symmetric contest between an organized interest that stands to benefit versus an organized interest that stands to lose.

Wilson's typology was developed for legislative and bureaucratic politics, so it is not always a perfect fit for the context of direct democracy elections. Recalls, initiatives, and referendums can be instruments of broad or narrow interests, but inherently they involve a "socialization of conflict" (Schattschnei-

---

1. There are two voting mechanisms by which the public can directly vote on proposed legislation. A referendum is a direct vote by the people on a proposed law or amendment; these propositions are usually placed on the ballot by state legislatures or city councils. An initiative is a means by which citizens, usually after collecting a specific number of signatures of voters, can propose legislation or amendments to be decided by a legislative body or by the people in a referendum. Both of these mechanisms were used in the cases we examined, but for the sake of simplicity we will refer to either mechanism as a "referendum."

der 1960) in that the decision is in the hands of the voters rather than a few elected officials.

Interviews conducted by the authors while researching the 1996 sports stadiums referendum (Brown and Paul 1999) suggested that the earlier strong-mayor campaign had influenced and conditioned the 1996 sports stadiums campaign. It appeared that local organized interests had engaged in an instance of "social learning" (Bandura 1977). Social learning theory posits that individuals and organizations learn from the consequences of past behaviors as well as by abstract modeling the behaviors of others in similar situations. Subsequent investigation of the two referendums found strong evidence of social (political) learning on the part of the campaign activists (Brown and Paul 2000). A major purpose of this research is to see whether political lessons learned in earlier referendums carried over to subsequent elections.

The authors (Paul and Brown 1999), following the theoretical lead of Zaller (1992), have investigated the influence of political elites in more than thirty-five referendums that have occurred in the United States since 1984 which involved public funding of the construction of new sports stadiums and arenas. Zaller (1992) posits that elite unity impacts public opinion regarding ballot issues: The greater the degree of elite unity in favor of such sports facilities, the greater will be the public support at the ballot box because voters receive consistent messages from elites. Our research found a strong, positive relation between the degree of elite unity and the percentage of the electorate supporting public subsidization of sports facilities in referendum elections.

With these theoretical insights in mind, an examination of the four referendum campaigns follows.

Battle #1: The 1995 Strong-Mayor Campaign[2]

Cincinnati has a tradition of progressive politics and good government initiatives. Much of Cincinnati's progressive movement was in response to the "Boss" Cox political machine that dominated the politics of the city and Hamilton County in the late nineteenth and early twentieth centuries (Miller 1968). After World War I, Cincinnati reformers set out to clean up the city's government through a program of business-like management and nonparti-

---

2. The account that follows in this section draws on our earlier work. We keep citations to archival newspaper sources to a bare minimum in the text here; they are fully documented in Brown and Paul (2000).

san professional administration. In 1924 a coalition of reformers, the City Charter Committee, proposed and won approval for an amendment that provided a system of proportional representation, at-large, nonpartisan council elections, and a city manager.

Since 1926, because of the Charterites, Cincinnati has used a council-manager form of government, one of three basic forms of municipal government in the United States. The council-manager plan was championed by the Progressive movement and was adopted by many cities in the early twentieth century.[3] A majority of cities in the United States use the mayor-council plan, a second form of government. Two variants of this type of government exist: the weak-mayor-council plan and the strong-mayor-council plan. The strong-mayor plan gives mayors increased administrative responsibilities to conduct policies and oversee city operations. This form of government places a greater emphasis on political leadership, especially executive leadership.

In April 1995, a group of the city's business elite launched a strong-mayor campaign (Roberts 1997). Organized as Taxpayers for Accountability in Government (TAG), the group's proposal significantly strengthened the mayor's position.[4] Andrew White, a local attorney and Republican Party activist, was tapped as the cochair and spokesperson for the group (White 1997). Three months earlier the local Republican Party had come out in favor of the direct election of the mayor and staggered four-year city council terms. A *Cincinnati Enquirer* poll in April reported that 68 percent of city residents favored the direct election of the mayor, while 19 percent favored the existing system and 6 percent favored the council selecting the mayor (Wilkinson and Green 1995).

Business interests spearheaded the proposal because "corporate leaders [had] grown increasingly alarmed with the squabbling and missteps by city council on such issues as downtown development" (Green 1995b). At the cen-

---

3. In most cities, the council is small (usually between five and nine members) and is responsible for policy making. A professional manager, who is hired by the council, is responsible for the administration of city functions and services. The city manager usually hires city department heads and lower administrative positions are usually chosen by civil service merit examinations. The mayor normally "performs only ceremonial functions and presides over council meetings, has no administrative powers except in emergency, and no veto" (Adrian and Fine 1991, 200).

4. The plan included the following provisions: The mayor would have the power to hire and fire the city manager and veto council actions; the nine-member council could overturn a veto with six votes; an at-large field election would be used to select the council members; a separate race would determine the election of the mayor; and the mayor's salary would be $90,000.

ter of this effort was an association of the twenty-six most powerful local CEOs, the Cincinnati Business Committee (CBC). Business leaders felt that Cincinnati was falling behind comparable cities in terms of general economic development.[5] In the eyes of the corporate community, the city council was "dysfunctional" and "unaccountable."

The proponents and their allies argued the plan would increase the responsiveness of city government and provide greater political leadership on economic development issues by strengthening the agenda setting and legislative powers of the mayor. A strong mayor would help the business community shepherd development projects through the council.[6] Although not stated, but widely understood by political observers, the plan would increase the odds of a Republican winning the mayoralty (Burke 1997; Roberts 1997).[7] Finally, some contended that the reduced role of the city manager would increase business influence in city hall.[8]

---

5. Several specific issues were of concern: (1) Fountain Square West, a city block of undeveloped prime downtown real estate, remained up in the air after a decade of planning; (2) the city was in danger of losing the Reds and the Bengals; (3) major department stores and retailers were leaving the central business district; and (4) the county and the city were squabbling over management of the Metropolitan Sewage District and its impact on suburban development (Roberts 1997; White 1997).

6. Urban politics scholars have increasingly used the concept of "urban regime" to understand the policy-making process in contemporary American cities. Stone (1989, 6) has defined a "regime" as "the informal arrangements by which public bodies and private interests function together in order to be able to make and carry out governing decisions." From this perspective, urban development policy depends on the interactions of economic actors who control investment and public officials who control local government. Pelissero, Henschen, and Sidlow (1993) review four "regimes" types (political machine, corporate, progressive, and caretaker) in terms of their willingness to support sports development. The corporate regime (see also Elkin 1987) is dominated by downtown business interests.

7. A Republican had not been elected mayor since 1971. By not requiring a partisan election with primaries or a runoff, it was more likely that a single, unified Republican might win against a set of Democratic contenders.

8. Because of its progressive history and the autonomy granted the city manager, the Cincinnati city manager position traditionally has been viewed as one of the most attractive manager positions in the country. There is evidence, however, that the reputation of the position has diminished in the last decade as a secession of four city managers have found themselves at odds with the political ambitions of council members, the impatience of business leaders, and the rivalries of neighborhoods. The current city manager, John F. Shirey, hired in 1993, said he felt "betrayed" by the CBC plan to strip the position of its powers.

TAG began a petition drive to have its proposal placed on the ballot. Business leaders promised a well-financed, visible media campaign. A coalition of Democrats, Charterites, blacks, labor leaders, and community activists quickly organized to oppose the strong-mayor plan, calling itself Citizens Coalition for Cincinnati (CCC). The county Democratic Party assigned its Executive Director, Aaron Herzig, to manage the opposition effort, while Tim Burke, the Hamilton County Democratic chair, served as the principal spokesperson for the group (Burke 1997; Herzig 1997). Although not united on every detail, opponents opposed the perceived desire by moneyed interests to control city government by means of a strong mayor. Many Democrats and blacks objected to the lack of a partisan primary and a run off as much as or more than the prospect of a strong mayor or a weak city manager. The strong-mayor proposal as crafted struck at the fortunes of individual Democratic politicians, as well as demographic and economic groups supportive of the local Democratic Party. The opponents complained about not having been consulted in the development of the proposal and TAG's uncompromising "get on board or get left behind" attitude.

Throughout the summer, both groups tried to frame the political debate. TAG argued that their proposal would increase accountability and leadership and decrease council chaos. CCC warned that the plan would destroy the council-manager form of government and that the CBC was trying to gain control of city politics (Goldberg and Michaud 1995).

In what later would be credited by many as the major turning point in the campaign, preelection campaign reports were filed on August 19, 1995. The reports showed that TAG was outspending CCC by a ratio of four-to-one. In addition, all of the $253,000 raised by TAG had come from major Cincinnati companies: none of the money had come from individuals. The total amount raised by CCC ($57,941) was less than the single largest donation ($60,000 from Procter & Gamble) received by TAG. Strong-mayor supporters chose to run a corporate-backed, media campaign and to dispense with grassroots activity (White 1997). In doing so, it followed a decades-old "standard operating procedure" that the CBC had used for local levies and school board elections. Major corporations had funded "90% of these campaigns for the last 15 years" and "the business committee had to pledge dollars or no one would do the issue" (Roberts 1997). But whereas corporate support had not been an issue before, it was this time.

Opponents of the strong-mayor plan pounced on the information in the campaign reports (Burke 1997). The group stressed in its radio ads that all of the strong-mayor financial supporters were corporations and that business was behind the ballot initiative. They warned that the proposal would do away with the city manager and that the mayor would be elected without a majority vote. Damning at the time, the ads also linked the strong-mayor proposal with the proposed sales tax increase for stadium construction.

Because low voter turnout was expected, both sides in the final week of the campaign focused on finding supportive voters and getting those voters to the polls. Both groups invested in telephone banks, and CCC also used the phone operations of groups that made up the coalition. Herzig (1997), campaign manager of CCC, said the campaign received a major boost when large numbers of volunteers came forward after the campaign finance report revelations. Black voters were encouraged by ministers on the Sunday before the election to vote against the charter amendment, and mobilization efforts included bus rides to the polls.

On August 30, voters rejected the strong-mayor charter amendment. Voter turnout, 26.5 percent, was higher than expected. Advocates of the strong-mayor proposal complained that opponents ran an antibusiness "smear campaign" but credited them with running a "smart" campaign that capitalized on the campaign finance reports as evidence of a "corporate takeover" (Wilkinson and Goldberg 1995; Roberts 1997). Organized opposition by the black community and municipal employees was seen a critical in defeating the proposal.

Postelection campaign finance reports showed that TAG spent $350,000 on the failed amendment. All but $3,000 of that money came from major corporations. CCC spent nearly $79,000; most of its money came from individuals, with the largest contribution being $19,755 from the International City/County Management Association (ICCMA).

Battle #2: The 1996 Campaign for Sports Stadiums[9]

At the same time that the strong-mayor proposal was being debated, a second business-supported issue developed. The two tenants of Cincinnati's Riverfront Stadium, built in 1970 and operated by the city, had voiced complaints about the facility for several years. Mike Brown, owner and general manager of the Cincinnati Bengals Football Team, and Marge Schott, owner of the Cincinnati Reds Baseball Club, each wanted a new facility. By Decem-

---

9. This section draws upon material in Brown and Paul (1999). Again, reference to newspaper documentation is kept to a bare minimum in the chapter.

ber 1994, both owners were hinting they would move their team out of Cincinnati in order to get a new stadium.

Although political and business leaders expressed dismay about losing one or both of the teams, there was no consensus on how to pay for a new stadium (and possibly two stadiums). A poll of Cincinnati residents found little support for public financing. Nearly 60 percent opposed the construction of a new stadium for the Reds and Bengals, with 37 percent favoring such a project; 17 percent supported the construction of two new stadiums; and just 19 percent supported a tax increase to pay for such projects (Green 1995a).

On June 22, Hamilton County Commissioner Bob Bedinghaus unveiled a plan to finance new stadiums for the Reds and the Bengals. A 20-year sales tax increase of 1 percent would pay for a $540 million stadium complex on the riverfront, a 300-bed county jail, and for an emergency communication center. Key features of the plan were a proposed 18 percent rollback in property taxes, the projection that non-Hamilton county citizens shopping at beltway malls would pick up about 50 percent of the tab, and the transfer of the stadiums' ownership and management to the county.[10]

After days of around-the-clock negotiations between the city and the county mediated by the business community, the City Council approved a revised plan by a 5-4 vote on June 29. The plan allowed the city to keep the Metropolitan Sewer District and included a provision of $10 million a year to the local public schools for capital improvements. Shortly thereafter, Hamilton County commissioners followed suit, voting 2-1 to pass the sales tax increase.[11]

---

10. "Good" politics, i.e., shifting a significant portion of the cost of paying for the new stadiums to non-Hamilton County voters and providing a property tax rebate so that Hamilton County voters would be more likely to vote for it, can also be "good" municipal finance. As Fuchs (1992, 192) has pointed out, some city governments have used legal arrangements involving "special districts, authorities, commissions, and county governments [to] provide services which would otherwise remain the city's obligation." These functional consolidations can be important to cities during times of financial crisis such as occurred during the mid-1970s in the United States. Spreading the financial burden beyond the city and the county by means of the sales tax takes some financial pressure off local public budgets.

11. It is important to note what is transpiring with these votes regarding the city and county governments. At the time, the stadium was owned by the city and leased to the Reds and Bengals. By the votes taken, the city was getting out of the stadium business and the county was taking over. As a consequence, the sales tax would be levied county-wide, raising substantially more revenue. Also, it would be the county electorate, not just the city voters, who would decide whether the sales tax increase would be allowed to stand. The two jurisdictions are different demographically. In 1996, according to U.S. Census figures,

At the insistence of the Bengals, county commissioners ignored the pleas of opponents that the tax increase be put to the voters. Incensed that the plan was not going to be put to a public vote, Tim Mara, a local attorney and antitax activist, organized a repeal campaign (Mara 1997). The repeal effort, called Citizens for Choice in Taxation (CCT), was supported initially by antitax activists, libertarians, teachers, organized labor, suburban government officials, and black ministers. The Cincinnati Federation of Teachers, concerned that the tax increase would make it more difficult to pass future school levies, was vehemently opposed. One black minister objected to "more millions for millionaires," a sentiment which become the opposition's campaign theme.

Tax opponents faced an arduous task. A tax had never been repealed by direct election in Hamilton County history. Because state law did not permit a full penny sales tax increase, Hamilton County commissioners proposed two half-cent increases. Therefore, CCT needed to collect 27,000 valid signatures on two different petitions within 30 days. Despite these obstacles, CCT collected nearly 90,000 signatures by the August 25 deadline with the help of 700 volunteers. The frenzied petition drive occurred in the days immediately before the strong-mayor vote on August 30, a terrible stroke of bad timing for TAG. A vote on the sales tax increase, Issue 1 as it was designated, was set for March 19, 1996.

With a citizen vote now required, proponents of the sales tax increase assembled a campaign organization. David Milenthal, the creative mind behind the "Ohio—The Heart of It All" state tourist campaign and chairman of HMS Partners of Columbus, Ohio, was selected in November as the chief strategist and organizer of the pro-sales tax campaign. A few weeks later, the group selected Jeff Berding, a Democrat who had congressional campaign experience in Cincinnati, to manage and direct the campaign. Neil Newhouse's Virginia-based Public Opinion Strategies was hired to do the tracking polling. The group became known as Citizens for a Major League Future (CMLF). Bed-

---

Cincinnati's population was 345,000, Hamilton County 866,000, and the surrounding Metropolitan Statistical Area 1,597,000. The 1990 Census reported that Cincinnati was 60 percent White, that 35 percent of housing units were owner-occupied, and that the median household income was $21,000. In contrast, the county statistics (including Cincinnati) were as follows: 70 percent of the population was White; 55 percent of housing units were owner-occupied; and $29,500 was the median household income. Voter registration figures are not very meaningful in Ohio since individuals register with a political party only by voting in primary elections. For the four presidential elections between 1984 and 1996, the city voted 57 percent Democratic, while the rest of the county tallied 69 percent for the GOP. Not surprisingly the more populous out-county residents are whiter, richer, and more Republican than their city counterparts.

inghaus called the newly formed group a "grass roots effort" even though it closely resembled TAG in composition.

Prostadium organizers resolved to learn from their mistakes in the strong-mayor campaign. First and foremost, they were determined to run a grass-roots campaign that was better organized and funded than their last effort (Berding 1997). The corporate community would assume its more traditional role by remaining behind the scenes this time (White 1997). While the CMLF raised significant amounts of money from corporations, the group also so-licited small donations to lower the amount of the average contribution. Like-wise, in an attempt to minimize the backlash toward the large corporate do-nations seen in the previous campaign, a $300,000 donation from the Bengals was conveniently received the day after the preelection campaign finance re-port deadline. In addition, CMLF brokered meetings with groups, especially teachers, labor, and blacks, in an attempt to gain their support or minimize their opposition. This decidedly more open decision-making process was de-signed to reduce feelings among the community that the proposal was being "crammed down peoples' throats" (Berding 1997).

Amid concern that voters would reject the sales tax increase, pressure mounted through the fall and into the winter to revise the ballot issue. In a significant move, the Hamilton County commissioners modified the ballot issue on January 5 to make the tax increase more palatable to voters. The new proposal cut the tax increase in half by dropping one of the two one-half cent sales tax increases, with 70 percent ($35 million annually) of the increase going to fund new Reds and Bengals stadiums and 30 percent ($15 million) to lower property taxes. The next day Mayor Roxanne Qualls and four other Cincin-nati council members backed the new plan, and the Baptist Ministers Con-ference and the Cincinnati Federation of Teachers softened their opposition.

It should be noted that the difference between the resources of the two cam-paigns was enormous. While the protax group had the support of major cor-porations and businesses, the antitax group had no large underwriter. By Elec-tion Day, according to campaign finance reports, CMLF had spent more than $1.1 million to defend the sales tax increase. In contrast, CCT reported hav-ing spent less than $30,000. The protax campaign received substantial contri-butions from the Bengals ($300,000), Cincinnati-headquartered Procter & Gamble ($77,000), the Northern Kentucky Chamber of Commerce ($35,000), the Cincinnati Area Board of Realtors(r) ($30,000), and home-based compa-nies Kroger ($23,000), Cincinnati Bell ($16,000), and Cincinnati Gas & Elec-tric ($13,000). Forty-two major ($5,000 or more) contributors to the protax campaign accounted for 73 percent of the funds raised by CMLF.

Despite their large resource advantage, CMLF's nightly polling showed that the campaign was having difficulty convincing at least half of the voters to support Issue 1 (Green 1996; Berding 1997). Of critical importance to the stadium supporters was showing the public that Brown, Schott, and the business community would help finance the stadiums' construction. In January and February, Hamilton County leaders held secret negotiations with the Reds and Bengals in hopes of reaching an agreement to defray some of the costs of building the stadiums.

Several steps were taken in the final months of the campaign in order to help persuade county residents to vote for Issue 1 and pacify some opposition groups. In late January Hamilton County commissioners pledged $5 million a year for 20 years to help Cincinnati Public Schools. While this move helped in the city of Cincinnati, it upset other school districts in the county. Promises were made to the black community that minority contractors and minority labor would be used in the construction of the stadiums. Later, the Hamilton County Commission voted to extend the property tax relief to nearly 4,000 additional properties. Mara (1997) felt that "money was spread around" to help buy off opponents of the stadiums proposal.

As the campaign entered into its final three weeks, each side earnestly attempted to sway voters. Both camps argued over the benefits that the project would bring to the Cincinnati area. CCT stressed that the teams would not leave Cincinnati if the referendum was defeated and that there would be time to devise another less expensive stadium plan (what they called "Plan B"). Supporters of Issue 1 stated there was no "Plan B" and the Bengals would leave Cincinnati if the measure failed. CMLF combined their economic development theme with appeals to civic pride, arguing that Cincinnati was on the verge of becoming a minor league town.[12]

Others credit two events in the final weeks of the campaign with convincing a majority of Hamilton County voters to pass Issue 1 (Michaud and Green 1996). First, on March 9, and after months of negotiations, the Bengals offered to pay $25 to $35 million to offset the costs of building a new stadium. While the offer was nonbinding and could potentially be withdrawn, it helped convince some

---

12. The prostadiums force's argument was given a credibility boost when the Cleveland Browns jumped ship and moved to Baltimore. Suddenly, the civic pride issue became more salient when it was rumored that the Bengals might move to Cleveland. While we think it is too neat to claim that this development alone cast the die as some do (Roberts 1997), it is hard to imagine a lower blow to Cincinnati pride than for Cleveland to steal away its team.

voters that the Bengals were willing to contribute to their stadium (Wilkinson 1996). Second, a media blitz of "heavy-hitters" was launched to squash the CCT's bid for finding another stadium plan. Governor George Voinovich came to town to insist that there was no "Plan B"; instead the Bengals, and possibly the Reds, would move and Cincinnati would lose its status as a major league city. In order to reinforce Voinovich's message, NFL Commissioner Paul Tagliabue stated that Issue 1 was Cincinnati's last chance to keep the Bengals. Mara (1997) felt his side took a "pounding" in the media during the last ten days of the campaign.

The overwhelming share of CMLF's budget went for paid media. By the end of the campaign, CMLF would run four orchestrated waves of TV commercials costing more than $600,000. However, the CMLF's campaign was more than just a media effort. Unlike TAG, it included direct mail, radio, telephone contact, yard signs, and voter-identification and get-out-the vote mobilization efforts. CMLF also gave the opposition no quarter; their goal throughout the campaign was "to set the terms of the debate, shut them down at every opportunity" while maintaining "complete credibility" (Berding 1997).

CMLF's efforts paid dividends when Issue 1 passed with 61 percent approval. The turnout, despite heavy rains, was 49.5 percent—a record for a local primary election.

Battle #3: The 1998 Baseball at Broadway Commons Campaign[13]

Passage of the sports stadiums sales tax increase raised the money to build two new facilities but did not resolve the issue of where to build them. The football team was the more pressing concern since their Cinergy Field lease was near expiration. After prolonged and acrimonious discussions among the Bengals, the city, and the county, an acceptable location on the western edge of downtown on the Ohio River was found. During the football stadium location negotiations, the city repeatedly found itself at odds with the county and the Bengals.

The new Paul Brown Football Stadium is part of a very ambitious effort pushed to redevelop the Cincinnati riverfront. The plan entails a major redesign and reconstruction of the downtown interstate highway system, the

---

13. The *Cincinnati Enquirer*, at <www.enquirer.com/editions/1999/04/07/loc_stadium-stories.html>, provides a full archive of its newspaper stories on the Broadway Commons vote. We minimize citations in the text.

erection of a multimodal transportation center, the establishment of a National Underground Railroad Freedom Center, the construction of an entertainment and commercial district, the building of massive underground garages for game and workday parking, and the creation of a park system on top of the garages to link the various parts together. The cost overruns associated with the Bengals facility and the highway construction, plus the limited space available on the riverfront given the other projects eventually led to the question, Where should the new Reds baseball stadium be built?[14]

Initially the county offered the Reds two alternatives: Broadway Commons, a downtown site on the eastern edge of the business district or Baseball on Main, also known as the "Wedge," a site east of Cinergy Field and west of an existing indoor sports arena on the Ohio River. The Reds wanted a stadium on the riverfront but were not enamored with the Wedge location. The Reds started looking at suburban sites, and in October 1997 the county broke off negotiations regarding the new stadium and threatened to force the Reds to abide by their Cinergy Field lease until 2010. A third alternative, renovation of Cinergy Field, was considered.

By March 1998 the Reds had decided that the "Wedge" site was feasible and were engaged in protracted negotiations with the county. Shortly thereafter, the Cincinnati City Planning Committee endorsed Broadway Commons, and the city offered the Reds $20 million in incentives to build there. The "Wedge" site was seen not only as tricky in terms of construction but also expensive because it would involve the partial demolition of Cinergy Field while it was still in use for baseball in order to find enough physical space to build a new baseball stadium. The Broadway Commons location was seen as a space slightly less expensive, as a space where a stadium would take less time to build, and as a potential for redeveloping a portion of town known as Over-The-Rhine that was a bit seedy. Giving Cinergy Field a facelift was criticized by all sides because it would not result in a new stadium.

As the Baseball at Main talks dragged on, Broadway Commons supporters looked for means to mandate construction at Broadway Commons. After considering a recall petition against one of the county supervisors and enacting prohibitive city zoning regulations, they settled on the novel mechanism of creating a Charter for Hamilton County government. Article I maintained that all the features of the current county government would continue, and Arti-

---

14. See Brown (1999) for a discussion of the implementation aftermath, including riverfront development, of the Cincinnati sports sales tax referendum.

cle II would require that the new Reds Stadium be built at Broadway Commons. On August 26, 1998, the Broadway Commons forces, led by City Councilmen Jim Tarbell (C) and Todd Portune (D), delivered 45,000 signatures to get the Charter proposal on the ballot (DiFilippo 1998).[15] The petition language prohibited the spending of revenues collected by the 1996 sales tax increase for any major league baseball stadium not at Broadway Commons. The proposal was put on the November 1998 ballot as Issue 11 to be decided by the Hamilton County electorate.

The policy debate was engaged on many fronts (May 1998c). Citizens for a County Charter for Baseball at Broadway (CCCBB) argued that a stadium on their preferred site would cost less than one on the Wedge site because it could be built more quickly. Construction could start immediately (work at the Wedge site could not start until the interstate renovation was completed) and did not require partial demolition of Cinergy Field. They also argued that the Wedge site was too tight a space for a good stadium. Move Greater Cincinnati Forward (MGCF), the anti-Issue 11 group, stressed the importance of the Baseball on Main as one bookend, along with the Bengals' stadium, of the riverfront development. They asserted that the costs concerning the two locations were not all that different and that no land costs would be involved at the Main site because the public sector already owned the land, unlike the Broadway Commons situation.[16] They contended that the Charter approach to resolving the baseball stadium location controversy was unnecessary and inappropriate. Rather, voters opposed to a stadium on the riverfront should defeat the current incumbent and select a county supervisor in the November election who favored Broadway Commons.[17] They also opposed the creation

---

15. Jim Tarbell, a Charterite, had recently been appointed to the City Council as the replacement for long-time Charterite City Councilwoman Bobbie Sterne. Tarbell, a flamboyant and popular owner of a restaurant near the proposed Broadway Commons location, had been the most prominent advocate of the site since passage of the sales tax increase. Todd Portune is the challenger against Bob Bedinghaus' reelection as county supervisor in the 2000 General Election, where delays and cost overruns in the riverfront development projects are expected to be a major campaign issue.

16. Most of the land at Broadway Commons is owned by Robert Chavez and is used for parking. Chavez and his associates would in October offer to sell 18.2 acres of land at Broadway Commons for $26.4 million. It should be pointed out that many of the property owners along 3rd and 4th Streets in downtown Cincinnati closest to the planned riverfront development favored and contributed to the Baseball on Main group.

17. The County Commission was divided 2-1. First term Republican incumbent Tom Neyer was part of the majority and was up for reelection on the same ballot as Issue 11.

of charter governance as a threat to the power of local townships and municipalities. Ironically, forces that had argued for stronger city government during the strong-mayor vote and for stronger county leadership on the sports stadiums sales tax increase vote were now expressing objections to the increased power that charter government might give the county. All of these points, plus a concern for public safety given the current deterioration of the neighborhoods surrounding Broadway Commons, would come out during the course of the campaign.

The campaign was compressed into about six weeks; its political similarity to the 1996 sales tax increase issue was noted (May 1998a). The political cleavages occurred along predictable lines. Supporters of Issue 11 included the Cincinnati City Council, the city and county planning commissions, one of the three county commissioners, the Democratic and Charter parties along with a small Republican group, the Over-The-Rhine Chamber of Commerce, and various neighborhood associations in the Broadway Commons vicinity. The Democratic candidate for county supervisor did a flip-flop on the issue during the last two weeks of the campaign, supporting, opposing and then again favoring Broadway Commons. The opponents were the Cincinnati Reds, two county commissioners, the Republican Party, the Greater Cincinnati and African-American Chambers of Commerce, Downtown Cincinnati, Incorporated (an association of business property owners), the Hamilton County Township Association (all township trustees opposed Issue 11), and the Over-The-Rhine Community Council.

Both sides ran comprehensive campaigns (May 1998b) in addition to participating in about twenty public debates. The Broadway Commons campaign distributed thousands of yard signs mailed to 150,000 likely voters, ran radio ads featuring Republican Hamilton County Commissioner John Dowlin, and television ads. One ad highlighted the nostalgia of the Reds' old Crosley Field, and the second featured paper-bag-headed "suitboys" wheeling and dealing with Cincinnati's future. The Baseball on Main group ran four waves of TV ads. The first promoted a vision of riverfront development, the second had an Over-The-Rhine woman expressing NIMBY-sentiments, the third listed group endorsements, and the fourth showed a post-2003 computer-generated view of the riverfront. The group also distributed 2,000 "Vote NO Issue 11" yard signs, sent out 200,000 pieces of mail, and ran radio spots talking about their Riverfront vision.

His opponent was Democratic challenger Marilyn Hyland, a critic of the county's stadium agreements.

MGCF ended up outspending CCCBB $580,000 to $215,000. The anti-Issue 11 group received major contributions from the Reds ($300,000), Bengals ($50,000), the Chamber ($32,500), P&G ($30,000), Reds part-owner and millionaire Carl Linder ($10,000), and Fifth Third Bank ($6,000), as well as $5,000 contributions from Cincinnati Bell, Cincinnati Milacron, Cinergy, ComAir, and Star Bank. About half of the Broadway Commons group's resources came in the form of a $100,000 loan from Robert Chavez, his family, and associates. The losing side ended the campaign $150,000 in debt.

In heavy voting (voter turnout was 47.6 percent), Issue 11 was rejected overwhelmingly. The defeat of 35 percent to 65 percent was much larger than anyone had expected going into Election Day. The issue lost big both inside and outside the city.

Battle #4: The 1999 Campaign for a "Stronger Mayor"[18]

The defeat of the strong-mayor plan in 1995 did not put a stop to efforts by the business community and the local GOP to restructure the organization of city government. By June 1998, two petition campaigns to alter the system of electing city council and increase the power of the mayor had failed to make it onto the ballot and a third effort was underway. A group, Build Cincinnati (BC), headed by Republican city council candidate Pat DeWine, Democratic Party operative and sports stadium tax campaign manager Jeff Berding, and NAACP Vice President Johnathan Holifield, devised a strong-mayor plan that called for the direct election of a mayor with increased administrative and legislative powers by means of a nonpartisan primary with a runoff, and district elections for city council positions (Goldberg and Wilkinson 1998). The group held over 100 public meetings to solicit citizen input on the proposal and promised they would not go forward unless a bipartisan plan could be formulated.

Opposition to the plan came from Charterites who wanted to maintain the role of an independent professional city manager in the day-to-day operation of the city, from Democrats who favored partisan elections, from African-

---

18. With a little bit of extra work, newspaper cover can be found at <www.enquirer.com/backissues/apr99.html> and <www.enquirer.com/backissues/may99.html>. Unlike the Broadway Commons vote, a single list does not exist. We continue our practice of keeping newspaper citations to a minimum in this section.

Americans who feared the run-off provision, and from Republicans who opposed district elections of city councilors. Build Cincinnati's plan appeared dead for at least another election cycle when a last-minute deal was brokered in city council in late February and early March 1999. Votes were found in the city council at the very last moment to put a "stronger" mayor plan, Issue 4, on the May 1999 ballot. Faced with the prospect of doing nothing or reverting to the pre-1987 system of having the city council select the mayor from among its own members, Build Cincinnati, under the auspices of the Greater Cincinnati Chamber of Commerce, held emergency meetings with leaders of the three political parties. The breakthrough came when key Charterite leaders and officeholders decided to support the plan (Wilkinson 1999a). The issue called for (1) the direction election of a mayor who would no longer be part of the city council, (2) a nonpartisan primary with a runoff if necessary between the top two vote-getters, (3) expanded legislative, budgetary, and executive powers for the mayor, (4) at-large first-past-the-post election of the nine-member city council, and (5) a professional city manager who would serve at the pleasure of the mayor.

Advocates of the plan touted it as an example of political compromise and consensus building. By maintaining the city manager position (important to Charterites) and leaving city council elections unchanged (important to Republicans and current incumbent officeholders), the charter amendment would change only the election of and powers of the mayor. The result, the advocates claimed, was a pared-down version of the original BC plan in that it would create a "stronger" mayor, not a "strong" mayor. Some Democrats who reasoned that they would elect one of their own to the top post under the proposed system and Republicans who felt the proposal would improve their slim chances of electing a mayor were attracted to the plan, as were others who simply felt there was a need for greater political leadership and accountability in city affairs.

Passage of Issue 4 became the goal of Coming Together for Cincinnati (CTC). CTC spokespersons in the press were quick to point out the differences between this effort and the previous failed effort of 1995 (Wilkinson 1999b). They pointed to the outreach efforts of BC in developing the compromise proposal that the city council placed on the ballot. They disavowed any power grab by the corporate community by stressing their broad-based community support. In addition to the BC leaders and the chairs of the Democratic, Republican, and Charterite political parties, five former mayors and current Mayor Roxanne Qualls endorsed the plan. The NAACP, a black city councilor, the AFL-CIO, and the teachers union blessed the effort. Herzig, a

Democrat, who had led the anti-strong-mayor forces in 1995, was the manager of the pro-stronger mayor campaign. In major news outlets, Herzig stressed, "We are going to run a positive, grass-roots campaign and get as many people as possible involved." The campaign professionals that the business community had hired for the sports stadium sales tax increase campaign (Milenthal and Newhouse) were retained by CTC, and a six-figure campaign was planned, with the money to be raised from the business community and from hundreds of citizens.

The group Citizens Against Issue 4 (CAI4) was headed by City Councilman Tyrone Yates. He, along with two other black incumbent city council members, opposed the plan because of its electoral features, as did the powerful Baptist Ministers Council. Some prominent Charter Party activists and four former Democratic mayors opposed the expanded powers the plan gave future mayors. The Hamilton County Democratic Central Committee on a close vote opted not to endorse the proposal. The Urban League, the United Auto Workers, and the Buildings Trade Council came out against the plan.

The constellation of political forces was much different this time than in the first strong-mayor vote in 1995. While the Republicans and business community remained united, the formerly united opposition was severely fractured this time around. Democratic, Charterite, labor, and black political elites were divided, with prominent representatives of these important political blocs on both sides of Issue 4 (Wilkinson 1999c). Members of these reference groups would not be able to utilize normal sources of information to guide their votes in this election.

The CTC raised and spent $250,000. Most of the money came in large donations from Cincinnati-based corporations, with Procter & Gamble ($46,500) leading the way, supplemented by 300 individual contributors. The opposition camp was able to raise only $14,000.

In a relatively close election, marred by a voter turnout of 18.2 percent, Issue 4 passed by a margin of 53 to 47 percent. The first "stronger" mayor will be elected in November 2001 and will take office on New Year's Eve.

Discussion

What can explain the outcomes of these four elections? Why did the corporate/GOP coalition lose the first strong-mayor referendum and win the three subsequent referendums? On the basis of the public record and personal interviews, we conclude that the business forces pushing a redevelopment agenda for downtown Cincinnati learned significant lessons from the first election that carried over to subsequent contests. The linkage between mistakes made and lessons learned was clearest in the first two referendums. Accordingly, we start there and work in comments about the other two elections where appropriate.

The key to understanding the outcomes of the first two referendums is to realize that they involved two different types of policy issues and two different types of politics. In the Wilsonian framework, the sports stadiums sales tax increase was "client politics" and the strong-mayor charter amendment was "interest group politics." The second referendum was a battle over hundreds of millions of dollars while the first was a contest over raw political power.

First, the sales tax increase referendum fits the classic mode of an organized set of interests benefiting substantially, while a largely unorganized, even partially disenfranchised, public pays for it one-half penny at a time. While there might have been legitimate public interest considerations involved, the referendum was also very much a political contest over money, with the team owners, corporate interests, land developers, financiers, and downtown hotels and restaurants winning subsidies for a large-scale public works project that would directly and indirectly put money into their pockets. The antitax forces were simply overwhelmed by the other side's resource advantage. In this instance there was no credible countervailing power.

The strong-mayor referendum turned out to be a more pluralistic contest between two organized opponents. It was an instance of "interest group politics" but not with the traditional configuration of two interest groups pitted against each other. Because fundamental political power in the form of the "rules of the game" was at stake, the contest took on a partisan dimension. The CBC and its junior partners, the local GOP, the local Chamber of Commerce and other businesses, with technical help from the NAHB, were effectively stymied by a status quo protecting coalition led by the local Democratic Party with support from the black community, Charterites, labor and women's groups, with financial assistance from the ICCMA. Furthermore, the politics of the strong-mayor amendment was so confounded with partisan politics that it lacked many of the defining characteristics of referendum politics.

In addition to policy type, there were a number of other factors that differentiated the two contests, including the constituencies involved, the campaigns conducted, the level of interpretative dominance achieved, and relationship of the specific proposals to the broader culture that also were relevant to the two later referendums. First, the strong-mayor issue was put to voters of Cincinnati while the sales tax increase measure was decided by the Hamilton County electorate. This is significant because Cincinnati is overwhelmingly Democratic with a substantial black population, while Hamilton County is just as overwhelmingly Republican with a greatly diluted black presence. The demographic and partisan realities of the two jurisdictions affected the strategies used and went a long way towards determining the outcomes.

Second, the sports stadiums sales tax campaign was a much "smarter" campaign than the strong-mayor campaign. There is abundant evidence from the interviews conducted that the business-coalition managers of the second campaign learned important lessons from the first losing campaign. There is no doubt that political (social) learning of the most direct sort occurred between the two campaigns. Most significantly, in terms of political learning, the sports stadiums campaign had a real grassroots component (phone canvassing, yard signs, rallies, small individual contributors, etc.) to complement its media effort. Likewise, the sports stadiums leadership was more inclusive, making specific overtures to blacks and teachers. This strategy contrasts completely with the "take it or leave it" attitude of the pro-strong-mayor campaign. Rather than feeling a proposal was being shoved down their throats, significant political groups and individuals felt consulted during the development of the stadiums proposal. The flexibility of the prostadiums forces also contributed to the sense of inclusion. The inflexibility of the first effort alienated some portions of the community, especially the black Baptist ministers, and increased their resolve to defeat the strong-mayor proposal.

With its attention to developing a grassroots image, the sports stadiums campaign rectified the two biggest mistakes of the strong-mayor campaign. First, it dealt with the "business is trying to buy the election" charge by assuring that it had hundreds of small donors. While undoubtedly symbolic in many respects—the campaign raised the bulk of its funds from the same corporations that supported the first CBC effort—it defended itself from the criticism that doomed the strong-mayor campaign. Furthermore, it strategically used the timing of the campaign finance disclosure reports to hide until after the election the $300,000 Bengals' contribution that certainly would have become a bone of contention if it had been known. Second, it utilized local political talent to manage the campaign rather than an outside group, thereby eliminating the "outsiders are trying to take over" accusation.

The first strong-mayor loss was a real eye-opener for the local corporate community. They learned important lessons that led them to modify their campaign operations in the second race. These practices were followed to good effect from their perspective in the next two campaigns.

The organizers of the "stronger" mayor campaign never tired of talking about the lessons they learned from the first two campaigns. In fact, it often seemed that their campaign was as much about demonstrating inclusiveness as it was about improving city governance. The Build Cincinnati organization reached out to and consulted with many political groups. By engaging in the art of the practical, the proposal for limited reform of the mayor's office found support from political elites of all stripes. Issue 4 was not a repeat of the extremely partisan "issue group" politics of Issue 1 in 1995, but took on the "majoritarian" politics style usually associated with governance issues. Given the very visible cross-cutting divisions among political elites (politicians for the various political parties and demographic groups were on both sides of the issue), it is not surprising that almost four-fifths of the voters stayed home on Election Day.

The Broadway Commons vote is not as pure as the other three votes in terms of Wilson's typology. It was mostly "interest group" politics with elements of "entrepreneurial" and "majoritarian" politics thrown in. The issue did not involve additional taxes or direct benefits to the public. Costs and benefits were real, however, for the Reds and the land developers that would have benefited from the alternative locations. This consideration is evident in the interests that bankrolled the two sides. Some Broadway Commons advocates, such as Jim Tarbell, were probably motivated partially by civic considerations and, therefore, acted as policy entrepreneurs championing neighborhood development that was at odds with the Reds' preference for a riverfront location. Although Broadway Commons organizers may not have had any other alternative, the Charter government mechanism to force construction at Broadway Commons was unfortunate from their perspective because many voters opposed the means more than the end. It generated unanimous opposition from the township trustees, an important political jurisdiction in Ohio, who perceived county charter government as a threat to their political autonomy.[19] Ultimately, the contest was probably decided by thousands of voters who reflected upon where they would have to park to attend a night game.

Third, the business-backed camps always had more financial resources than their opponents. The clearest instance was the stadiums tax issue where the pro-side outspent the con-side by 36.7 to 1. With the hundreds of thousands of dollars it spent on media, the stadiums sales tax increase campaign achieved interpretative dominance. Even more important was the lack of commercial

---

19. Marilyn Hyland running 22,000 votes ahead of the Issue 11 pro-vote provides credence to this interpretation.

time by the opposition, who were not "on the screen" since they lacked the funds to compete. Still, the campaign contribution fiasco of the first strong-mayor campaign had shown the strength of a potent counterissue. The prostadiums forces did not make the same mistake again: They got their message out while neutralizing their opposition at every turn. A lopsided financial advantage also characterized the stronger-mayor vote in 1999, where the ratio was 15.4 to 1. Financially, the Broadway Commons vote was the most competitive but only because the Baseball at Broadway group went deeply into debt.

The level of interpretative dominance achieved can be affected also by the degree of political elite unity. As has been noted, opposition to the stadiums sales tax increase was limited to an ad hoc antitax group that had almost no support from local political elites. On the other hand, local political elites were much divided along partisan lines on the first strong-mayor vote, and divisions along partisan and geographical lines characterized the Broadway Commons vote. Local political elites, especially Democratic and Charterite leaders, were divided in unconventional ways on the stronger-mayor vote, resulting in the hypothetically pleasing outcome of greater electoral support for passage and lower voter turnout when compared to the earlier strong-mayor vote. The outcomes of these four votes generally conform to Zaller's hypothesis regarding the positive relationship between local political elite unity and support for an issue's passage.

Fourth, there is a difference between the issues that cannot be ignored. Professional sport holds an almost revered status in American society, while politics is increasingly disdained. While sports is part of the popular culture, politics has less saliency for most citizens and has increasingly become an "insider's game" played by politicians and special interests. The public took notice of the stadium referendums and almost half of the eligible electorate participated in those elections. On the other hand, the two charter amendment referendums involving the power of the mayor generated much less interest in the citizenry. The voter turnout for sport stadiums referenda was about two times higher than for the strong-mayor contests.

It is too early to know what these referendums mean for the future of Cincinnati as an urban regime. Clearly, from the corporate perspective, Cincinnati city government has the elements of a "caretaker" regime that fails to deal effectively with major development issues. The strong-mayor proposal was an attempt to get more energetic city government that would be more sympathetic to the corporate agenda for downtown redevelopment. When that failed, business interests turned to county government as a more favorable political arena to achieve their ends. The interviewees were unanimous in voicing this view, and all expect that county government will become more powerful in the future as city government fades in importance. As such, it is possible that the sports stadiums referendum represents the beginning of a new "corporate" regime for the Cincinnati area based on not on city government but county government. Passage of the stronger-mayor system is movement in the direction that the business community favors, but it is too soon to know whether it will provide them with more decisive political leadership in municipal affairs in the ways that they desire.

Cincinnati's referendum wars have had a couple of short-term effects. Greater than projected spending (more than one billion dollars and counting) on the stadiums and associated riverfront construction has made it difficult to find funding for other pressing social problems. Two victims of the opportunity costs involved are the local public schools and the city's convention center. The city has struggled with finding ways to fulfill its promise made during the sports stadiums sales tax campaign of $5 million dollars a year for the school system. Various proposals to raise additional funds via increased hotel and entertainment taxes were quickly withdrawn in the face of angry taxpayers and the threat of citizen repeal petitions. Currently, the money is slated to come out of general revenues. By everyone's estimation, the most serious unresolved public works project on the drawing board is the expansion of the convention center. The project is estimated to cost hundreds of millions of dollars, but it is expected to have a much greater economic return for the region than the stadiums. As of this writing, convention center funding is stymied by a lack of political will on the part of local elected officials, as well as the corporate community, to propose additional taxes and to fight the inevitable referendum battle that such action would provoke. A half-decade of quick and easy recourse to referendum politics to resolve difficult public issues has resulted in battle wariness and political paralysis on spending issues in Cincinnati.

The corporate community and its allies had a good chance to win but lost the strong-mayor campaign because it limited itself to a corporate-funded media campaign and it directly threatened the interests of the governing Democratic coalition in Cincinnati. The latter guaranteed the campaign organized opposition and the former exposed it to serious criticism. Social (political) learning by local business interests allowed them to correct their previous blunders when organizing the sports stadiums sales tax campaign. The second time around, they ran a campaign that was more inclusive, more flexible, and more complete in that it included a grassroots component. The lessons learned from those campaigns affected the subsequent campaigns. In sum, our conclusion is that the stakes involved, the lessons learned, and the quality of the campaigns conducted largely determined the outcomes of the referendums.

References

Adrian, C., and M. Fine. 1991. *State and local politics.* Chicago: Lyceum Books/Nelson-Hall Publishers.

Ansolabehere, S., R. Behr, and S. Iyengar. 1993. *The media game.* New York: Macmillan.

Bandura, A. 1977. *Social learning theory.* Englewood Cliffs, NJ: Prentice-Hall.

Berding, J. 1997. Interviewed by authors, March 11, Cincinnati.

Brown, C. 1999. The devil is in the details: The implementation aftermath of the 1996

Cincinnati sports stadia referendum. Paper presented at the Midwest Political Science Association annual meeting, Chicago, April 15–17.

Brown, C., and D. Paul. 1999. Local Organized Interests and the 1996 Cincinnati Sports Stadia Referendum. *Journal of Sport and Social Issues* 23: 218–37.

_____. 2000. The campaign by Cincinnati business interests for strong mayors and sports stadia. *Social Science Journal* 37.

Burke, T. 1997. Interviewed by authors, August 6, Cincinnati.

DiFilippo, D. 1998. Broadway vote a step closer. *Cincinnati Enquirer,* 27 July, B1.

Donovan, T., S. Bowler, D. McCuan, and K. Fernandez. 1998. Contending players and strategies: Opposition advantages in initiative campaigns. In *Citizens as Legislators,* edited by S. Bowler, T. Donovan, and C. J. Tolbert. Columbus: Ohio State University Press.

Elkin, S. 1987. *City and regime in the American republic.* Chicago: University of Chicago Press.

Fuchs, E. 1992. *Mayors and money.* Chicago: University of Chicago Press.

Goldberg, L., and A. Michaud. 1995. Strong words exchanged in debate over strong-mayor plan. *Cincinnati Enquirer,* 28 June, A1.

Goldberg, L., and H. Wilkinson. 1998. Bipartisan group attempts overhaul of city government. *Cincinnati Enquirer,* 2 June, B4.

Green, R. 1995a. City poll shows most oppose new stadium. *Cincinnati Enquirer,* 27 April, A4.

———. 1995b. Big business seen as bogeyman. *Cincinnati Enquirer,* 31 August, A1.

———. 1996. Sales tax had near-death experience. *Cincinnati Enquirer,* 22 March, A1.

Herzig, A. 1997. Interviewed by authors, August 4, Cincinnati.

Lowi, T. 1964. American business, public policy, case studies and political theory. *World Politics* 16: 677–715.

Magleby, D. 1984. *Direct legislation.* Baltimore: John Hopkins University Press.

Mara, T. 1997. Interviewed by authors, March 12, Cincinnati.

May, L. 1998a. Ballot issue déjà vu. *Cincinnati Enquirer,* 12 October, B1.

———. 1998b. Broadway Commons or Baseball on Main: You decide. *Cincinnati Enquirer,* 18 October, A1.

———. 1998c. Ballpark site battle a slugfest. *Cincinnati Enquirer,* 1 November, B1.

Michaud, A., and R. Green. 1996. Stadium campaign lauded. *Cincinnati Enquirer,* 24 March, A1.

Miller, Z. 1968. *Boss Cox's Cincinnati.* Chicago: University of Chicago Press.

Paul, D., and C. Brown. 1999. The impact of elite opinion at the local level: A test of Zaller's RAS model using sports stadium referenda. Paper presented at the Western Political Science Association Annual Meeting, Seattle, March 25–27.

Pelissero, J., B. Henschen, and E. Sidlow. 1993. Community development or business promotion? In *Community economic development,* edited by D. Fasenfast. New York: St. Martin's Press.

Roberts, Ron. 1997. Interviewed by authors, August 20, Cincinnati.

Rochefort, D. A., and R. W. Cobb. 1994. *The politics of problem definition.* Lawrence, KS: University of Kansas Press.

Schattschneider, E. E. 1960. *The semi-sovereign people.* New York: Holt, Rinehart and Winston.

Stone, C. N. 1989. *Regime politics.* Lawrence, KS: University of Kansas Press.

Stuckey, M. E., and F. J. Antczak. 1995. The battle of issues and images. In *Presidential Campaign Discourse,* edited by K. K. Kendall. Albany, NY: State University of New York Press.

White, A. 1997. Interviewed by authors, August 14, Cincinnati.

Wilkinson, H. 1996. Sales-tax support cuts across all lines. *Cincinnati Enquirer*, 21 March, A10.

_____. 1999a. Deal puts mayor plan on ballot. *Cincinnati Enquirer*, 8 March, B1.

_____. 1999b. Team's aim: Get mayor's job changed. *Cincinnati Enquirer*, 18 March, C2.

_____. 1999c. Issue 4 divides interest groups. *Cincinnati Enquirer*, 3 May, B1.

Wilkinson, H., and L. Goldberg. 1995. Strong mayor fails. *Cincinnati Enquirer*, 31 August, A1.

Wilkinson, H., and R. Green. 1995. Poll: 60% want direct mayor vote. *Cincinnati Enquirer*, 27 April, A1.

Wilson, J. Q. 1973. *Political organizations*. New York: Basic Books.

Zaller, J. 1992. *The nature and origins of mass opinion*. New York: Cambridge University Press.

Zisk, B. 1987. *Money, media and the grass roots*. Newbury Park, CA: Sage.

CHAPTER 10

Orange Crush: Mobilization of Bias, Ballot Initiatives, and the Politics of Professional Sports Stadia

Dan Smith, University of Florida-Gainesville[1]

On March 9, 1998, less than two months after the Denver Broncos won their first Super Bowl, principal owner Pat Bowlen announced for the second straight year that his team would not raise ticket prices for the upcoming football season. Bowlen stated, "A ticket price [increase] looks wrong to me because we're sitting in Mile High Stadium, and I'm not really giving the fans any more there." He added, "It doesn't make sense to me to ask fans to pay the freight while we're still in the old stadium." At the time of the announcement, critics charged that the move was politically motivated to promote the passage of a tax that would finance a new football stadium. Bowlen responded, "I want them to vote for me, but I want them to think they were treated right. That's the bottom line. I don't think it's in the best interest of the Denver Broncos to try to take advantage of our fans because we won the Super Bowl" (Schefter 1998). On February 19, 1999, a little more than three months after the voters approved a tax to publicly finance a new stadium and only a few weeks after the team repeated as Super Bowl champions, the citizens were reminded that professional sports is, above all else, a business. Broncos fans were treated to a 25 percent price increase at Mile High Stadium for Broncos' games for the 1999 season (Latimer 1999).

---

1. The author wishes to thank Sure Log, University of Colorado-Boulder, for assistance in a previous version of this paper.

Denver is just one more example of a city enticed into providing public funding for a sports facility. The recent construction explosion of stadia engulfed several cities across the United States. Anaheim, Arlington, Atlanta, Baltimore, Boston, Chicago, Cleveland, Green Bay, Miami, Minneapolis, Nashville, New York, Oakland, Philadelphia, Phoenix, Portland, Salt Lake City, San Antonio, San Jose, Seattle, and St. Louis have had at least one new facility built or an old facility significantly remodeled for a major league franchise during the 1990s (Rosentraub 1997). In many other cities, proposals for new facilities are currently being considered. Some economists predict that before 2006 more that $7 billion, most of it coming from public sources, will be spent on the construction of new sports facilities (Noll and Zimbalist 1997).

Despite the proliferation of new stadia being built across the country, there are good reasons to expect that stadium referendums would be routinely defeated if put before the voters. First, most voters when surveyed say they are against publicly financed stadia. A nationwide poll conducted in 1996 by Media Research and Communications found that 80 percent of Americans opposed the use of public funding for sports facilities (Keating 1996). Indeed, such was the case during the 1970s and 1980s, when voters rejected 13 out of 15 stadium referendums. Second, the scholarly community has shown rather convincingly that publicly financed stadia are generally raw deals for taxpayers. The economic argument that professional franchises commonly advance during campaigns for new stadia—that a new stadium has a positive economic impact on the community—holds little water. A bevy of scholars have firmly documented that the economic benefits accrued to a city or metropolitan area publicly financing a new sports facility are at best marginal (Rosentraub 1997; Noll and Zimbalist 1997; Danielson 1997; Euchner 1993).

But are citizens voting on stadium referendums listening to scholars, or for that matter, public opinion polls? During the 1990s, there has been a stunning reversal in the public's response to ballot measures that provide for the public financing of new stadia. When asked to vote directly on whether or not to publicly finance a new sports facility for their *own* home team, citizens have more often than not voted for the new facility. Between 1990 and 1996, voters approved 12 out of 17 measures put to them (Danielson 1997, 271). The 1998 vote for the new Broncos stadium seemingly only furthers the recent trend.

What, then, explains the apparent disjuncture between the negative public opinion and the scholarly economic arguments against publicly financed stadia, and the recent popular votes in favor of stadia referendums? In this chapter, we analyze the structural, symbolic, and political factors that contributed to the Broncos' victory for a new football facility. While a majority of metro

Denver voters approved the measure, Referendum 4A, with 57 percent of the vote, the victory did not come easily for the Broncos. Well before the November 1998 election, the Broncos used their tremendous structural advantage as a member of the NFL, as well as their symbolic place in Denver, to mobilize political support for the ballot measure. Then, during the ballot campaign, the Broncos mounted a vigorous political operation, spending millions of dollars on their campaign efforts.

In our lengthy examination of the passage of Referendum 4A, we first survey the scholarly literature that indicates that professional sport franchises have a privileged position—structural and symbolic, if not economic—when bargaining with communities for publicly financed stadia. We then trace the history of the Broncos' drive for a new stadium, including their lobbying efforts in the state legislature, their push for a metropolitan stadium district, and their courting of influential Denver Mayor Wellington Webb. We then turn to the actual political campaign for the stadium referendum. We examine the rhetoric used by the Broncos in support of Referendum 4A and the "citizen" organizations that supported and opposed the measure, including their campaign contributions and expenditures, and we focus on how the media portrayed the new stadium. We examine the depiction of the stadium referendum on the radio and provide a content analysis of all the related articles on the stadium in Colorado's two largest papers. We conclude by arguing that the Broncos' well-oiled political machine was able to mobilize support in the community for the referendum well before the November vote.

The Privileged Position of Professional Sport Franchises

Although he is not credited, scholars of the public financing of professional sport franchises invariably build on the work of political economist Charles Lindblom. Lindblom (1977) argues that business has a privileged position in the political realm. He reasons that because jobs, prices, production, growth, the standard of living, and economic security rest in the hands of business, government officials cannot be indifferent to how well business performs. Consequently, Lindblom contends that a government must offer inducements to business interests in order to effectively carry out its function in society. He states, "In the eyes of government officials, therefore, businessmen do not appear simply as representatives of special interests as representatives of special interest groups do. They appear as functionaries performing functions that

government officials view as indispensable" (Lindblom 1977). While he con-
cedes that business does not get everything it wants from the government,
Lindblom maintains that business does have a privileged relationship with
government.

At first blush Lindblom's argument does not seem relevant to the realm of
professional sports. Political economists generally agree that professional sport
franchises provide little to no economic benefit to a local economy (Baade
1996; Danielson 1997; Noll and Zimbalist 1997; Rosentraub 1997). Numerous studies have shown that projected economic benefits from publicly financed stadia are largely exaggerated, optimistic, or simply incorrect. Growth
and development generally do not accompany the construction of new stadia.
Rather, the overall distribution of jobs in a community is essentially un-
touched by the presence of a new sports facility. Baade (1996) indicates that
money spent on building new sports facilities is not connected to local economic growth. Swindell and Rosentraub (1998) find minimal economic return to cities and downtown communities is generated from sports facilities.
Although new sports facilities may attract visitors to previously ignored areas,
there is no evidence that the facilities change employment or residential location patterns (Swindell and Rosentraub 1998). Furthermore, political economists agree that the income spent by fans is merely discretionary money which
would be spent elsewhere if a team left the community (Rosentraub 1997).
Local revenues are not increased unless a team is able to draw spectators from
outside of the community, and professional teams do not draw many outside
visitors (Rafool 1997).

If professional teams generally do not bring economic benefits to a community, politicians should not be beholden to them. The privileged position
of business, then, should not pertain to professional sport franchises. Why,
then, do professional teams seem to hold such a strong hand over local governments in stadium negotiations? Turning Lindblom on his head, Charles
Euchner (1993) suggests that professional franchises have even more political
and economic leverage than other businesses because they have so little impact on the local economy. Since professional sport franchises have a negligible economic impact, there are no natural constituencies that can emerge to
oppose the owners of the teams when they lobby for a new stadium. Ironically, then, the "privileged position" of professional teams is perhaps even
greater than traditional businesses because their economic impact is so marginal.

Instead of their economic importance, professional teams seem to have
leverage over politicians for structural and symbolic reasons. On the struc-

tural side, not every city or state has a professional team. Because professional sports leagues operate essentially as monopolies, cities must compete among one another for teams in a zero-sum game. Team owners have the ability to limit the number of teams in their league, even if the demand for new teams is high. By intentionally limiting the number of teams in a league, the owners are able to attain a structural advantage over local government officials in the stadium negotiation process. Euchner (1993) points out that during the late 1980s and early 1990s, nearly every professional sports team threatened to move to a different city in order to gain more benefits. Cities not only compete with the franchises in stadium negotiations; they are also forced to contend with other cities. If cities currently housing professional franchises are unwilling or are unable to provide newer, greater revenue generating stadiums, then there are many cities willing to provide the services sought after by the owners. By prohibiting cities to buy the teams, owners are given free reign to move their teams once their leases with cities expire. Hence, professional team owners have a privileged position in politics more than other businesses in America because of the monopolistic power of professional leagues. Because of this structural advantage, teams are accorded much leverage vis-à-vis public officials during stadium negotiations.

Coupled with the structural advantage of professional sport franchises is the symbolic import of professional teams in the United States. Although politicians often say that professional franchises serve an important economic role for the city they represent, local officials want to ensure that their city has a professional sport team more for symbolic reasons than for economic ones. Professional teams are seen by elected officials as a valuable addition to a city's entertainment, recreational, and leisure activities (Danielson 1997). Moreover, politicians frequently claim that sports teams foster civic pride, enhance the image of the city, and strengthen the sense of community. Professional teams can bring about a feeling of unity that politicians cannot create with other civic venues. In 1998, for example, over 650,000 people from all races and economic classes congregated in Denver to celebrate the Broncos' victory over the Green Bay Packers. Politicians tout not only the economic benefits associated with the public funding of stadia but also the social benefits. As such, sport franchises maintain a structural as well as an attendant symbolic advantage over cities during stadium negotiations. Politicians do not want to lose teams because of the prestige associated with having a professional franchise.

When examining the Denver stadium case, we see the familiar pattern followed by the Broncos during their negotiations with the city. The Broncos argued that if they did not receive a new stadium from the city, the team would be forced to leave. To make this point clear, the Broncos hired twelve lobbyists to reinforce their position to the city and the state legislature. In the end, the strong-arm tactics of the team succeeded, and the Broncos got nearly everything they had demanded from the city, the state legislature, and ultimately metro Denver voters. During the stadium negotiations, the Broncos had structural and symbolic advantages—if not the economic arguments and the support of public opinion—and they used them to the fullest.

The Bronco's First Drive for a New Stadium

The push for a new football stadium was a long and calculated endeavor by Pat Bowlen, the principal owner of the Denver Broncos, and his associates. In 1984, Bowlen and his partners bought the Denver Broncos from Edgar Kaiser for a little more than $70 million, and nearly every year afterward, Bowlen argued for replacing the antiquated stadium. According to Bowlen, Mile High was "if not the worst stadium, one of the worst stadiums in the league from the standpoint of comfort and amenities" (Adams 1994). Bowlen and the Broncos argued that Mile High needed to be replaced if the team wanted to be competitive on the field, because the team lacked the stadium revenue necessary to compete against the rest of the teams in the National Football League.[2]

---

2. While the NFL generates more revenue than any other professional sports league, football teams also share more revenue than any other sports league. Nearly all of the merchandising and television revenue is split equally among NFL teams. Game day revenue generated by ticket sales is divided up between the two competing teams with 60 percent going to the home team and 40 percent going to the visiting team (Rafool 1997). However, each team is allowed to keep all revenues from their own stadium. Consequently, stadium revenue is more important for NFL team owners than for team owners in the three other major sports leagues. The Broncos and many other owners in the league argued that high-revenue-generating stadia are important because of the league's salary cap adopted in 1993 that determined the minimum and maximum amount of money a team can pay its players. To benefit most from the salary cap limitations, teams began offering large signing bonuses to highly coveted free agents. Because only the wealthiest franchises were able to offer hefty signing bonuses, owners across the country cried out for new stadiums (Rafool 1997). In particular, Bowlen was upset with the terms of his team's lease with the city of Denver, as the Broncos had one of the league's lowest-revenue-generating stadia. Excluding ticket sales, stadium revenues on average comprise 10 percent of an NFL team's total revenue. The Broncos, who had an existing lease that ran until 2018, did not receive stan-

In February 1994, the city of Denver and the Broncos hired LONCO, Inc., a Denver architectural firm, for $156,000 to conduct a structural study of Mile High Stadium. While the Broncos believed that Mile High needed to be replaced, city officials believed that the facility could be used for another thirty years. Porter Wharton III, a chief spokesperson for the Denver Broncos stated, "I think [the report] assists both sides, regardless of the answer. If it's 30 years, then we'll plan accordingly. But if it's a short period of time, then obviously we need to be planning for that as soon as possible" (Lopez 1994d). Bowlen's stance on a new stadium was clear. He stated, "We think the intelligent thing to do, for ourselves and the city, and perhaps the state for that matter, is to get a long-range plan for the replacement of Mile High Stadium" (Adams 1994).

At the time, public opinion polls showed Denver-area voters overwhelmingly opposing the public financing of a new stadium for the Broncos. A *Denver Post*/News 4 poll of residents in the intended stadium district revealed that 84 percent of the respondents would vote against a proposed stadium tax if the election were held at the time, while 14 percent said they would favor the proposal (Lopez 1994a). Many people were upset by the escalating prices and broken promises that had accompanied the Coors Field tax for the expansion Colorado Rockies baseball team. Voters were initially told that they would be asked to pay $50 million in sales tax, including interest. Later, the projection was increased to $97 million, plus interest. The taxpayers were ultimately liable for $161.3 million, plus $39 million in interest from stadium bonds, in the form of a one-tenth of one-cent sales tax in the Denver metro area. Voters had been promised that private areas within Coors Field, such as luxury boxes, club seats, private restaurants, and private lounges would be paid for with private money. Later, stadium officials decided taxpayers would finance the cost of those amenities, adding $40 million to the stadium bill. During construction of Coors Field, the Rockies lobbied to increase stadium capacity by 7,000 seats, promising that they would cover the cost of any expansion. Ultimately, it did not work out that way as taxpayers were asked to foot the bill (Hutchinson 1995). With the memories of Coors Field fresh in their minds, the voters would have resoundingly rejected a new stadium for the Broncos had the election been held in 1994. Wharton responded to the negative poll numbers, stating, "I think it's like asking a jury to decide a case before they hear the evidence. I have complete confidence that we can make a compelling

---

dard stadium revenues from parking, concessions, and advertising, meaning the Broncos lost that 10 percent in revenue.

case for a new facility" (Lopez 1994a). Confident they could make their case; the Broncos pushed their case for a new stadium forward.

The LONCO study was released on July 21, 1994, apparently confirming Bowlen's claims. The Broncos interpreted the study as stating that preserving and upgrading Mile High Stadium over the next thirty years would cost $100 million more than building a new stadium. The Broncos estimated that the cost of building a new stadium would be about $160 million, while the study cited the cost of maintaining and improving the old stadium to be $264 million over the next thirty years. While admitting that there would be maintenance and upgrade costs associated with the new stadium, the Broncos reasoned that the costs to preserve the nearly fifty-year-old Mile High Stadium would be much greater. However, the city officials did not abandon their position that Mile High could be operational for the next thirty years. Mike Flaherty, deputy manager of parks and recreation, stated, "From our perspective, we can continue to maintain and make Mile High a serviceable stadium for some time into the future." Broncos' spokesman Wharton responded, "We do not disagree that it is possible to keep Mile High Stadium open for an indefinite period. But is that a wise expenditure of tax payers' money?" (Lopez 1994b). Still, the city maintained its stiff negotiating posture. Denver's Mayor Wellington Webb firmly believed that Mile High Stadium could be salvaged and used for years to come.

On December 20, 1994, the Denver Broncos outlined their proposal for a new stadium to a sports advisory task force created by Webb. The Broncos wanted to obtain operating control of Mile High Stadium while the Broncos played there for a few more years, after which they would lobby for a new stadium by extending the Coors Field tax. The team cited that control of the stadium was necessary to procure revenues from stadium concessions, advertising, and parking. The Broncos reiterated that this revenue was important so they could field a competitive team (Lopez 1994d).

Over the next year, Wharton claimed that the negotiations were progressing favorably (Wharton 1998). According to Wharton, "The negotiations that we're having with the mayor's task force are going very well. We think we're going to be able to arrive at a play that works well for the city and the Broncos" (Lopez 1995). By the start of the 1995 football season, the Broncos hoped to control about 7,000 parking spaces owned by the city. However, the team did not receive control of the parking spaces and began a more hard-nosed approach in negotiations with the city. In September 1995, the Broncos demanded that the city complete millions of dollars in repairs and upgrades for Mile High Stadium. The team argued that the city had failed to live up to its obligations of maintaining the facility as a condition under the current lease.

Wharton said of the situation, "The lease is an obligation that both parties need to live up to, and if one side isn't living up to their end, then you look at what your options are" (Lopez 1995). City officials claimed that the Broncos were posturing themselves for a new stadium by trying to show that the upkeep of the old stadium was too costly. Furthermore, officials claimed that the Broncos were trying to escape their existing lease by claiming that the city failed to uphold its end of the contract by allowing the stadium to deteriorate. Dan Muse, the city of Denver's attorney, responded to the Broncos' actions by saying, "All I know is, we have them under contract 'till 2018" (Lopez 1995).

As negotiations between the city and the Broncos proceeded, public opinion was still decidedly against the Broncos. A poll conducted by Talmey-Drake Research and Strategy, Inc., taken during the last two weeks of 1995, revealed that only 33 percent of voters in the six-county Denver metro area would support an extension of the Coors Field tax to pay for a new football stadium. Paul Talmey, president of the firm, noted that the extending the tax to support the Broncos lacked the appeal of approving the tax to bring in Denver's professional baseball team, the Colorado Rockies. Talmey stated, "Voters look at the stadium and they say, 'Mile High's OK, and if we tax ourselves what do we get? We still get the Broncos'" (Brown 1996). Still, the Broncos remained undaunted in their push for a new stadium.

Lobbying the Colorado General Assembly

In January 1996, the Broncos took their case for a new stadium to the state legislature. Initially, many legislators were unimpressed with their demands for a new stadium. Republican Senator Tom Blickensderfer remarked, "I'm not really in favor of it at all and I can't imagine they'd find support in the legislature to extend the tax [for Coors Field]." Senate Minority Leader Mike Feeley added, "I think we've gone to the voters too much recently for public financing of larger facilities. I think it's going to be real tough for the Broncos to persuade the legislature to send this to a vote of the people." Senator Pat Pascoe agreed with her fellow legislators: "I'm beginning to wonder how many stadiums we need? I know that they will blackmail us with 'We're going to leave Denver,' but I just don't know how many teams we can support in light of how many teams are here." Despite the negative early reaction from legislators, the Broncos political machine remained convinced that it could sway the position of many legislators. Wharton responded, "We're confident that once we've explained the situation and people see the facts, they'll be receptive" (Lopez 1996).

The Broncos presented their proposal for a new stadium to the legislature on February 7, 1996. They wanted a retractable dome stadium, hoping that the structure would attract major events, including the Super Bowl and Big XII Championship. Broncos team president Bob Hampe reported that the new stadium would cost between $250 million and $260 million. The Broncos offered to pay 25 percent of the cost, with the remaining balance for the stadium coming from an extension of the Coors Field tax (Lopez 1996a). Mayor Wellington Webb's sports advisory task force endorsed the Broncos' proposal, recommending to the mayor that he allow the team to pursue a new stadium. Webb immediately responded that he would support the recommendation but that he would not personally campaign for a new stadium. "Let the people decide what they want to do with this," Webb said (Lopez 1996b). With the support of the Mayor's task force, the Broncos' political machine went to work.

The Broncos hired well-known lobbyists Poncho Hays, Wally Stealey, and Bill Artist to work over the state legislature. Moreover, they hired campaign strategist Rick Reiter to influence public opinion over the issue. Reiter was the strategist behind the campaigns to build Coors Field and Denver International Airport (Lopez 1996c). Many legislators were still reluctant to support placing a stadium referendum for a public vote. Early in the process, legislators did not step forward to introduce a bill to support the proposal. House Speaker Chuck Berry stated, "There's not a whole lot of support in the House to go ahead with this. I'm personally not persuaded the Broncos need a new stadium." Representative Jeanne Faatz said that 70 percent of her constituents opposed continuing the sales tax to build a new stadium for the Broncos. She said, "Most feel like the Broncos are a profit-making entity and it's not really the taxpayer's responsibility to provide them with a new stadium" (Frank 1996). It was not the sort of support the Broncos had hoped for in their drive for a new stadium.

In April 1996, the Broncos revealed a new proposal to the state legislature. The proposal called for the creation of the football stadium authority similar to the Denver Metropolitan Baseball Stadium District used to build Coors Field. The stadium authority would be used to raise $180 million from residents in the six-county Denver metro area, with a one cent tax per each $10 purchase to pay for a new $240 million dollar stadium, with the Broncos paying the remaining balance (Lipsher 1996). The sales tax would take effect in Adams, Arapahoe, Boulder, Denver, Douglas and Jefferson counties if the voters approved the measure. Later that month, the Denver Broncos found a stadium bill sponsor when Representative Vickie Agler introduced House Bill 1374. The bill pushed for the creation of the nine-member stadium authority. Agler conceded that the proposal likely meant that fans and the city would be financial losers if the ballot passed. The measure entailed higher ticket, concession, and parking prices and less revenue for the city. However, she defended the bill stating, "The city of Denver is going to have to come to grips with the facts that they could lose the team. They can have a drop in revenue, or they could lose it all" (Lipsher 1996b). Some lawmakers not only questioned the loss of funds by the city but also the seemingly arbitrary district boundaries being taxed to fund the new stadium. Representative Bill Swenson, a Republican from Longmont remarked, "We are using the RTD [Rapid Transit District] boundaries for the convenience of taxing other districts, whether or not they are benefiting from these services" (Lipsher 1996b). After a series of amendments, on the final day of the legislative session, the House approved the final version of the bill 33-32, with the Senate voting 19-16 for the measure (Frank and Lipsher 1996). The Metropolitan Football Authority was created and the drive for a new stadium was on (Lied 1998).

The Metropolitan Football Stadium District

The Metropolitan Football Stadium District was designed to be a fact-finding entity, separate from the Denver Broncos. The District was given certain responsibilities for the construction of a new football stadium. First, the stadium authority needed to confirm the need for a new stadium. Second, they needed to determine an appropriate site for building the stadium. Third, the authority needed to break the Broncos' lease with the city while securing a new long-term deal where revenue would be divided among both the team and all the counties involved in funding the new stadium. Finally, the authority was responsible for collecting enough signatures to place the referendum on the November 1997 ballot (Lipsher 1996a).

On July 18, 1996, the nine-member stadium board was assembled. The Stadium District authority was an overtly political body. Then-Governor Roy Romer selected two members for the board, and a third member came from the baseball stadium authority. The remaining six members came from the six Denver metro-area counties, with Mayor Webb selecting the member from Denver. In November, the football authority started investigating different financing possibilities for a new stadium. The board discussed possibilities such as a ticket tax, seat licenses, and lottery money. Several board members expressed reservations about extending the Coors Field tax to finance a stadium for the Broncos on the grounds of fairness. "The ultimate hardship is whether this can be financed equitably without hardships on people who don't get any benefit from the stadium," said board member Jim Carrigan. Later in their investigation, the board brought in representatives from Smith Barney, Prudential Securities, and Deloitte & Touche to hear how public money was being used to pay for other stadia across the country (Snel 1997). In addition to exploring different financing options, the board authorized an eighteen-member subcommittee to begin searching for a site for the new facility. Board member Chris Romer, a son of Governor Romer, believed that it was not cost effective to renovate Mile High Stadium and that the time had come for the city to push for a new stadium (Snel 1996c). It appeared that the drive for a new stadium had gained momentum within the stadium committee—that is, until a plan to modernize Mile High resurfaced because of a Denver architect.

Stuart Ohlson, whose uncle designed the original Mile High stadium (Snel 1997b), proposed a $189 million plan to renovate Mile High Stadium. Ohlson was not new to the architectural game, having designed 260 athletic and fitness facilities in forty-two states and six foreign countries (Sinisi 1997). The proposal called for attaching 600,000 square feet of offices, housing, and stores to the stadium, as well as covering the aging stadium with a dome. Ohlson saw little need to build a whole new stadium when the interior structure of Mile High was stable. Ohlson reasoned, "The most cost-efficient route to a new stadium appears to keep the bones and simply add new flesh to Mile High." Bowlen was less than receptive to the idea, stating, "Any refurbishment of Mile High would cost so much money relative to what you ever get out of it that it would be impractical" (Snel 1997a). A *Denver Post*/9News poll found that 61 percent of the respondents favored rehabilitating Mile High over building a new stadium, whereas only 31 percent favored building a new stadium (Obmascik 1997). Despite the Broncos' opposition to the proposal, the debate about improving Mile High stadium had resurfaced with most metro-area residents approving the renovation plan.

City officials promised that the renovation plan would get an honest look. In March, the city commissioned HOK Sport, the nation's largest sports architectural firm, for $200,000 to conduct a study on the rehabilitation of Mile High (Snel 1997c). In June, Dennis Wellner, a representative of the firm, reported that Mile High could be effectively transformed into a modern football facility, but at a cost of $202 to $211 million. Wellner contended that an extensive upgrade of Mile High was essentially asking for "a new stadium on an existing site." Furthermore, he reported that a new stadium could be built in Denver for about $200 million (Snel 1997e). On August 19, 1997, Mayor

Webb openly opposed the renovation of Mile High, saying that it was a "waste of taxpayer dollars" (Snel 1997f). Ohlson hoped the mayor would soften his stance on the rehabilitation project. However, Ohlson's plan was ultimately defeated. Three days later, the metropolitan stadium authority unanimously decided it made more sense to build a new stadium than upgrade the archaic Mile High. Board member Pat Hamill stated the renovation of Mile High was too risky, was not cost effective, and would be a bad investment (Snel 1997g). While the stadium authority was weighing the costs of renovating Mile High against the expense to build a new stadium, its subcommittee was actively searching for the best site for a new stadium.

Mayor Wellington Webb had declared that he would not allow the Broncos to escape their lease unless the new stadium was built in Denver, which limited to the site committee possible locations for the new stadium. In April 1997, the metro stadium site committee also hired HOK Sport to facilitate its search for the best potential stadium location. Odell Barry, a former Broncos player and chairman of the committee, hoped that the search would be concluded by May; however the search took much longer (Snel 1997d). The committee reviewed sites at two primary locations—one the current location of Mile High Stadium and the other the former Stapleton Airport. Mayor Webb endorsed the current location of Mile High as the best location for a new stadium, citing the added costs for road improvements and utilities associated with building the new facility at the Stapleton location. Dan Muse reported that the cost of road and utility improvements at the Stapleton site would run between $60 and $100 million (Katz and Snel 1997). On July 25, the site committee settled on the Mile High location as the site for the new stadium. It was argued by the Urban Land Institute, the group that recommended the sites for Coors Field and the Colorado Convention Center, that the Denver Sports Complex would spur more economic development and require less time and money to develop.

On July 30, 1997, the stadium authority announced that there was not enough time to stage a referendum for the issue on the November ballot. Stadium opponents hailed the announcement, saying that it would give legislators more time to come up with an alternative stadium funding method to the sales tax of one cent for every $10 in purchases. The Broncos expressed disappointment. According to Wharton, "We're disappointed. The longer we play in Mile High Stadium the more difficult it will be to remain a competitive franchise" (Snel 1997f).

The following February, the Metropolitan Stadium Authority selected Turner Construction Co./Empire Construction Co. to serve as contractor for the new stadium. The general contractor's role was to work with the architect to keep stadium costs on budget. Also, the general contractor was responsible for giving a guaranteed maximum cost for the facility as well as for hiring sub-contractors for various construction projects. The Turner-Empire team was se-lected from five competing construction firms after the several board members visited Ericsson Stadium in North Carolina and were impressed with their work (Snel 1998b). Later that month, the stadium authority selected the firm HNTB/Fentress, Bradburn and Associates as the stadium's architect. HNTB was chosen over HOK Sport. The stadium board picked the HNTB, which had designed the Colorado Convention Center and Denver International Airport, because of its Denver roots. Furthermore, the firm pledged to hire 80 percent of its consultants from the Denver area (Snel 1998c). Having selected a site and contractors for the new stadium, the stadium board awaited passage of a new Broncos stadium bill in the legislature and the release of the team from its cur-rent lease by the city. Once both tasks were completed, the stadium authority only had to collect enough signatures to put the stadium tax on the November ballot and secure a new lease between the Broncos and the city.

On August 31, 1998, the stadium authority, with the help of the Denver Broncos, secured enough signatures to qualify the measure on the ballot. One day later, the board finalized a new lease with the Broncos. The deal gave Bowlen access to nearly all the revenues from the new stadium, including tick-ets, parking, concessions, and luxury suite rentals. Additionally, the taxpay-ers share would pay 75 percent of the stadium costs and the Broncos would pay 25 percent. In return, the Broncos promised to stay in Denver for thirty years, with two five-year options to renew afterward. The team would be re-sponsible for certain costs, such as $20 million dollars to be paid to the city to escape its current lease, operating and maintenance expenses at the new stadium which would cost $4 million to $5 million annually, and rent at the stadium which would total $70 million over the term of the lease. The sta-dium district would receive revenues from the sale of the stadium naming rights and from non-NFL events that would increase from 20 percent to 50 percent over the length of the lease. Moreover, if Pat Bowlen sold the team, the new owner would be bound by the lease and be prohibited from moving the team. Wharton said of the deal, "This is not a great deal for the Broncos. This is a fair deal." He added that of the past thirteen football stadium deals, only two had more money from the NFL franchises going into the projects (Martinez 1998). With the Broncos' stadium deal finally secure, the team needed only to secure passage of the ballot in the November election for the facility to be built.

Lobbying the Legislature, Again

In January 1998, Bowlen for the first time used words strongly suggesting that if Denver-area voters did not approve a stadium ballot, the team would be moved. Bowlen said that while he would never personally move the team, he would be forced to sell the Denver Broncos and the new owner would move the team after seeing the team's financial restraints. Bowlen told a Los Angeles newspaper, "It would be too heart-wrenching for me to move this team...but if we do not get a new stadium, I cannot continue to own the team. Somebody else will buy this team...and I will maximize whatever I can get—not on the basis of what they're going to do in Denver but what they're going to do somewhere else" (Snel 1998). Critics claimed that it would be impossible for Bowlen or any new owner to move the team because of the twenty years remaining on the current lease. The Broncos deflected those arguments by claiming that the city failed to live up to its end of the lease by allowing the stadium to deteriorate beyond the terms of the lease. Wharton (1998) stated that when the stadium drive first began, lawyers believed that the lease was airtight; however, that perception changed when the LONCO study was released.

After the Denver Broncos won the Super Bowl in 1998, polls revealed that the citizens were warming up to the idea of publicly financing a new football stadium. Furthermore, by February 1998, the stadium cost projections had climbed to $300 million. With the public only liable for a $180-million contribution, the Broncos sought to increase the taxpayers' share. Bowlen mounted an extensive lobbying effort in the Colorado legislature. The Broncos hired three of the largest lobbying firms in the Colorado for their stadium push: Brownstein, Hyatt, Farber & Strickland, Stealey & Associates, and Hays, Hays & Wilson (Lowe 1998d). Additionally, the Broncos retained the services of lobbyists Porter Wharton and Bill Artist, the two men largely credited with making the campaign a success up to that point (Wharton 1998).

Many legislators told the *Denver Post* that the Broncos employed a one-on-one lobbying tactic, where the lobbyists would choose people or interests groups to spread their message who were particularly friendly with individual lawmakers. Representative Gloria Leyba of Denver said of the Broncos' lobbying effort, "They have been really strategic and have been able to identify individuals who are able to influence certain legislators." Mike Feeley added, "It's a real intense lobbying effort. They really know what they're doing" (Lowe 1998d).

In their effort to raise the maximum contribution of taxpayers, the Broncos received quick support from State Senator Elsie Lacy from Aurora. Lacy took charge of the new stadium drive in the Senate, pushing for an increase in the taxpayers' contribution and a special May election. The early election attempt ultimately failed, but on February 11, Lacy introduced a bill to increase the taxpayers' maximum contribution to $265 million (Snel 1998a). This figure was later raised to $266 million. Lacy and the Denver Broncos claimed that the $180 million initially passed by the legislature would be insufficient to cover the rising cost of building a new stadium. "The economics of (the old stadium deal), with the escalating costs for the stadium simply doesn't work for the franchise," Wharton said (Lowe 1998). Lacy and the Broncos faced early difficulty in their push to increase the taxpayers' share. Senator Stan Matsunaka of Greeley reported that the bill was stalled on three issues: 1) an amendment to reduce the cap back to the original $180 million; 2) an amendment to consider a domed stadium; and 3) lawmaker concerns that Bowlen would be the sole beneficiary from a new stadium (Brown 1997). Ultimately, the push for a domed stadium failed when the stadium board recommended that the project be dismissed, but the $266 million cap was approved in the Senate after Matsunaka and Senator Peggy Reeves of Fort Collins, who both held out early, gave their votes to the higher cap. Matsunaka and Reeves gave their support only after two amendments were approved. One required that, should Pat Bowlen ever sell the Broncos, the team must contribute $1 million to youth charities and return two percent of the team's net sales to the stadium authority. The other asked for at least a twenty-year commitment by the Broncos to stay in Denver (Lowe 1998a).

In the Colorado House of Representatives, Bowlen again responded to charges that the stadium bill would only increase his fortunes at the expense of taxpayers. "This is not about the money. This is about keeping the Broncos in the state of Colorado," he reiterated. Representative Ron Tupa of Boulder proposed an amendment to expand the stadium taxing district to include all of Douglas County, more of Adams and Arapahoe County, and a small part of Weld County. The proposal included the new Park Meadows mall and Castle Rock Factory Shops. While the expansion would have increased tax revenue, allowing the stadium to be paid off more quickly, it also would have increased the number of voters (Lowe 1998c). Artist said of the expanded tax district, "We're concerned that we might bring in so many no votes we can't get the issue passed" (Brown 1998a). Fearing that an expanded voting district would be detrimental to the stadium ballot, Bowlen's lobbyists went to work. When the bill finally cleared both houses, the Denver Broncos' lobby secured a district expansion that increased the amount of taxes generated without adding a single voter (Lowe 1998e). On April 21, 1998, the final bill was approved by the General Assembly. In addition to the expanded district, the measure held onto the $266 million cap, specified that the Broncos were responsible for 25 percent of the stadium costs, limited taxpayer overrun costs to $75 million, and gave the stadium board the right to sell the stadium naming rights to lighten the taxpayer burden (Lowe 1998g). Governor Roy Romer hailed the passage of the bill, stating, "We need to keep the Broncos in Denver. They are an important part of our community. This step will ensure many more good years of football" (Lowe 1998h).

The Changing Face of Denver's Mayor

The Colorado General Assembly was not the only political institution whose opinion changed regarding a new stadium. Over the course of four years, there was a gradual shift in the attitudes of Denver's Mayor Wellington Webb. At the beginning of the stadium drive, the mayor was very skeptical of Bowlen's plans. Webb presented himself as an advocate of the taxpayer. Later, the attitude shifted to one of neutrality. In the end, Webb presented himself as an outspoken supporter of the stadium tax. He lobbied for the passage of the stadium bill in the legislature, prompted the stadium board to hurry its work, and allowed the team to escape its current lease from the city. Webb became an active force in the passage of the Broncos stadium referendum.

When the Denver Broncos brought up the stadium issue in 1994, Webb showed little interest in building a new facility for the Broncos. Webb asked, "Is the need for a new stadium tied to a need for more revenue or do the Broncos want a new stadium just to have a new stadium?" (Hutchinson and Lopez 1994). After the release of the LONCO report in 1994, Webb still saw nothing wrong with Mile High Stadium. "Mile High Stadium has a lot of use left in it," he stated. "Structurally, the stadium is sound. I think we can take revenue and enhance Mile High if that's the issue" (Lopez 1994c). For much of the early stadium negotiating process, the mayor maintained a very hard-nosed approach.

In early August 1994, Mayor Webb announced that the Broncos and the Nuggets, who were also seeking a new arena, would have to meet four conditions if they wanted new sports facilities. First, both teams needed to demonstrate that their current facilities were obsolete and unable to meet their current needs. Second, both teams needed to show long-term commitments to staying in Denver. Third, Webb said that the city was unwilling to lose any revenue it was currently getting in its leases with both teams. Finally, Webb said that he would not support recommendations for new taxes or the use of revenue bonds by the city. While Webb did not dismiss supporting a six-county stadium district like the one used to build Coors Field, he was not entirely sold on the tax for several reasons. Denver would not have control over the team if the new stadium were to be financed by the stadium district. Furthermore, Webb stated that taxpayers were promised that Coors Field tax would expire after the stadium was built (Lopez 1994c).

When the Denver Broncos made their presentation to Webb's sports advisory task force in December of 1994, Webb was still reluctant to support any stadium proposal. Webb, who did not attend the meeting, said, "I would be very cool on a new stadium because I don't know where the money would come from" (Lopez. 1994d). By the time the Broncos made their push for a new stadium in the legislature in 1996, though, Wellington Webb had softened his stance. He stated that he would not impede passage of a stadium bill as it worked its way through the legislature. He maintained that if the Broncos wanted a new stadium, they would have to make their own case to the people and he would not actively lobby for them. Webb at the time stated that the "the people of the metro area have the right to vote on this" (Hodges and Lopez 1996).

By 1997, the mayor still did not actively support the Broncos' stadium drive, but he supported many positions favored by the team. In May of that year, Webb publicly endorsed tearing down McNichols Arena—the city's basketball and hockey arena—to clear way for building a new football stadium. For the first time, the mayor suggested his favorite site for building a new stadium and dismissed the possibility of renovating Mile High Stadium (Katz and Snel 1997). In August 1997, Webb had become openly opposed to any stadium renovation plan, in particular Stuart Ohlson's plan. He proclaimed that Mile High was not worth rebuilding, a move that pleased Bronco representatives (Snel 1997g). The stadium authority, which claimed to have no official stance on the stadium-rebuilding project at the time, agreed with Webb's position and dismissed the rebuilding plan three days later.

Despite continuing negotiations over the Broncos' lease and the new stadium, in October of that year, Wellington Webb and his wife Wilma accepted an invitation to attend a Monday Night Football game in Denver with Bowlen. Webb defended the move saying, "We weren't talking about a new stadium. Nobody was talking business." Wharton claimed that the invitation wouldn't "have one iota of influence on what is ultimately done in terms of the new stadium." He continued, "It was a social situation with a bunch of people who enjoyed a terrific football game. There was no stadium business being discussed at all" (Snel 1997i).

On January 27, 1998, in front of 650,000 people attending the Denver Broncos Super Bowl rally, Mayor Webb declared his support for a new stadium and his actions afterward indicated such. During the spring Webb did some last minute campaigning in the House of Representatives shortly before passage of the final stadium bill (Lowe 1998f). The mayor's administration agreed to lease the eighty-acre proposed stadium site to the Broncos for $1.00 in exchange for a promise from the team to stay in the city for twenty-five years. After the twenty-five years, the land would be returned to the city (Martinez 1998a). Furthermore, despite earlier claims that Webb would not allow the team to escape its lease if the city lost revenue it was currently receiving from the stadium, the final deal gave the Broncos the stadium operations and its profits. On August 24, 1998, the city council approved an agreement to release the Broncos from their existing lease, allowing the stadium district to complete its lease negotiations with the city. With the mayor's help, the new stadium measure was on its way to being placed on the November ballot.

The Campaign for a New Stadium

Ideally, laws passed via referendum will closely reflect the preferences of the average voter (Gerber 1996; but see Lascher, Hagan, and Hochlin 1996). As it relates to stadium politics, a referendum helps to legitimize the public financing of sports facilities because it can reflect voter preference on the issue (Fort 1997). In most cases, when a stadium issue comes up for vote, a referendum has been hammered out by the legislature and the team owners in a complicated negotiation process, as was the case for the Denver Broncos stadium. In a best case scenario, committees on both sides of a given ballot proposal are able to freely disseminate their positions, and the voter is able to make an educated vote on the issue. In the case of the Denver stadium, though, the Broncos were able to spread their message much more easily because of a huge campaign chest and because the media coverage was biased in favor of a new stadium.

Citizens Opposing the Stadium Tax

In 1996, two veterans of the Denver Democratic Party, William and Shirley Schley, organized a campaign against the public financing of a new stadium. Shirley, a former chairwoman of the Denver Democratic Party, argued, "Taxpayer money should not be used to enrich the corporate giants of this city" (Hodges 1996). The group was initially called the Citizens Against the Stadium Tax. This name was later changed to the Citizens Opposed to the Stadium Tax (COST) (Burness 1998). The group was miffed at some of the "myths" that were being circulated by the media and the Denver Broncos in favor of the stadium. COST challenged the figure that taxpayers would only be responsible for $266 million to build the stadium, when real costs could be as high as $467 million once interest and overrun costs were included, and it tried to counter the arguments that a new stadium would benefit the city economically (Citizens Opposing the Stadium Tax 1998).

COST had a difficult time raising money for its campaign (Burness 1998). While it received 415 contributions to its opposition campaign in 1998, most were small individual contributions. COST's campaign was not well supported by the business community. It only received five contributions from businesses, the largest of which was for $500. The Schleys, themselves, made contributions to the campaign on fourteen separate occasions, totaling $685. Also of note, Stuart Ohlson, the architect behind the failed attempt to remodel Mile High, contributed $500 to the campaign on October 29, 1998. In all, COST was only able to raise $26,078, a paltry sum given the mammoth task in front of them (Colorado Office of Secretary of State 1998). (See Appendix 10A.)

COST was unable to prevent the Broncos from getting what they wanted in the state legislature and subsequently the election. In the Colorado General Assembly, the group could not make a major move to prevent the passage of the stadium bill. Bill Schley said, "We feel in lobbying, we're at such a disadvantage there. And while we've been treated cordially, I think the Broncos' lobbyists have a tremendous advantage" (Lowe 1998b). The Broncos ultimately got nearly everything they wanted from the stadium bill. During the stadium campaign, COST was simply unable to mount a very affective campaign with so little funding. COST spent a large portion of its funds on general campaign material: buttons, flyers, and signs, for example. The group managed to air three different radio ads on the Denver stations KYGO, KOOL, KVOD, KOSI, and KNUS. The ads on the five radio stations cost the group $12,815 (Colorado Office of Secretary of State 1998). Each ad conveyed a different message. In one ad, COST personalized its attack on Pat Bowlen, portraying him as a selfish owner bent on reaping all the benefits from the new stadium. In another ad, the group tried to dissuade public fears that the team could be the next Cleveland Browns by pointing out the existing twenty years remaining on the stadium lease. In the third ad, COST pointed to new stadia built in San Francisco, Washington D.C., and North Carolina, where public financing was much lower (Obmascik 1998).

With its resources limited, the group relied less on paid media to further its cause and more on other methods for campaigning. Volunteers wrote numerous letters to the editor to both major Colorado newspapers. COST took to the streets to convey its message, organizing rallies through out the city. In one stunt, a member of the group dressed up to look like Pat Bowlen holding a sign that read, "Help! Hungry. Will work for luxury boxes. Can you spare $467 million?" (Lowe 1998i). Additionally, COST members were very vocal at public hearings on the stadium, shouting out their arguments as stadium board representatives tried to present the stadium proposal to the public. In all, it was a valiant, yet futile campaign against a stronger more powerful opponent.

Citizens for a New Stadium

Direct democracy scholar Cronin (1989) writes, "Effective use of the media may often make the difference between failure and success at the polls, and effective use of the media is often a function of money." Given the overwhelming campaign contributions to Citizens for a New Stadium (CFANS), stadium supporters were more effectively able to make use of the media than their opponents. CFANS effectively used its money to hire campaign consultants and to buy expensive television time.

CFANS did not organize as early as COST. However, its campaign was well funded and better organized. As the Broncos had shown previously during the stadium drive, they were not about to take chances with the campaign and got an early start. Lobbyist Bill Artist directed the CFANS campaign. Artist said that the campaign would be "grassroots and very broad-based." He added, "This is going to be a community based effort and we'll be soliciting a lot of volunteers. This will be mostly a nuts and bolts campaign" (Lowe 1998i).

The message CFANS conveyed to the voters was that everyone in the community would benefit from a new stadium. The group's slogan was, "We All Win." CFANS tried to communicate that even if some citizens were not Broncos fans, they would benefit from the new stadium. It wanted to point out that the Broncos were important to the community not only for providing civic pride but also for their charity work (Brown 1998). CFANS argued that building a new stadium was a good deal, stating that renovating Mile High would cost nearly as much as building a new facility. The group argued that the costs to each family were minimal, possibly less than one dollar a month per family. Furthermore, the team wanted the fans to know that they would win with a new stadium, because it would allow the Broncos to be competitive with other NFL teams (Citizens for a New Stadium 1998). For CFANS, conveying its message to voters was relatively easy.

While CFANS received only 260 contributions to its campaign, 155 less than COST, the total value of contributions greatly exceeded that of the COST campaign. The campaign received 53 donations of $5,000 and greater, 32 donations of $10,000 and greater, 22 donations equaling $25,000 or more, and 10 contributions of $100,000 or greater. It was able to secure support from area and national businesses. The campaign received 70 business contributions from companies such as Norwest Bank, Bank One, United Airlines, U.S. Bank, KeyBank, the Gart Companies, Land Title Guarantee Company, Robinson Dairy, the Public Service Company, Coors Brewing Company, and U.S. West Communications. Additionally, CFANS received donations from HNTB Corporation and Turner Construction Company, the two companies that won contracts to build the stadium—of $25,000 and $30,000, respectively. However, support for the campaign did not come just from businesses, since wealthy and influential Colorado residents also made important contributions. Bill Daniels, a local cable television tycoon, and area businessman Charles Gallagher each contributed $100,000. Denver Broncos players contributed a combined $27,340, with John Elway's $10,000 donation leading the way. Mike Shanahan, head coach of the Denver Broncos, also contributed $5,000. The largest contributions to the CFANS war chest, however, came from Pat Bowlen himself. Bowlen made contributions to the campaign on six different occasions, totaling $1,960,000. In all, the campaign raised over $3 million to help pass the Broncos' stadium referendum (Colorado Office of Secretary of State 1998). With virtually a blank check from Bowlen at its disposal, CFANS launched an all-out media assault on the Denver voters. (See Appendix 10B.)

CFANS was a well-functioning political machine. The group had a paid staff and employed temporary help when needed. Working with the stadium authority—and using a combination of volunteer and paid signature gathers—the group, unlike many proponents of ballot measures (Garrett 1999), had little difficulty collecting the 28,705 signatures by August 31 to secure the measure on the November ballot. The group paid over $70,000 for polling work and data analysis. It hired consultants for nearly $160,000, including the firm of Reiter & Associates, as well as individual consultants such as Eric Morgan, Will Fox, and Bill Artist. With its consultants, CFANS devised a media campaign that would appeal to all voters while specifically targeting females, who were less supportive of the stadium tax than males. It wanted to send the message that the stadium tax was not a new tax but merely a continuation of an existing tax. The group spent $1,334,270.81, nearly half of its money, on television commercials and commercial production (Colorado Office of Secretary of State 1998).

The campaign to attract female voters was in full swing by October 1998. That month, Janet Elway, Annabel Bowlen, Peggy Shanahan, and Olympic gold medal swimmer Amy Van Dyken all appeared at what was called "A Women's Town Hall: Why We All Win." At that event, the women focused on the team's charitable contributions to the community. COST was also targeting women, believing that they would make up the swing vote. COST volunteers attended soccer games to talk to "soccer moms" (Lowe 1998m). However, COST's work could not match the media blitz staged by CFANS. In the first of three television commercials, a spokeswoman appeared, reminding the voters of the civic pride enjoyed by the city after the Broncos won the Super Bowl and telling them that "we can make sure the metro area remains a world class-city by building a world-class stadium that we'll all own without raising taxes" (Lowe 1998k). In the second ad, one seemingly designed to appeal to sports fans, a mock news conference was held by Mike Shanahan where he told a group of reporters that building a new stadium would ensure that pay-per-view would never be used for Broncos telecasts and that the stadium could be used for other events such as rock concerts and soccer games. Shanahan also claimed in the ad that the new stadium would be built without raising new taxes. In the final stadium ad, the Broncos used their key spokesperson, John Elway. Again, CFANS stated in the ad that the new stadium was going to be built without raising taxes. Elway said of the new stadium in the commercial, "It's the best solution for everyone. That's why I'm asking you to vote yes for a new stadium. It's about keeping the Denver area special" (Obmascik 1998).

In ballot contests, the group that best utilizes paid radio and television advertisements often holds an advantage (Cronin 1989). However, effective use of radio and television ads is often related to money. COST had limited financial backing and was unable to make effective use of the media. While the group did produce three radio ads, its campaign consisted largely of grassroots efforts such as rallies and letter writing. CFANS, on the other hand, received tremendous support from the business community and from Pat Bowlen himself. It used the money to effectively present its arguments through the most frequently utilized media outlet, television. CFANS bombarded citizens with a multimillion dollar advertising campaign that helped the Broncos win support for a new stadium.

The Media and the Stadium

The media, of course, play an important role in the process of direct democracy, since they are a major source through which people gain information about ballot issues (Bowler and Donovan 1998). However, as Noll and Zimbalist (1997) write, "The relationship between the media and sports is synergistic: sports coverage sells newspapers and increases audience rating, but it also enhances interest in sports." Hence, there is an inclination on the part of the media to favor stadium referendums. In the Denver case, reporting on the stadium tax proposal certainly favored Pat Bowlen and the Broncos. Not only did Denver's largest radio stations urge listeners to vote in favor the stadium tax, but an analysis of the coverage in the *Denver Post* and *Rocky Mountain News,* Colorado's two largest newspapers, reveals a stadium bias by staff writers as well as the editors. In the end, the radio and newspaper media served as a valuable ally for the Denver Broncos.

Radio Coverage and the Stadium Issue

Jacor Broadcasting Company owns eight Denver-area radio stations and controls nearly 40 percent of the listening audience age 12 and older (Lowe 1998j). Jacor did not withhold the fact that it was prostadium. Robin Bertolucci, manager of two Jacor stations in Denver stated, "We've had a 30 year partnership with the Broncos, so we're not impartial. We're supporters and cheerleaders, and it's something we're very proud of, actually. We don't hide the fact that we have a close association with the team and we support the stadium" (Lowe 1998j). For a thirty-second ad on KOA during a Broncos game, the company receives $1,700. Mason Lewis, station manager of KRRF, stated, "This is a money deal. The Broncos bring a lot of money and a lot of stature to that station. It's in the best interest of the radio station to make sure that whatever involves the team is done in a positive light" (Lowe 1998j). While the company did not mandate that its radio personalities support the stadium drive, most did. Support for the stadium by radio personalities could be found on nearly every Jacor station, including Lewis and Floorwax from KRFX, as well as its sports director, Rich "The G-Man" Goins; KOA talk show hosts Mike Rosen, Reggie Rivers, Dave Logan, Scott Hastings, Dan Caplis, and Tom "Lou from Littleton" Manoogian; Jay Marvin from KHOW; and KTLK's Irv Brown and Joe Williams (Lowe 1998j).

Radio personalities did more than just voice their opinions on the stadium tax over the airwaves. Some participated in the stadium push in other ways. The company encouraged its employees to participate in the stadium petition drive. Rich Goins disrupted a COST rally, calling COST supporters "a bunch of soccer fans" (Lowe 1998j). Additionally, Rosen (1998), also a columnist for the *Denver Post*, wrote a series of articles supporting the stadium. "The city will reap the economic benefits of having a new stadium here, just as it did with Coors Field," Rosen wrote. "If we don't subsidize an NFL team with a stadium, we'll eventually lose the team to a city that will." It was the free circulation of these kinds of arguments on the radio that infuriated some stadium opponents.

State Representative Ron Tupa said that the Jacor stations were "presenting it [the stadium referendum] as a very one-sided issue, that there's no other option. It's simply not true." Tupa took offense when he believed that many of the radio personalities did not have their facts on the stadium correct, particularly the claim that the Broncos would leave if not given a new stadium. Tupa noted that the lease with the city prohibited the Broncos from leaving. Shirley Schley reported, "We're finding that's the number one issue. People are saying they're going to vote for the stadium because they're afraid Bowlen's going to move the team" (Lowe 1998j). Despite pleas from COST supporters that the fear of the team's moving was unfounded, the stations still articulated that position.

Newspaper Coverage and the Stadium Issue

A cursory look at the newspaper coverage might lead one to believe that the two largest newspapers in Colorado slightly opposed building a new stadium. Of the 546 stadium-related articles printed in the two newspapers from January 1 through November 3, 1998, 50 percent of the news stories were unbiased, 24 percent were favorable towards the stadium, and 26 percent were unfavorable towards the stadium. (See Appendix 10C.) In the *Denver Post*, 50 percent of the articles were neutral, with 23 percent and 27 percent of the articles having biases for and against the stadium, respectively. In the *Rocky Mountain News*, half of the news articles were unbiased towards the building of the new stadium, with the other half split equally between favorable and unfavorable stories. Breaking the articles down by their respective types, we find that 32 percent of the articles concerning the Broncos stadium were either letters to the editor or op-eds, articles not written by staff writers of the two newspapers. Of these citizen-submitted articles, 58 percent were unfavorable towards the stadium, 30 percent favored building a new stadium, and 12 percent were unbiased. This reflects COST's letter writing campaign against the stadium in the face of limited financial recourses. Of the articles written by the staff writers and columnists for each paper, there was definite support for the Broncos stadium. Of the straight news stories with a discernible bias, 64 percent favored building the new stadium, while only 36 percent of the articles were unfavorable towards the stadium. Of the editorials in both papers, 70 percent favored building a new stadium, with only 30 percent unfavorable to the stadium.

By disaggregating over time all the stories on the stadium issue, another interesting pattern emerged. There were four crucial time periods for the stadium referendum in 1998: 1) January 1 until January 25, from the start of the year to the Broncos' Super Bowl win; 2) January 26 to April 22, the date from the Broncos' Super Bowl win to the date Roy Romer signed the stadium bill; 3) April 23 to August 31, from the day Romer signed the bill to the day the petition signatures were collected; and 4) September 1 to November 3, from the date the signatures were collected until the election. During the first three time periods, a majority of articles with a discernable bias were unfavorable toward the stadium tax. During the first three time periods, 56 percent, 53 percent, and 64 percent of the articles with a discernable slant came out against the tax. However, as the drive for the new stadium neared election day, the bias flipped. During the last period, from the day the signatures were collected to election day, 59 percent of all biased articles were favorable toward the stadium. The newspaper staff and editorial writers, as well as citizens writing letters to the editor and op-eds, littered the newspapers with articles supporting the new stadium. Our content analysis indicates that the during the crucial final campaign leading up to the November vote, newspapers and their writers were generally in favor of the new stadium, and this medium was a valuable Broncos ally.

Did the Broncos and the Media Influence Voters?

Direct democracy scholars Shaun Bowler and Todd Donovan (1998) note that when spending on media advertising in initiative campaigns is high, more potential voters become aware of the supporters and opponents of a ballot measure. Additionally, they suggest that television "is the vehicle that might be best suited to influencing the opinions of the less-educated voters—voters who we know are exposed to fewer sources of information and who are particularly less likely to utilize print information." Well-organized interests groups of stadium proponents generally outspend the opposition by enormous amounts. In San Francisco, pro stadium campaigns spent 25 times more money than the campaigns of their opponents. In Washington D.C., proponents outspent the opposition by 80 to 1 (Noll and Zimbalist 1997). Both campaigns won by slim margins. While it would be inaccurate to state that there is causation between campaign spending and the final stadium vote, it would not be wrong to suggest that a one-sided political debate could swing the vote in close elections. We found the same trend occurring in Denver.

During the stadium drive, voters were bombarded with information through all of the major media sources, which were largely one-sided in their presentations. While it is fair to say that the general public was more educated on the Broncos' stadium ballot than many of the other ballot issues, given the enormous press coverage and campaign advertisements, most of the information came from groups supporting the new stadium. Determining precisely how much influence the media and the Broncos had over the voters is difficult; however we speculate, based on professional polling data in the days leading up to the election and on our own election day exit-polling data, that the Broncos and the media influenced the voters.

A Ciruli Associates telephone poll revealed that three days before the election, 53 percent of the citizens supported building a new stadium, 40 percent opposed it, and 7 percent were undecided. The final stadium vote was 57 percent in favor and 43 percent opposed. Of the people who said they would support building the stadium, 33 percent said they would vote for the stadium because they were fans who loved the Broncos; 28 percent said that the city needed a new stadium; 15 percent voted for it because they believed it would be good for the economy; 9 percent feared losing the team; 6 percent believed that a new stadium was a good deal for the city; 5 percent supported it because the final estimated cost for building the stadium was small; and 3 percent said they voted for it because they voted for baseball (Ciruli 1999). (See Appendix 10D). During the stadium drive, the Denver Broncos used each of these arguments in their paid and free media outlets to gain popular support for a new stadium. Standing alone, though, these statistics reveal little about the media's impact on the stadium vote.

To get at this question, an exit poll of 524 metro Denver citizens who voted on the stadium ballot was conducted. In the sample, 57 percent said they voted for the stadium and 39 percent said they voted against it. While the exit poll asked questions similar to those in the Ciruli poll, it was more specifically tailored to analyzing the media's influence on Denver area voters. Voters were asked what the major source of information they used to make their decision on the stadium vote. In addition to the reasons provided in the Ciruli poll, voters were asked if they voted for the stadium referendum to "keep the Denver area special." As mentioned earlier, John Elway appeared in the last pro-stadium commercial leading up to the election, reminding viewers that "Colorado was a special place to live and raise a family" and that voting for the new stadium was about "keeping the Denver area special" (Obmascik 1998). Of the people we polled who voted for the stadium on election day, 27 percent said they did it to keep Denver special, 24 percent believed in the economic benefits, 18 percent feared that the Broncos would leave, 10 percent were just Bronco fans who loved and supported the team, while 21 percent cited another reason or did not know. While the exit poll results differed from those of the Ciruli poll, the results indicated that keeping the Denver area "special" was the primary reason citizens approved the new stadium. (See Appendix 10E.)

Of the people who responded to the question about the major source of information they used to cast their vote on the stadium referendum, 30 percent said they used the newspaper; 23 percent responded that they used television; 7 percent replied that they used information from family and friends; 6 percent stated that radio was their major source of information; another 6 percent used the legislative voting guide or another voting guide; and 27 percent said they used other resources. In total, nearly 60 percent of those who responded said that they used either the newspaper, television, or radio as their primary source of information for voting on the stadium issue.

While it would be careless to contend that there is a causal relationship between the media's representation of the stadium issue and the results of the 1998 November vote, we speculate that the media played an important role in the passage of the stadium referendum. The Denver media had a financial stake in seeing the stadium pass, so the Denver media outlets allied with the Broncos during the stadium drive. Denver area voters were blitzed with over $1.3 million in paid television advertisements that glorified the need for a new stadium. Radio personalities from Denver's largest stations regularly extolled, for free, the virtues of a new stadium. Additionally, two-thirds of the slanted articles written by staff writers in both papers supported building the new stadium. Since 60 percent of the voters relied on one of these outlets as their major source of information on the stadium issue, the majority of metro area voters were subjected to either biased or misleading information.

Conclusion

In the years leading up to the stadium vote, a majority of metro area residents and most politicians opposed building a new stadium for the Denver Broncos. The team was under an existing lease to stay in the city until 2018 and the residents were already subjected to broken promises from the Coors

Field tax. However, over the course of five years, the team successfully controlled the stadium debate in the legislature and in the media. The Broncos argued that they needed a new stadium to remain competitive with other NFL teams. They claimed that the deteriorating conditions at Mile High were unpleasant for the fans. They asserted that the new stadium would benefit everyone in the community. They threatened that the team would move if a new stadium was not built. The Broncos spent millions of dollars to promote their cries of poverty and the Denver media supported their message.

The Denver Broncos' "Orange Crush" demonstrates how some professional team owners are able to persuade community leaders and residents of the need for a new stadium, for structural and symbolic reasons rather than economic ones. Because the Broncos were the only game in town, their structural advantages helped to pave the way for their subsequent political campaign. The Broncos commissioned architects to belittle Mile High. They hired an army of lobbyists to push their proposals through the Colorado General Assembly. They used public relations consultants and polling data to maintain a positive image within the community. Finally, the team paid millions of dollars in advertising to promote their message to the voters. As journalist Ann Imse (1998a) remarked two days after the election:

> The Broncos spent $5 million over four years to win a $360 million new stadium. The bulk of Bowlen's funding went into years of political maneuvering leading up to the vote. He hired architects to denigrate renovation of Mile High Stadium and plan his dream stadium. He hired political strategists to push the subsidy through the legislature. He hired market researchers to learn how much fans would pay for luxury seats. Finally, he gave $1.4 million [Bowlen's final contribution total was actually $1.96 million] to the Citizens for a New Stadium, the campaign that won 57 percent of the vote.

It turned out to be a good investment for Bowlen. According to experts on the value of sport franchises, the value of the Broncos increased roughly $100 million after voters approved the stadium measure (Imse 1998a).

The stadium drive also demonstrates the perceived symbolic importance of the team. While the team itself brings in little economic growth and development to the city, major businesses in Colorado deem the Broncos to be an important asset to the community. Local and national corporations financially backed the drive for a new stadium. Moreover, the local media had a vested interest in seeing the Broncos win their new stadium, and they responded in kind. Radio stations with promotional contracts with the Broncos encouraged their radio personalities to support the team, and most did. In addition, as the content analysis of the newspaper articles indicates, newspaper staff writers wrote articles and editorials overwhelmingly supporting the new stadium.

The victory for the Broncos is a good example of how the privileged structural position of professional sport teams in a community, combined with their symbolic advantages, plays a crucial role in the initiative process. The passage of the stadium referendum also underscores the political and financial clout of professional teams and their supporters and how professional teams have a built-in advantage in mobilizing the bias of the media and the public in support of publicly funded sports facilities. While it was the citizens who ultimately approved the public financing of the new stadium, Pat Bowlen's money and the media's biased coverage of the Broncos were essential in mobilizing popular support for the measure. Economic arguments—that the stadium would benefit the local economy—had little play during the Broncos' campaign to promote the ballot measure. Rather, the Broncos' political machine (with the complicity of the media) was able to disseminate information and saturate the airwaves with propaganda favorable to the new stadium. As with other ballot measures, emotional rhetoric and even misinformation played an integral part in the direct democracy campaign (Smith 1998). While citizens ultimately shoulder the responsibility for the decisions they make on ballot measures, in the case of the Broncos' bid for a new stadium, the process of direct democracy was quite susceptible to the symbolic arguments advanced by a structurally privileged professional franchise.

Appendix 10A

COST Campaign Contributions, 1998

	# of Total Contributions	% of Contributions	$ Total Contributions	% of Contributions
Individual	409	99	24,671	94
Business	5	1	907	4
Association	1	0	500	2
Total	415	100	26,078	100

COST Campaign Expenditures, 1998

	$ Total Expenditures	% Expenditures
General Campaign Materials	13,973	47
Advertising	12,815	43
Postage	1,843	6
Services/Paid Employees	176	1
Other	891	3
Total	29,698	100

Appendix 10B

CFANS Campaign Contributions, 1998

	# of Total Contributions	% of Contributions	$ Total Contributions	% of Contributions
Individual	180	69	334,597	11
Business	70	27	624,060	21
Association	4	2	47,804	2
Pat Bowlen	6	2	1,960,000	66
Totals	260	100	2,966,461	100

CFANS Campaign Expenditures, 1998

	$ Total Expenditures	% Expenditures
Advertising (TV, Radio and Print)	1,577,882	51
Paid Employers including Consultants	678,508	22
General Campaign Materials (Buttons, Posters, Signs, etc . . .)	673,236	22
Postage	52,981	2
Other	112,370	4
Totals	3,094,977	100

Appendix 10C

Content Analysis of Newspaper Coverage

To analyze newspaper coverage of Referendum 4A, we conducted a content analysis of all newspaper articles covering the measure that appeared in the state's two largest newspapers, the *Rocky Mountain News* and the *Denver Post,* from January 1, 1998, to November 3, 1998. Each of the 546 articles was coded by source, type, and date. To determine a bias within each article, we used the arguments outlined by both COST and CFANS flyers. When a paragraph in any given article contained an argument by either side, the paragraph was flagged as either favorable or unfavorable toward the stadium. Paragraphs not containing either a CFANS or COST argument were marked unbiased. We counted the number of favorable, unfavorable, and unbiased paragraphs in each article, and if an article had twice as many favorable paragraphs as unfavorable, then the article was coded as supporting the stadium, and vice versa. If an article did not meet the two-to-one criteria, then the article was coded as unbiased.

Appendix 10D

Ciruli Poll Data
Polling Responses on Referendum 4A, October 30, 1998

Definite Support	Somewhat Support	Somewhat Opposed	Definitely Opposed	Don't Know
47%	6%	4%	36%	7%

Why do you support the new Bronco stadium?

Broncos fan/love Broncos	33%
Need a new stadium	28%
Good for economy	15%
Don't lose team	9%
Broncos pay part/good deal	6%
It's a small amount	5%
We did it for baseball	3%
Don't know	2%

Why do you oppose the new Bronco stadium?

Bowlen should pay more/subsidy for Bowlen/Welfare for rich	36%
Other needs more important	19%
Don't need a new stadium	17%
Don't watch/not interested in football	10%
Don't like Bowlen's threats	4%
Don't care if Broncos leave	3%
Can't get tickets	1%
Other	6%
Don't know	3%

Bronco stadium support: Demographics

	Total	Men	Women	Democrat	Republican
Support	53%	58%	49%	51%	57%
Oppose	40%	39%	42%	47%	34%
Don't know	7%	3%	9%	2%	8%

Appendix 10E

Election Day Poll
November 3, 1998

Did you vote for the new stadium?

Support Stadium	Oppose	Don't Know/Didn't Answer
Stadium 57%	39%	4%

Do you consider yourself a fan of the Broncos?

Strong Fan	Moderate Fan	Not a Fan
39%	42%	19%

	Support Stadium	Oppose Stadium	Don't Know/Didn't Answer
Strong Fans	79%	19%	1%
Moderate Fans	67%	32%	1%
Not a Fan	26%	72%	2%

Have you ever been to a Broncos' game at Mile High?

Attended Game	Have not Attended a Game
76%	24%

	Support Stadium	Oppose Stadium	Didn't Answer
Attended Game	70%	28%	2%
Have not Attended	43%	57%	0%

What was your major source of information in making your decision?

Newspaper	30%
Television	23%
Family/Friends	7%
Radio	6%
City Voting Guide	4%
Another Voting Guide	2%
Other	27%

Appendix 10E (*continued*)

How did you vote, given your major source of information?

	Support Stadium	Oppose Stadium	Didn't Answer
Newspaper	57%	43%	0%
Television	69%	29%	2%
Family/Friends	90%	10%	0%
Radio	70%	30%	0%
City Voting Guide	57%	43%	0%
Other Voting Guide	50%	50%	0%
Other	67%	33%	0%

What was your major reason for voting for the stadium tax?

Keeping Denver a Special Place/ 1st Tier City	27%
Economic Benefits	24%
Prevent the Broncos from Leaving	18%
Broncos fan	10%
Other	21%

What was your major reason for voting against the stadium tax?

Bad Deal for Metro District	32%
Don't like Taxes	27%
Too Costly	8%
Dislike Pat Bowlen	4%
Dislike Broncos	0%
Other	29%

References

Adams, Samuel. 1994. Bowlen unhappy with Mile High. *Denver Post*, 16 February.

Baade, Robert A. 1996. Stadium subsidies make little economic sense for cities, a rejoinder. *Journal of Urban Affairs* 18.

Bowler, Shaun, and Todd Donovan. 1998. *Demanding choices: Opinion, voting, and direct democracy.* Ann Arbor: University of Michigan Press.

Brown, Fred. 1996. Voters unwilling to shell out for Broncos, Poll: 33% favor stadium tax. *Denver Post*, 8 January.

_____. 1998. Stadium bill stalls in Senate: Sponsor makes plea for 2 votes. *Denver Post*, 24 February.

_____. 1998a. Broncos stadium bill heads back to Senate. *Denver Post*, 25 March.

Brown, Mark. 1998. CFANS. Personal interview. Denver, 12 October.

Burke, Amy. 1997. Skyboxed in. *American Prospect*, September/October.

Burness, Jim. 1998. Personal interview. Denver, 19 October.

Ciruli Associates. 1998. *Final election tracking survey*. Available: <http://www.ciruli.com>.

Citizens for a New Stadium (CFANS). 1998. Flyer. *Stadium benefits*. Denver.

Citizens Opposing the Stadium Tax (COST). 1998. *Pro-stadium myths*. Denver.

Colorado Office of Secretary of State (CSOS). 1998. *Reports for expenditures and contributions for CFANS and COST*. Denver: Colorado Office of Secretary of State. January-December.

_____. 1998a. *Reports on lobbyist income*. Denver: Colorado Office of Secretary of State, January-December.

Conner, Chance. 1995. Mile High Stadium Magazine: Broncos' deal stinks. *Denver Post*, 18 November.

Cronin, Thomas. 1989. *Direct democracy: The politics of initiatives, referendum, and recall*. Cambridge: Harvard University Press.

Danielson, Michael. 1997. *Home team: Professional sports and the American metropolis*. Princeton: Princeton University Press.

Euchner, Charles. 1993. *Playing the field*. Baltimore: John Hopkins University Press.

Fort, Rodney. 1997. Direct democracy and the stadium mess. In *Sports, jobs, and taxes*, edited by Roger Noll and Andrew Zimbalist. Washington: Brookings Institution Press.

Frank, Thomas. 1996. Support for stadium weak. *Denver Post*, 20 February.

Frank, Thomas, and Steve Lipsher. 1996. Stadium now up to voters. *Denver Post*, 9 May.

Garrett, Elizabeth. 1999. Money, agenda setting, and direct democracy. *Texas Law Review* 73:(forthcoming).

Gerber, Elisabeth. 1996. Legislative response to the threat of popular initiatives. *American Journal of Political Science* 40: 99–128.

Henderson, John. 1997. Steelers' stadium flop send ripples to Denver. *Denver Post*, 6 December.

Hodges, Arthur. 1996. New stadium vote gets council's OK: Lukewarm support could hurt Broncos' chances in the legislature. *Denver Post*, 5 March.

_____. 1996a. Group to fight tax for new stadium. *Denver Post*, 3 August.

Hodges, Arthur, and Christopher Lopez. 1996. Webb stays neutral on field tax. *Denver Post*, 26 January.

Hutchinson, Paul. 1995. Broncos dream of stadium: Rockies string of broken promises chills chances. *Denver Post*, 3 January.

Hutchinson, Paul, and Christopher Lopez. 1994. Broncos kick around stadium plan. *Denver Post*, 29 April.

Imse, Ann. 1998. Broncos gain $36 million: New television pacts bring dollar deluge, but team still expects taxes to build new stadium. *Rocky Mountain News*, 14 January.

_____. 1998a. Bowlen says cash paid off in votes. *Rocky Mountain News*, 5 November.

Katz, Alan, and Alan Snel. 1997. Webb backs bulldozing McNichols, Mile High revamp, sites at Stapleton too costly. *Denver Post*, 28 May.

Keating, Raymond J. 1996. Pitching socialism. *National Review*, 22 April.

Latimer, Clay. 1999. Broncos, Avs hit fans with hikes. *Rocky Mountain News*, 20 February.

Lascher, Edward, Michael Hagen, and Steven Rochlin. 1996. Gun behind the door? Ballot initiatives, state policies and public opinion. *Journal of Politics* 58: 760–75.

Leid, Kelly. 1998. Personal interview. Denver, 5 October.

Lindblom, Charles E. 1977. *Politics and markets: The world's political economic systems*. New York: Basic Books.

Lipsher, Steve. 1996. Broncos unveil new sales-tax strategy. *Denver Post*, 10 April.

_____. 1996a. Bowlen booed as no-show at hearing on stadium plan. *Denver Post*, 25 April.

————. 1996b. New Stadium called a sucker bet for fans. *Denver Post*, 26 April.

Lipsher, Steve, and Thomas Frank. 1996. Stadium plan squeaks along. *Denver Post*, 7 May.

Lopez, Christopher. 1994. Stadium study planned: Broncos, city want facts on Mile High's health. *Denver Post*, 11 February.

————. 1994a. Taxpayers would spurn stadiums. *Denver Post*, 20 July.

————. 1994b. New stadium cheaper in the long run. *Denver Post*, 22 July.

————. 1994c. Webb stiff-arms arena deals: No bonds or taxes for new facilities. *Denver Post*, 2 August.

————. 1994d. Broncos outline proposal for new stadium. *Denver Post*, 21 December.

————. 1995. Broncos 'blitz' on stadium: Game plan revealed on Mile High Status. *Denver Post*, 7 September.

————. 1996. Broncos rush legislature. *Denver Post*, 19 January.

————. 1996a. Broncos offer to pay 25%: Team details stadium plans. *Denver Post*, 8 February.

————. 1996b. Webb OK's Broncos' bid: Stadium plan moves to legislature. *Denver Post*, 14 February.

————. 1996c. Broncos' vote strategist scored on Coors, DIA. *Denver Post*, 12, May.

————. 1996d. Stadium board's unisex makeup triggers wrath. *Denver Post*, 20 July.

Lowe, Peggy. 1998. Stadium decision postponed. *Denver Post*, 21 February.

————. 1998a. Two moderate Democrats provide winning play for stadium subsidy. *Denver Post*, 25 February.

————. 1998b. Stadium foes ready to take on Goliath. *Denver Post*, 16 March.

————. 1998c. Stadium bill adds two cash cows. *Denver Post*, 24 March.

————. 1998d. Stadium teems with lobbyists. *Denver Post*, 5 April.

————. 1998e. Stadium district expands: Committee votes to include mall. *Denver Post*, 17 April.

————. 1998f. House taps Park Meadows: Mall added to stadium tax district plan. *Denver Post*, 21 April.

————. 1998g. Stadium bill goes to governor. *Denver Post*, 22 April.

_____. 1998h. Romer quickly signs stadium bill. *Denver Post*, 23 April.

_____. 1998i. Stadium campaigns get an early kickoff. *Denver Post*, 13 May.

_____. 1998j. Stadium fans get airtime: Jacor radio hosts back Broncos' cause. *Denver Post*, 2 August.

_____. 1998k. Stadium ads to air. *Denver Post*, 3 October.

_____. 1998l. Stadium backers court female vote. *Denver Post*, 14 October.

Lowe, Peggy, and Julia Martinez. 1998. Stadium issue nearly ready for vote: Backers gather more than enough signatures. *Denver Post*, 1 September.

Martinez, Julia C. 1998. Bowlen scores stadium control. *Denver Post*, 2 September.

_____. 1998a. Broncos, city plan a trade: Team to swap vow to stay for $1 site. *Denver Post*, 4 August.

_____. 1998b. Broncos score with city council: Approval of stadium bills paves way for new lease. *Denver Post*, 25 August.

Noll, Roger G., and Andrew Zimbalist, ed. 1997. *Sports, jobs, and taxes*. Washington: Brookings Institute Press.

Obmascik, Mark. 1998. Stadium ads fumble ball on both sides of the line. *Denver Post*, 28 October.

_____. 1997. Poll on Mile High has 61 percent favoring renovation of stadium. *Denver Post*, 21 February.

Rafool, Mandy. 1997. Playing the stadium game. *Legislative Finance Paper*. March.

Rosen, Mike. 1998. Stadium naysayers line up. *Denver Post*, 9 January.

Rosentraub, Mark. 1997. *Major league losers*. New York: Basic Books.

Schefter, Adam. 1998. Bowlen won't raise ticket prices in '98: Owner says move isn't political one. *Denver Post*, 10 March.

Simonich, Milan, and Dan Pacheco. 1994. NFL stadiums. *Denver Post*, 14 August.

Sinisi, J. Sebastian. 1997. Stadium designer sees beauty in refurbishing. *Denver Post*, 8 June.

Smith, Daniel A. 1998. *Tax crusaders and the politics of direct democracy*. New York: Routledge.

Snel, Alan. 1996. Stadium board background alarms some, five members have land-development ties. *Denver Post*, 8 September.

_____. 1996a. Stadium panel to hear from the top NFL chief, owner to push for new Bronco venue. *Denver Post*, 23 October.

_____. 1996b. Board takes first stadium tour; members' reactions mixed. *Denver Post*, 26 October.

_____. 1996c. Stadium board goes to work: Sit, financing steps taken in bid for new Broncos field. *Denver Post*, 21 November.

_____. 1997. Stadium finance lesson: Firms outline funding options. *Denver Post*, 17 January.

_____. 1997a. Plan 'tops' Mile High, architect sees new structure encasing the old. *Denver Post*, 20 February.

_____. 1997b. Stadium remodeler is driven, Ohlson aims to finish job his uncle started. *Denver Post*, 16 March.

_____. 1997c. Broncos enter heated debate over stadium. *Denver Post*, 21 March.

_____. 1997d. Stadium panel to hire architect to study sites. *Denver Post*, 5 April.

_____. 1997e. Denver council gets estimates on Mile High: Up to $211 million needed for renovation, designer says. *Denver Post*, 2 June.

_____. 1997f. Stadium-vote timing: Election to be in May or Nov. 1998. *Denver Post*, 31 July.

_____. 1997g. Mile High not worth renovating, Webb says. *Denver Post*, 20 August.

_____. 1997h. Board opts for new stadium: Proposal to rehab Mile High fails to gain support. *Denver Post*, 22 August.

_____. 1997i. No charge for Webb to watch Broncos: Mayor denies stadium discussed with owner. *Denver Post*, 8 October.

_____. 1998 If he can't sell voters, he'll sell team: Let new owner move Broncos, Bowlen says. *Denver Post*, 2 January.

_____. 1998a. Stadium vote must wait: Senate also hikes tab for public. *Denver Post*, 12 February.

_____. 1998b. Football stadium board picks contractor. *Denver Post*, 20 February.

_____. 1998c. Local team wins stadium design pact: City had sued firm over DIA. *Denver Post*, 22 February.

Swindell, David, and Mark Rosentraub. 1998. Who benefits from the presence of professional sports teams? The implications for public

funding of stadiums and arenas. *Public Administration Review*,
January/February.

Wharton, Porter III. 1998. Personal interview. Denver, 28 September.

Zimbalist, Andrew. 1998. The economics of stadiums, teams and cities.
Policy Studies Review 15.

PART IV

Ballot Access, Initiative Reform, and the Question of Representation in the "Parallel Legislature"

CHAPTER 11

Direct Democracy in the Twenty-First Century: Likely Trends and Directions

M. Dane Waters, Initiative and Referendum Institute
and
David McCuan, Sonoma State University

The battle between the citizens who want a direct voice in the lawmaking process and politicians who are unwilling to share the power of government is an age-old struggle. This conflict has never been more evident than in the twenty-four states and thousands of cities across the United States where citizens have the ability to place laws directly on the ballot through the initiative process.

Since the first statewide initiative appeared on the ballot in 1904, academics have been debating the merits of such a process. Research abounds on this topic with most of it being written since the 1990s—the peak usage period of the initiative. However, most of this research, though extremely valuable to individuals interested in learning about the initiative process, has centered only on statewide initiatives and in high usage states like California and Oregon. Though this research has definite value, it has skewed the perception of the initiative process and has not painted an accurate picture of the initiative process all across the country. Fortunately, younger scholars are building upon the current research and are now taking a closer look at low usage states—like Idaho, Michigan, Ohio, North Dakota, South Carolina, Utah, and Montana—as well as looking past statewide initiatives and taking a closer look at how ballot measures have impacted the citizens at the local level. The differences between high-use and low-use initiative traditions, as well as between high-profile and low-profile ballot measures, are instructive about the state of initiative affairs in this country. This research is critical in creating a true and accurate picture of the initiative and referendum process in its entirety rather than giving the citizens only a small sampling of information.

But the following questions arise: What have we already learned? More specifically, based on existing research, what is the future of the initiative and referendum process? Finally, what are the likely trends and directions for state and local ballot measures that will be the basis for future research?

As we have read throughout this book, the initiative and referendum process has been a critical part of our lives for over a century. Almost every American has been impacted by an initiative or referendum on the ballot. Because of ballot measures, women have the right to vote; property owners have seen their property taxes reduced; union members have gained important bargaining rights; sports fans get the opportunity to see their favorite teams in new stadiums; lawmakers get to end their careers early because of term limits: and hunters are limited in what they can shoot and kill. Rich people, poor people, and the middle class have all been affected by ballot measures—no one is immune from them. Indeed, the process has become so pervasive that some argue it is has become a "parallel legislature" (McCuan 2002).

Some have argued that this method of lawmaking is an affront to our Founding Fathers, while others see it as nothing more than an extension of the principles of self-government that our nation was founded upon. But regardless of which school of thought each of us subscribes to, the initiative and referendum process is a fundamental part of our everyday existence.

Unfortunately, the process has become its own worst enemy. Not only will this chapter discuss the future trends of how the initiative process will be used in the twenty-first century, but it will also discuss the process itself and, in particular, how the use of the process has led to calls to limit it. We will examine recent trends from the 2000 and 2002 elections, while proffering some directions for 2004.

However, before we can undertake the discussion of the process's future, we must take a quick look at its past in order to have an appreciation of its future. As Plato said, "Past is Prologue."

"Past is Prologue"

Since the first statewide initiative on Oregon's ballot in 1904, citizens in the twenty-four states with the initiative process have placed approximately 1,987 statewide measures on the ballot and have adopted only 821 (41 percent). Even though the twenty-four states have some form of statewide initiative, almost

60 percent of all initiative activity has taken place in just five states—Oregon, California, Colorado, North Dakota, and Arizona. In 1996, considered by many to be the "high water mark" for the initiative process, citizens placed 102 initiatives on statewide ballots and adopted 45 (44 percent). In contrast, the state legislatures that same year in those same twenty-four states adopted over 17,000 laws.

Since the first statewide initiative, the initiative process in the United States has been through periods of tremendous use as well as periods in which it was rarely utilized. From 1904 to 1976, the use of the initiative steadily declined from its peak of 291 from 1911 through 1920 to its low of 78 in 1961–1970. Many factors contributed to this decline, but the distraction of two world wars, the Great Depression, and the Korean War is largely responsible. In California alone, from 1950 to 1960, as the practice of cross-filing disappeared during elections, the state witnessed just 14 measures submitted for Title and Summary, with 11 of these measures qualifying through the petition process. Only a single measure was passed which that decade put on the ballot through the petition process. However, in 1978, with the passage of California's Proposition 13 (an initiative that cut state property taxes by nearly 60 percent), initiative entrepreneurs, activists, and interest groups began to realize the power of the initiative process once again, and its use began to climb. Since 1978, the two most prolific decades of initiative use have occurred: 1981–1990 (with 289 initiatives) and 1991–2000 (with approximately 396).

However, contrary to conventional wisdom, since 1996 the number of initiatives actually making the ballot seems to be decreasing. In 1998, only 66 initiatives actually made the ballot—the lowest in a decade. In 2000, a total of 76 initiatives found their way to statewide ballots. Though more than 1998, this number is still off the pace of the past two decades. As recently as 2002, this trend accelerated upward, with 202 statewide ballot measures in forty states.[1] Of these measures, 149 were legislatively referred measures, while 53 were placed on the ballot through the petition process. Voters passed almost half of those measures placed on the ballot through popular petition (47 percent). This percentage is somewhat high historically, since the average is about 41 percent. Measures referred from state legislatures continue to be passed at higher rates—a historical trend—with almost two-thirds (66 percent) passing in 2000. In 2003 (odd-year elections are historically light on the number

---

1. While twenty-four states have the statewide initiative process, all fifty states have the legislative referendum process.

of statewide ballot measures), voters decided on 22 statewide ballot measures in eight states. Voters passed 14 of these measures (64 percent). However, while 2003 was a "light year," typical of odd-year electoral trends, the recall of Governor Gray Davis and his replacement by bodybuilder/actor-turned-politician Arnold Schwarzenegger dominated the domestic political scene throughout the summer and fall.

The use of the ballot to deal with important issues is far more prolific at the local level than at the state level. As discussed in the introduction, ballot measures at the local level have been a highly overlooked area of study. Fortunately, this seems to be changing as a younger generation of academics take a closer look at how local ballots are utilized. Moreover, as states and localities struggle with balancing quality of life issues such as growth and development alongside revenue generation, including taxing and spending within local communities, local ballot measures will continue to be the battleground. Cities throughout the nation, for example, are struggling with issues around fiscal governance and values in their communities. Local governments find themselves asking whether building residences or commercial development is a drain on local coffers. Additionally, as conditions of fiscal stress percolate from states down to local authorities, municipalities find themselves casting about for avenues to generate revenue. These issues increasingly spill over into the arena of local direct democracy.

Though much of the research on local ballot measures is still in its infancy and deserving fuller attention, it seems from an initial review that the local process is being used extensively on issues that impact the daily lives of the citizens. Issues concerning zoning, taxes, education, and the environment seem to be the most prevalent.

But what are the issues at the statewide level that the citizens have been addressing? And have these issues set trends for future initiative usage?

In one recent election, November 2000, the voters in seventeen states spoke out on 72 statewide initiatives dealing with some of the most emotional and controversial issues—abortion, drugs, gay rights, taxes, animal welfare, education, and the environment. The voters adopted 35 of them—48 percent. The overriding theme of the election when discussing initiative results is that the voters were cautious. The citizens voted down almost every measure that could be labeled "progressive," "far-reaching," or even "radical." Don't get us wrong: There were definitely big winners and losers, and the voters did pass a few measures whose impact will be long lasting. But, overall, voters chose to take a very cautious and moderate approach to reform. This has been the case for the last several election periods (including 2000 and 2002) and is likely to remain so. Let's take a closer look at recent election results, at how the top issues fared, and what that means for future ballots.

Animal Protection: Initiatives dealing with animal protection were voted on in Massachusetts (banning dog racing), Montana (banning game farms), Oregon (banning traps and poisons) and Washington state (banning traps and poisons). Additionally, there was a popular referendum on the Alaska ballot concerning the legislature's attempt to allow hunters to use airplanes to land and shoot wolves on the same day they fly. The animal protection movement had an impressive win record with initiatives—primarily because of the support of the Humane Society of the United States and their growing knowledge and expertise in using the initiative process to accomplish their reform. This election cycle saw a continuation of that winning streak, though it was not as "perfect" as in previous elections. The animal protection movement won in Alaska, Montana, and Washington state but lost in Massachusetts and Oregon.

The animal protection movement has prided itself on using the initiative process at an increasing pace from election year to election year. However, after the 2004 cycle, we believe that the animal protection movement will return strongly with numerous ballot measures across the country, after having opted in 2002 to lessen the number of initiatives placed on the ballot in order to devote more resources to candidate campaigns.

Drug Policy Reform: The biggest recent "winner" in direct democracy occurred in November 2000 in the drug policy reform movement. The medical marijuana movement, supported by George Soros and friends and that dominated statewide ballots in 1998, was back. But with the exception of the medical marijuana initiatives that were voted on in Colorado and Nevada on November 7, drug policy reformers changed their focus to reforming asset forfeiture laws and how nonviolent drug offenders are sentenced. Initiatives dealing with these issues were voted on in California, Massachusetts, Oregon, and Utah. The reformers won in California (drug treatment), Colorado (medical marijuana), Utah (asset forfeiture reform), Oregon (asset forfeiture reform), and Nevada (medical marijuana). Their only defeat occurred in Massachusetts (drug treatment). The legalizing of marijuana for recreational use, which was not part of the drug policy reform efforts sponsored by George Soros, was defeated in Alaska.

There is no doubt that this movement will be around in 2004 and beyond. The movement is not as likely to have as many initiatives on the ballot as in previous years because it focused on some of the larger states in 2002—like Florida, Michigan, and Ohio. The ultimate goal is to create a groundswell of popular support for drug reform that can then be used to push Congress to take a new look at the nation's drug laws.

Education Reform: School choice advocates had hoped that this would be the year of redemption for them at the ballot box. There has never been a successful school choice initiative primarily because of the tremendous amount of time, energy, and money the teachers unions have spent against these measures. This year proved no different. The anticipated "Goliath versus Goliath" fights—pitting the millions of dollars of the unions against the increasingly well-heeled supporters of school choice initiatives (like billionaire Tim Draper of California, Microsoft billionaire Paul Allen in Washington state, and Amway founders Betsy and Dick DeVos in Michigan)—were exactly those kinds of fights. The campaigns of these three measures accounted for almost 50 percent of all the money spent pro/con on initiatives this election cycle—around $100 million. Indeed, in California's one recent special initiative election (not including the state's recent recall of incumbent Democratic Governor Gray Davis), Proposition 174 (1993) witnessed forty-five ballot measure committees opposed to the measure who raised almost $25 million dollars to successfully defeat that proposition (McCuan 2002).

These losses, coupled with victories in California (lowering the threshold for passing local school bonds), in Colorado (increased funding for public education), in Oregon (increased funding for public education), and in Washington state (increased teacher's pay and class size reduction), constituted a good year for the advocates of additional funding for public education.

In the aftermath of electoral defeat in 2000 and 2002, the school choice movement was declared "dead" at the ballot box. However, new groups are said to be considering initiatives for the sole purpose of pushing school choice initiatives again at the ballot box. On the other side of the aisle, the teachers unions are trying to figure out what to do with the millions of dollars they are collecting in their initiative fund. As many of the readers of this article may remember, the teachers unions increased each member's dues by $5.00 in order to create a fund to fight "antipublic education" initiatives in 2000. The increase is scheduled to continue for a few years, and many unions are trying to decide whether to put that money into new initiatives of their own or save it to fight initiatives they do not like. In any case, we believe that there will be several education-related initiatives floating around in the next several election cycles, including 2004, but spreading to other battleground states.

Guns: The NRA was largely silent during the 2000 election cycle concerning regulations on guns. Gun control advocates won big victories in Colorado and Oregon on measures requiring that persons purchasing guns at gun shows be subject to background checks.

These victories have emboldened the advocates of gun control and will no doubt lead to other gun control measures in the very near future. However, there is little doubt that the NRA and other gun owner groups will continue to fight these initiatives, opposing ballot measures after battles are fought in the legislative arena.

Health Care Reform: Many people have placed the defeat of universal health care in Massachusetts as a big blow to the health care reform movement, but in reality it was a victory for it. The mere fact that the measure was on the ballot served as the 800-pound gorilla that prompted the state legislature to pass a watered-down version of the measure. That the legislature was prompted to act in Massachusetts has spurned activists in other states to push for health care reform in the hope that the legislature's action would prompt legislators in other states to enact similar legislation.

Physician-Assisted Suicide: This issue has had its ups and downs at the ballot box—big victories in Oregon and a devastating loss in Michigan in 1998. It looks as though advocates in this policy area have been dealt another blow. Voters in Maine chose not to adopt their proposed death-with-dignity law. While not down for the count, the movement is examining alternate venues, including traditional legislative channels, for policy adoption.

Same-Sex Marriage/Gay Rights: The ban on same-sex marriages is *the new trend* to watch at the ballot box. The issue was first tested in Hawaii and in Alaska in 1998, and in California in March 2000. From these victories, the proponents of this ban moved inland, placing the issue on ballots in Nebraska and Nevada, where the measure passed handily, giving rise to the possibility that this ban is here to stay. With these two victories and the failure of a measure in Maine prohibiting discrimination based on sexual orientation, 2002 was not a good year for gay-rights advocates.

There is little doubt that the movement to ban same-sex marriage will continue to be fought in state legislatures and at the ballot box. The measure that was adopted in Nevada was up again for voters to examine in 2002. In the 2004 electoral cycle, the use of gay and lesbian marriage as a "wedge issue" in states such as Pennsylvania and Michigan plays an important role in drawing voters to the polls. However, it is hard to say how opponents of same sex-marriage fare when placed head-to-head with pocketbook issues, such as jobs and the state of the economy. In five states (Georgia, Kentucky, Mississippi, Oklahoma, and Utah), measures were placed on the fall 2004 ballot seeking to ban same sex-marriages in these states' constitutions. In at least eight other states, opponents of same-sex marriage were mobilized to gather enough signatures to place a similar constitutional ban before state voters. These states included Arkansas, Montana, Ohio, and Oregon. Actions in state legislatures to place constitutional amendments banning same-sex marriage before voters have been taking place in more than a dozen other states, principally in the South and Midwest. If one were to examine a map of the United States, however, activists on both sides of this issue throughout the country have been participating in both the legislative arena and the "parallel legislature" of direct democracy, seeking to get this issue before voters. The issue seems to have spilled over, like the tax reform movement of the late 1970s, across the nation, reverberating both in state capitals and down to local communities. Indeed, after November 2004 when all 11 measures appearing on state ballots passed, the issue of banning same sex marriage appears likely to be on ballots in the next electoral cycle.

Taxes: Tax reform has recently had a mixed bag of results as well. As we all know, this reform has been an issue on the ballot since the initiative process was first established, but its dominance has grown since 1978's Proposition 13 in California. Tax cutters suffered some big defeats with voters in Alaska (property tax relief), in Colorado (lower taxes on certain items), and in Oregon (allowing for the full deduction of federal income taxes from one's state taxes) choosing not to vote in favor of these changes. However, these losses were offset by big victories in Massachusetts (reducing income taxes), in South Dakota (abolishing the inheritance tax), and in Washington state (declaring null and void certain tax or fee increases adopted without voter approval by state and local governments).

Regardless of these outcomes and continued fiscal strife in states and localities across the country, the tax revolt is here to stay and will almost certainly be a permanent fixture on state ballots. Questions remain about the types of measures placed before the voters and in what states/localities these measures will appear on the ballot. Much depends on the future of the economy. Tax activists are waiting to see what happens concerning the economy, as well as how competitive the 2004 presidential race shapes up, before acting in any substantial way. However, there has already been serious talk among some tax groups to push for replacing state income taxes with a universal sales tax in the hope of turning this mandate into ammunition to push Congress to adopt such a change.

Additionally, there has been a lot of talk about what to do with all the tobacco settlement money that numerous states are receiving. This last election saw numerous initiatives—as well as legislatively referred measures—that allocated the tobacco money in various ways. With most of these payoffs due to take place over twenty years, many people who want either to cut taxes or to increase spending in certain areas will be looking at the tobacco money as a clear target to accomplish their goals of either reducing the size of government or increasing it.

Bilingual Education: Arizonans voted overwhelmingly to eliminate bilingual education in their state. This strong showing, coupled with all the positive reports associated with the passage of a similar measure in California and the impact it has had on education in that state, has given rise to the strong prospect that this reform will be voted on in future elections. The chief architect of this movement, Ron Unz, has been seriously eyeing certain high-profile states, like Florida and Colorado, for 2004 and beyond. Unz also gave serious thought to putting the issue before the voters of New York City back in 2002.

Environmental Reform: Environmental initiatives took a beating in 2000, with defeats in Colorado (growth limitations), in Arizona (growth limitations), in Maine (clear cutting), and in Missouri (banning billboards). Their only major victory seems to have occurred in Florida with the passage of the initiative creating a statewide high-speed rail system. However, legislative referenda dealing with increased funding for environmental and conservation efforts seem to have done well—as they do in most election cycles.

Even though these initiative defeats may give pause to environmental reformers, there is no doubt that this type of measure will be a frequent visitor to a ballot near you. However, it is likely that this movement may move toward using the local initiative process in greater numbers than statewide initiatives. Environmental reformers at the local level made similar attempts in the early 1980s with Nuclear Free Zones (NFZs)—primarily because most zoning laws are created by local governments and should be changed by local initiatives. Additionally, this local zoning law requirement may allow environmental reformers to focus their efforts on specific voting blocs that might be receptive to their measures rather than trying to convince an entire state to adopt a reform that only affects certain large cities and counties.

Campaign Finance Reform: In a surprise development, both campaign finance reform measures that appeared on the 2000 ballot were defeated overwhelmingly—one in Missouri and one in Oregon. It is hard to say exactly what these defeats mean to the reform movement, but after big victories in 1998, they will almost certainly slow some of the movement's momentum. However, much depends on the Supreme Court's treatment of the *McCain-Feingold* legislation. This issue seems to crop up time and again at the local level, and the applicability of *McCain-Feingold* to some arenas could reinvigorate efforts at the state level and prompt more initiatives and regulation in campaign finance reform.

Term Limits: One of the most successful movements using the initiative process put another measure in the win column in 2000. Nebraska became the nineteenth state to impose term limits on their state lawmakers. There are only two other states where term-limit laws concerning state legislators can theoretically be imposed using the initiative process—North Dakota and Mississippi—though it is doubtful that such an initiative will be placed on their ballots in 2001 or 2002. That 2002 was the first election cycle since 1988 without a term-limit initiative appearing on a statewide ballot is a testament to the current status of the movement.

Tort Reform: Tort reform did not appear on any statewide ballots in 2000 or in 2002, but there has been talk of numerous initiatives across the country dealing with this issue in 2004.

Based on the above analyses and on conversations with initiative activists, we believe that between 50 and 70 statewide initiatives will appear on the 2004 ballot—a continuation of the downward trend at the statewide level. At the local level, we expect the number of initiatives to be reduced as well, though not as drastically as at the state level primarily because local officials have not raised the bar for using the initiative process as drastically as state lawmakers have. Activity at the local level will continue, though, to be a function of the fiscal stress that cities and citizens may feel, based on the federal and state budget pictures, economic growth, and salient local issues like development.

Most of the initiatives that will be making their way to future ballots will most likely be those that have the backing of national groups providing the primary funding for them. As with previous elections over the last decade, fewer and fewer initiatives that are the product of one individual's vision within the state are making it to the ballot. Instead, more and more often, the initiatives appearing on state ballots reflect the visions of national interest groups that wish to place their reforms on state ballots all over the country as a way to increase the national debate on their issues and in hope of pushing Congress to adopt their reforms—be they term limits, drug policy reform, campaign finance reform, animal protection, or tax reform. But what is the reason for this trend? Is this recent "activism" a product of larger trends based on how the initiative process works in practice?

The Regulation of the Process
and Its Impact on Future Usage

Since 1990, states have increasingly regulated and restricted the use of the initiative process. These regulations have included raising signature requirements, limiting who can circulate petitions, shortening the circulation period, increasing the distribution requirement for signatures, and limiting access to places for collecting signatures. These regulations and restrictions have placed the initiative process out of the reach of the average citizen and have made the process only accessible to groups and individuals with access to money. This has forced citizens in the various states who seek reform to reach out to national groups for financial and organizational support.

New regulations have raised the cost of using the initiative process astronomically, and there is every indication that state legislators are only going to continue that trend. This means that more and more money will be ending up in the initiative process because no matter how many hurdles are placed to obstruct the process, those with access to money will be able to use the process and the everyday citizen will not. This is where "initiative entrepreneurs" and the "initiative industry" comes in (as discussed by David McCuan in Chapter 3 of this book). Initiative proponents have to seek the help of attorneys, paid signature gatherers, political consultants, and media consultants in order to jump these hurdles. Such a process takes place earlier and earlier in electoral cycles, making it difficult to predict what ballots will look like and causing the initiative process to become its own "parallel legislature."

One curious development, however, is that state legislators argue that the increasing amount of money in initiative campaigns being paid to the "initiative industry" is the reason for the need to additionally regulate the process— even though their actions are the cause of the increase in the amount of money being spent. Maybe the "initiative industry" should send thank-you notes to the state legislators for helping generate revenue for their businesses. This is certainly how many of the consultants we talk to feel, off the record. However, state legislators must realize that they can never take money out of the initiative process because the courts have consistently ruled that money in initiative campaigns cannot be banned or limited. Therefore, many people believe that state legislators should be finding ways to increase the average citizen's involvement in the initiative process rather than regulating the process to the point that the average citizen is completely excluded. This, in turn, would reduce the need for the initiative industry and would drastically cut its growth. We note that it is no accident that the initiative industry is less involved with initiatives in states where the requirements to use the initiative process are less stringent than in those states where the hurdles and compliance costs are high—including California.

There is no doubt that the initiative process is being utilized more and more by special interest groups—primarily large, national nonprofits with specific national policy goals. But this is nothing new. Since the beginning of the initiative process in 1898, national movements have used the process to accomplish a national agenda. The women's suffrage movement and the movement to require the direct election of U.S. Senators are just two examples of how the initiative process at the state level was used in the early 1900s to accomplish a national reform. The national nonprofits of today are just following in their footsteps. In addition to these nonprofits, for-profit companies are using the process as well. The gambling and insurance industries are perfect examples. Even though they have had mixed success at the ballot box, there is no doubt that they will be back. But is their use of the process a misuse of the process? Many people do not believe so, because for-profit companies, like everyday citizens, have the right to place issues directly before the people to decide when legislators have chosen to ignore them. It only makes sense that any issue that is proper for state legislators to adopt and/or ignore is a proper issue to be placed before the people using the initiative process—regardless of who is funding that effort.

There is also no doubt that legislating by initiative—or the "parallel legislature" track—is here to stay. Based on the issues noted above and presented throughout this book, the 2004 and even the 2006 election cycles will have numerous initiatives that could potentially have a tremendous impact on our daily lives. These initiatives will be derived from the brains of activists of all political persuasions—from the brains of those that wish to diminish the size of government as well as of those that wish to increase it. Everyone uses political professionals now; everyone begins using them earlier and earlier in the process; and interest groups of all persuasions are in this "parallel game." Regardless of which political party or philosophy is behind these initiatives, two certainties are an increase in the amount of money being spent on initiatives and a decrease in the number of successful initiatives launched by individuals within a state who have no support from individuals or groups outside the state. These certainties will only lead to the proliferation of the initiative industry, which has the expertise necessary to overcome the tremendous obstacles placed on the process. This reality is the result of state legislative action against a process that legislators do not like and/or want. State legislators should listen to the immortal words of William Jennings Bryan, who said in 1920: "[W]e have the initiative and referendum in Nebraska; do not disturb them. If defects are discovered, correct them and perfect the machinery.... [M]ake it possible for the people to have what they want.... [W]e are the world's teacher in democracy; the world looks to us for an example. We cannot ask others to trust the people unless we are ourselves willing to trust them." This statement is truer today than it was eighty years ago.

Conclusion

As this chapter has discussed, the future of the initiative and referendum process in the twenty-first century is unclear regarding its content but crystal clear regarding its implications. A key variable, however, to the future of the process is simply predicated on how far lawmakers are willing to go to try to hinder the use of the process through increased regulation. Moreover, the process continues to spill over to increased activism at the local level, with issues such as same sex marriage blossoming into national movements among interest groups on both sides of the issue. Much like the property tax reform movement of the late 1970s and the term limits movement of the late 1980s, the issue of same-sex marriage has the potential to dominate activities at the ballot box beyond just the direct legislation traditions of the twenty-four states with the initiative process.

Whether or not this increased regulation of the process is a good thing is up to the individual, but the impact of the regulation is undeniable. Only those with access to money and resources can utilize the initiative process. Those groups with limited resources will be shut out, just as they are shut out of the normal legislative process. Academics and books such as this can help us understand the implications of regulations and the costs of compliance, and can encourage further disclosure in order for all citizens to make more informed choices.

Money and its incumbent condition of resource allocation have become an unfortunate by-product or necessity for citizens and groups wishing to utilize the tools of the direct-democracy process. Research shows that money is critical in helping overcome the new regulations and restrictions being placed on the process (Bowler, Donovan, and Tolbert 1998; Donovan, Bowler, and McCuan 2001). This use of campaign resources, including access to dollars, now defines the process for all citizens and groups in order to be successful at all levels of the parallel legislature.

The number of initiatives making the ballot will, in our opinion, be reduced over the coming years from the historical highs of the last two decades.

Those issues that do make the ballot will be consistent with issues that have appeared on previous election ballots. In short, the issues citizens will be voting on will be the same—fiscal as well as social (or values) issues. Though some of the issues each may have a different nuance here and there, the issues in principle will be the same. But what about the players—the people who put issues on the ballot? For the most part, the players will remain the same as well—not because other groups and individuals do not want to jump into the fray, but because only the individuals and groups who know how to jump the hurdles and who have access to money can utilize the process. Does this fact violate the belief of purists that the initiative and referendum should be a tool of the average citizen and not of individuals and groups with money? Yes. But the fact is an unfortunate reality whose blame can be laid clearly at the doorstep of state legislators who are afraid of the process and, by extension, who are afraid of the people making laws. As has been discussed, the initiative and referendum process is not a tool to replace representative government, but only a complement to it. This fact state legislators are choosing to ignore.

As we enter the twenty-first century and the use of the initiative process continues, the battle between the citizens who want a direct voice in the lawmaking process and the politicians who are unwilling to share the power of government will continue. As of now, such politicians seem to be winning. They seem to be accomplishing their goal of reducing the number of ballot measures, but they have not been able to stop the flow of money into the process—a battle that they cannot and will not win.

We have just completed a century of citizen lawmaking. The only question for the next century is not whether important social and fiscal issues will appear on the ballots at the state and local level, but whether or not the divide between the government and the people will continue to grow regarding citizen lawmaking. It clearly takes many resources beyond just dollars to compete in the parallel legislature game. In the next century of citizen lawmaking, questions about "access" and the "process of the parallel legislature" will come to dominate the agenda as much as the policy questions placed before the voters.

References

Donovan, Todd, Shaun Bowler, and Caroline Tolbert, eds. 1998. *Citizens as legislators: Direct democracy in the United States.* Columbus, OH: Ohio State University Press.

Donovan, Todd, Shaun Bowler, and David McCuan. 2001. Political consultants and the initiative industrial complex. In *Dangerous democracy?: The battle over ballot initiatives in America,* edited by L. J. Sabato, H. R. Ernst, and B. A. Larson, 101–34. Lanham, MD: Rowman & Littlefield, 2001.

McCuan, David. 2002. *Grassroots democracy and the initiative wars: The professionalization of direct democracy in California.* Ph.D. diss., University of California, Riverside.

CONTRIBUTORS

Shaun Bowler, University of California-Riverside (Ph.D., Washington University)

Shaun Bowler is Professor of Political Science and is well published in the fields of direct democracy, state politics, voter behavior, and third-party politics. His research has appeared in numerous journals including the *American Political Science Review, American Journal of Political Science, Journal of Politics, State Politics and Policy Quarterly,* and *American Politics Quarterly.* He has published two books in the area of direct democracy: *Demanding Choices: Opinion Voting and Direct Democracy,* with Todd Donovan (Ann Arbor: University of Michigan Press, 1998), and *Citizens as Legislators,* with Todd Donovan and Caroline Tolbert (Columbus: Ohio State University Press, 1998).

Richard Braunstein, University of South Dakota (Ph.D., University of Colorado-Boulder)

Richard Braunstein is Assistant Professor with a joint appointment in the Department of Political Science and the W. O. Farber Center for Civic Leadership. He is also the founder and executive director of CIVIC, a nonprofit organization dedicated to providing citizens with access to a wide range of public voter information. His research interests include institutions, democratic theory and practice, as well as citizen and organized group behavior.

Clyde Brown, Miami University (Ph.D., University of Iowa)

Clyde Brown is Professor in the Department of Political Science and the author of many articles and works in the fields of American politics, state and local politics, and campaigns and elections. His primary teaching responsibilities are in the area of American government and Research Methods. His specific interests include the role of organized interests in political life, applied politics, including campaigns and elections, and methods of political analysis.

Todd Donovan, Western Washington University (Ph.D., University of California-Riverside)

Todd Donovan is Professor of Political Science in the Department of Political Science and has published extensively in the fields of state politics and policy, including the areas of direct democracy, electoral systems and representation, political behavior, and local economic development. His research has appeared in numerous journals, including the *American Journal of Political Science, Journal of Politics, Political Research Quarterly, State Politics and Policy Quarterly*, and *American Politics Quarterly*. He has published many books, including two in the area of direct democracy: *Demanding Choices: Opinion Voting and Direct Democracy*, with Shaun Bowler (Ann Arbor: University of Michigan Press, 1998), and *Citizens as Legislators*, with Shaun Bowler and Caroline Tolbert (Columbus: Ohio State University Press, 1998). He has also published *The Elements of Social Scientific Thinking* (New York: St. Martin's Press, now in its 8th edition).

Linda Lopez, American Political Science Association (Ph.D., University of Southern California)

Linda Lopez is APSA Director of Education and Professional Programs. Her interests are in the areas of Latino/Latina politics, public law, and criminal justice policy. She previously taught at Sonoma State University in the Criminal Justice Department and formerly was director of the Legal Studies program at Chapman University, where she taught courses in public law and researched the role of hate crime legislation and its impacts on minority communities.

David McCuan, Sonoma State University (Ph.D., University of California-Riverside)

David McCuan, Assistant Professor of Political Science and Graduate Coordinator of the MPA program, has interests in the area of American politics, specifically in the subfield of state and local politics. His research and publications concern the general impact of ballot measures or direct democracy on the state of California and across the nation and include chapters in other volumes as well as in peer-reviewed publications. He teaches in the fields of state and local politics, campaigns and elections, and political behavior, with a specific emphasis on direct democracy. He has used his expertise as an elections observer in Africa and formerly taught at California State University-Maritime.

Catherine Nelson, Sonoma State University (Ph.D., University of California-Davis)

Catherine Nelson is an Associate Professor in the Department of Political Science and has interests in the broad area of Political Theory, focusing on the politics of race, gender, and class. She also focuses on the interplay of these forces in the media and its coverage of gender and race. Her research expertise in political philosophy focuses on feminist theory. She has also conducted research on various dimensions of public opinion in times of war, from the Vietnam War to the first Gulf War and the new war on terrorism. Dr. Nelson teaches courses on American National Government, Political Theory, and Ethics. She has presented her research at regional and national conferences and has given commentary in her areas of expertise as a guest lecturer and commentary to the media.

David M. Paul, The Ohio State University-Newark (Ph.D., University of Illinois)

David M. Paul is an Assistant Professor in the Department of Political Science and specializes in direct democracy, campaigns, political parties, voting behavior, interest groups and lobbying. His current research projects include an examination of the power of business groups to influence public policy at the local level; an investigation on the effects of gender on voter turnout; and an analysis of the factors that contribute to the power of ethnic-American groups to influence public policy. He has published articles in *Political Research Quarterly, Social Science Journal,* and *Journal of Sports and Social Issues.*

Dan Smith, University of Florida-Gainesville (Ph.D., University of Wisconsin-Madison)

Dan Smith is an Associate Professor in the Department of Political Science. His research broadly examines the democratic process of American politics, with particular emphasis on institutions and patterns of political participation in the American states. His past research has led to the publication of more than two dozen articles in journals and to the publication of two books, *Tax Crusaders and the Politics of Direct Democracy* (New York: Routledge, 1998), and *Educated by Initiative: The Effects of Direct Democracy on Citizens and Political Organizations in the American States,* with Caroline J. Tolbert (Ann Arbor: University of Michigan Press, 2004). He serves on the Board of Directors of the Ballot Initiative Strategy Center Foundation (BISCF), a non-profit organization based in Washington, D.C. and is a member of the Board of Scholars with the Initiative and Referendum Institute at the University of Southern California.

Mark A. Smith, University of Washington (Ph.D., University of Minnesota)

Mark A. Smith is an Associate Professor in the Department of Political Science and joined UW in 1997. He is a specialist in American politics, with research interests in public opinion, interest groups, political communication, and public policy. His book, *American Business and Political Power: Public Opinion, Elections, and Democracy* (Chicago: University of Chicago Press, 2000) won the 2001 Leon Epstein award for outstanding contribution to the study of political organizations and parties. Smith has published articles in the *American Journal of Political Science* and the *Journal of Politics*. Smith teaches courses on American politics, interest groups, public opinion, and research design.

Stephen Stambough, California State University-Fullerton (Ph.D., University of California-Riverside)

Stephen Stambough is an Assistant Professor in the Department of Political Science and teaches courses in both national and subnational American politics. He has published articles in *Political Research Quarterly, Journal of Politics*, and *Policy Studies Journal*. His current research consists primarily of two aspects of state and local politics—a comparative state case approach to the area of direct democracy and a comprehensive analysis of the role of candidate gender in gubernatorial campaigns. The latter work is being turned into a book-length treatment on the subject.

M. Dane Waters, Founder and President, The Initiative and Referendum Institute

Dane Waters is founder, president, and cochairman of the Initiative and Referendum Institute, a Washington, D.C.-based, nonprofit, educational and research organization dedicated to educating the people on the initiative and referendum process. An expert on the initiative and referendum process, Mr. Waters has lectured extensively throughout the world on governmental and electoral issues and has advised foreign governments on the initiative and referendum process. Mr. Waters has written a monthly column on the initiative process for *Campaigns & Elections* magazine and has served on the board of the Appleseed Foundation's Electoral Reform Project, a joint effort between Harvard Law School and American University to improve American democracy through the reform of national electoral processes. He has a degree in political science from the University of Alabama at Birmingham.

Index

Affirmative action, 36, 107–9, 114, 123, 158, 161, 166–68, 170–83, 185

Alternative Media, 157–58, 161–63, 169

Ballot Access, 4, 6, 52, 78, 257

Bowler, Shaun, 7, 11, 73, 75, 113–17, 240, 250, 272–73, 275–76

Braunstein, Richard, 77, 275

Brown, Clyde, 189, 275

Campaign Finance, 62, 77–97, 104, 107, 109, 115, 195, 198, 208, 267–68

Campaign Spending, 7–8, 53, 69, 75, 77–78, 81–82, 86–87, 90, 92–95, 115, 217, 241

Candidate Attitudes, 9, 12–13, 20, 22

Candidate Campaigns, 35, 51–52, 54, 79, 103, 110, 263, 278

Cincinnati Reds, 195, 200, 202–3

Client Politics, 51, 57, 67–68, 70–71, 190, 207

Courts, 269

Crime, 101, 121–24, 133, 135–37, 141–44, 183, 276

Denver Broncos, 215, 219–25, 228–34, 236, 238, 241–43, 251–55

Donovan, Todd, 7, 11, 73, 75, 113–17, 240, 250, 272–73, 275–76

Electoral Context, 33, 39, 41, 45

Entrepreneurial Politics, 51, 57, 67–68, 70, 73, 114, 190, 209

Ethnicity, 103, 117, 119, 123–24, 126–27, 130, 133–36, 138, 140, 142, 146, 149, 171–72, 178

Ideological Compatibility, 97, 102, 108

Ideology, 30, 124, 128–29, 131–32, 135, 143, 149, 158–61, 163–64, 167–69, 172, 176, 182

Immigrants, 121, 132, 161, 165–66, 174

Initiative and Referendum Institute, 34, 37, 259, 277–78

Interest Group Politics, 51, 56, 67, 70, 190, 207, 209

Interest Groups, 6–7, 9, 17, 47, 51–52, 54–56, 69, 71, 82, 87, 207, 214, 217, 261, 268, 270–71, 277–78

Legislator Attitudes, 9, 22
Local, 5, 32, 59, 62, 121, 124, 127,
    129, 131, 137, 145, 187, 189–94,
    196–97, 200, 203–4, 207–8,
    210–13, 218–19, 236, 243–44,
    255, 259–60, 262, 264, 266–68,
    271–72, 275–78
Lopez, Linda, 121, 276
Los Angeles Literature, 119, 130

Mainstream Media, 157–58,
    161–63, 169–70
Majoritarian, 30–31, 51, 58,
    67–68, 70, 101, 104, 107, 109,
    190, 209
Mayors, 129–130, 189, 192,
    205–206, 212
McCuan, Dave, 3, 51, 73, 75, 114,
    116, 259, 269, 273, 276
Media, 5–6, 25–28, 35, 37, 39, 41,
    46–47, 52–53, 58, 77–79, 96,
    107–8, 157–185, 190, 194, 200,
    208–209, 211–212, 214–217,
    233–238, 240–244, 269, 277
Media Influence, 215, 240–241
Minorities, 5, 119, 123, 128, 131,
    139, 157, 161, 167, 171,
    173–175, 177–180
Minority, 4–5, 29, 33, 48, 52,
    121–124, 127–130, 137–139,
    144, 146–148, 199, 223, 276

Nelson, Catherine, 157, 277

Opinions, 9, 11–14, 16–20, 22–23,
    28, 98, 157, 238, 240

Parallel Legislature, 1, 3–7, 257,
    260, 266, 269–272

Paul, David M., 189, 277
Petitions, 38, 197, 211, 269
Political Parties, 9, 13, 49, 82,
    97–102, 112–113, 126, 205, 209,
    277–278
Political Professionals, 7, 51–52,
    54–56, 67–69, 71–72, 75, 116,
    270
Populism, 32
Professionalization, 51–56, 67–71,
    78, 273
Progressives, 4–5, 18, 32, 53
Proposition 13, 5–6, 37, 39, 42,
    106, 117, 261, 266
Proposition 187, 101, 103–105,
    111, 121, 123, 132
Proposition 209, 5, 36, 101,
    107–108, 111, 157–158,
    161–163, 166–178, 180–181

Race, 23, 30, 41, 43, 46, 103, 117,
    119, 123–124, 126–127,
    130–136, 138, 140, 142–143,
    145–146, 148–149, 157–185,
    192, 208, 266, 277
Referenda, 4, 33–35, 37–38, 40, 80,
    189, 210, 213, 267
Referendum, 6–8, 34, 37, 49, 62,
    73, 75, 77, 80, 95–96, 98,
    106–7, 113–14, 116, 146,
    189–214, 217, 224–25, 227, 231,
    233, 236, 239–42, 244, 247–248,
    251, 259–61, 263, 271–72,
    277–78
Reform, 5–6, 18–20, 22, 28,
    30–31, 48, 67, 81, 101, 106, 108,
    112, 116, 148, 166, 183, 209,
    257, 262–71, 278

Reforms, 1, 3–8, 26, 28–29, 33, 98–100, 268
Regulation of the Process, 257, 268–69, 271
Representation, 4, 12, 30, 128, 160, 162, 192, 242, 257, 276

Salience of Initiatives, 33, 36–39, 42–47
Smith, Dan, 97, 215, 277
Smith. Mark, 33, 278
Spillover Effects, 51–52
Stadia, 5, 212, 215–20, 226, 234
Stadium Tax, 195, 202, 204, 206, 215, 221–25, 227–28, 230–34, 236–38, 240, 250–53
Stadiums, 187, 189, 191, 195–96, 198–200, 203, 207–11, 219–20, 223, 253–54, 256, 260
Stambough, Stephen, 3, 278
Strong-Mayor, 187, 189, 191–92, 194–95, 197–98, 203–4, 206–8, 210–12

Three strikes, 63, 121–56
Turnout, 33–49, 97, 102–4, 107, 111, 113, 115, 117, 126, 138, 195, 200, 204, 206, 210, 277
Typology, 51, 53–56, 58, 67–69, 71, 81–82, 87–88, 101, 190, 209

Voter, 9, 11–14, 16–18, 20, 22, 24–28, 32–49, 57, 65, 88–90, 95, 97, 102–5, 115–16, 123–24, 126, 131–32, 137–38, 140, 145, 148, 195, 197, 204, 206, 210, 230, 233, 266, 275, 277
Voter Opinions, 9, 12–14, 16–18, 20, 22
Voters, 4, 9, 11–34, 36, 39, 45, 48, 53–54, 56, 79, 82, 85–88, 91–92, 94–95, 98–101, 110, 114, 122–23, 125, 131–32, 135–138, 140–141, 143, 149, 157, 190–91, 195–200, 202–3, 207, 209, 215–17, 220–21, 223–24, 229–30, 235–37, 240–43, 251, 255, 261–62, 265–67, 272
Voting, 5–6, 8, 17–18, 30–31, 33–35, 39, 41–42, 44, 47–49, 57, 59, 75, 77, 79–80, 92–93, 95–96, 99, 116, 121, 123–27, 130–33, 135–38, 140–41, 143, 146–49, 160, 190, 196–97, 204, 216, 225, 230, 242, 249–50, 267, 272, 275–77

Waters, M. Dane, 259, 278
Wedge Issues, 97, 107